THREE ANGELS, ONE MESSAGE

John T. Anderson

REVIEW AND HERALD® PUBLISHING ASSOCIATION

Since 1861 | www.reviewandherald.com

Also by John T. Anderson:
Investigating the Judgment
To order, call **1-800-765-6955**.

Visit us at **www.reviewandherald.com**
for information on other Review and Herald® products.

———————————

Review and Herald® titles may be purchased in bulk for educational, business, fund-raising, or sales promotional use. For information, e-mail SpecialMarkets@reviewandherald.com.

The Review and Herald® Publishing Association publishes biblically based materials for spiritual, physical, and mental growth and Christian discipleship.

The author assumes full responsibility for the accuracy of all facts and quotations as cited in this book.

Unless otherwise indicated, Scripture quotations are from the New King James Version. Copyright © 1979, 1980, 1982 by Thomas Nelson, Inc. Used by permission. All rights reserved.

Scriptures credited to NCV are from *The Holy Bible, New Century Version,* copyright © 2005 by Thomas Nelson, Inc. Used by permission.

Texts credited to NIV are from the *Holy Bible, New International Version.* Copyright © 1973, 1978, 1984, 2011 by Biblica, Inc. Used by permission. All rights reserved worldwide.

Bible texts credited to TEV are from the *Good News Bible*–Old Testament: Copyright © American Bible Society 1976, 1992; New Testament: Copyright © American Bible Society 1966, 1971, 1976, 1992.

This book was
Copyedited by Judy Blodgett
Designed by Mark Bond
Typeset: Minion Pro 12/15

PRINTED IN U.S.A.
16 15 14 13 12   5 4 3 2 1

Library of Congress Cataloging-in-Publication Data
Anderson, John T. (John Thomas), 1949-   .
   Three angels, one message / John T. Anderson.
      p. cm.
   ISBN 978-0-8280-2658-1
   1. Bible. N.T. Revelation XIV, 6-12—Criticism, interpretation, etc. 2. Seventh-Day Adventists—Doctrines. I. Title.
   BS2825.52.A53 2012
   228'.06--dc23

                              2012011336

ISBN 978-0-8280-2658-1

DEDICATION

To my dear wife, without whose patience and forbearance
this would not have been possible, and to my precious Savior,
whose love and forgiveness is immeasurable. It is my hope
that this endeavor will make His great plan of salvation
and the issues for these closing hours of earth's history clearer.

ACKNOWLEDGMENTS

The author gratefully acknowledges the assistance
of many whose ideas, concepts, and suggestions
have woven their way into his thinking and into this book.
Also, many lent their eyes in checking for typographical mistakes.

To Bob, Lance, Charlie, Kevin, Pat, Doug, John, and his wife,
Yvonne, the author wishes to offer his sincerest thanks.

CONTENTS

INTRODUCTION

What are the "three angels' messages"? They are found in the fourteenth chapter, the heart of the book of Revelation. But isn't Revelation a "sealed book," one not intended to be understood? No, in fact the very name of the book "Revelation" means "unveiling." It is by definition something "revealed." Sometimes we hear of the book of Revelation referred to as the Apocalypse, because the word in the original Greek is *apocalypses*, built on the root *calypse*, which means "covering," and the prefix *apo*, which means "from" or "away." Hence, an *apocalypses* is the removal of a covering, a "revelation." If you changed the prefix to *eu*, which means "good" (as in "eulogy," literally "good word"), you would have the name of a type of tree that makes a "good covering" or "good shade"—a *eucalyptus* tree.

Revelation is not a sealed book. Its very opening announces: "Blessed is he who reads and those who hear the words of this prophecy, and keep those things which are written in it" (Rev. 1:3). A closing admonition declares, "Do not seal up the words of the prophecy of this scroll, because the time is near" (Rev. 22:10, NIV). Instead of being closed, Revelation actually confers a specific blessing on those who read or hear and apply the words of this prophecy. Thus it is a book meant to be understood!

But isn't, as some suggest, Revelation intended only for the church following the rapture? No, John was told to "write the things which you have seen, and the *things which are*, and the things which will take place after this" (Rev. 1:19). In other words, its subject matter concerns things stretching from John's day to ours—from the First Advent (the "things which are") to the Second Advent and beyond. Think what

9

a great coup the devil could pull off if he could persuade people that one of the most important books in all of the Bible was either not intelligible or relevant to today's world. But for many people, he has done just that!

Breaking the Code

Some might debate the most significant event contributing to the successful completion of World War II. Was it the daring and desperate rescue at Dunkirk? the victory at Midway? the Battle of the Bulge? Or could it have been the triumph following D-Day? Actually, one could make a strong argument that the single most important factor in the Allied victory was not something that occurred on a battlefield at all, but what took place in a compound at Bletchley Park in Buckinghamshire, England. That was where Allied intelligence agents worked to decipher messages sent by using the Enigma Machine, the Nazi encoding device.

Before the war even began Polish forces had obtained one of the machines, and on July 25, 1939, the Polish Cipher Bureau shared it with the British and French forces. Throughout the war the Allies had the distinct advantage of being able to intercept and understand German military communications through a program they called "Ultra." Following the hostilities, Winston Churchill told King George VI of England, "It was thanks to Ultra that we won the war."[1]

God has given humanity information concerning the war between Christ and Satan, much of it in symbols within the book of Revelation. The very first verse of that book describes itself as "the Revelation of Jesus Christ, which God gave Him to *show* His servants—things which must shortly take place. And He sent and *signified* it by His angel to His servant John" (Rev. 1:1). The Greek word translated "signified" contains the root of the English word "semaphore," which means to "convey by signs." Indeed, much of the information in Revelation appears just that way. Notice that God gave His revelation "to show" His servants. Throughout the book John then relates the things he "saw." It was an audio and a video presentation.

While God may have employed symbols and codes to convey the book's message, through the study of the Scriptures and the enlightenment of the Holy Spirit we can decipher it. The code can be broken. In fact, God invites us to study the book so that we can know about His plan, what we can expect in the future, and most important, how to prepare for it. However, we should not expect that those in rebellion against God will grasp it. The Bible makes it clear that only the "wise" will understand (Dan. 12:10). It is a message solely for "His servants," that is, those who love and serve Him. If we comply with His requirement, we can be assured that He will provide the necessary wisdom.

We need to understand what's going on in our world. Imagine someone totally unfamiliar to Western culture coming to our shores and watching an American football game. "What's going on?" they might ask in their confusion. "Why are they doing that? Why is everyone cheering now? Why is that player celebrating?" Without knowing the purposes and strategies, a person would regard such a game as total chaos. I've ridden in trains across India and watched kids playing cricket, and I've tried to grasp that game's rules. Without knowing the nuances of strategy, it's hard to figure out what's happening. Observing a game like that without knowing the objectives is hard enough, but imagine finding yourself thrown onto the playing field without knowing what you're supposed to be doing.

Life on our planet can likewise appear confusing and perplexing, like the "wheels within wheels" that Ezekiel saw in vision (see Eze. 1). But God wants His message to be understood. He told Habakkuk to "write down the revelation and make it plain on tablets, so that a herald may run with it" (Hab. 2:2, NIV). The idea conveyed in the Hebrew of that text is not that a jogger can understand or share it, but "that a person may read it fluently," that is, smoothly and easily. We pray that this study will be of that character. The Bible is the book that opens our minds to see what is taking place behind the scenes. The Scriptures explain why our sad and troubled world appears as it does today. Thankfully, they also reveal to us that God has a plan for our planet. They tell us how we may receive salvation by grace and through faith, and thus one day be taken to heaven when Jesus returns. God loved us so much that He sent His divine Son, Jesus, to die for our sins. He really wants us to be saved and to live with Him!

Of all the important messages that Revelation contains, no passage has greater significance today than the messages of the three angels recorded in Revelation 14. Spotlighting the issues that face our globe as the era of sin comes to its close, they tell us how we may align ourselves with the winning team. That's of critical importance!

Furthermore, they are particularly geared for the period just prior to the return of our Lord to earth. Nothing could have greater and more urgent meaning to our world right now than the messages of those three angels. But if you went out on the street and asked passersby, "Do you know what the messages of the three angels in Revelation 14 of the Bible are?" how many would have any clue what you are talking about? Even how many preachers today could give you an answer?

Sad to say, it was not much different when Jesus came the first time. The prophetic clues were there, and the angels sang in the sky, but how many were paying attention? For the most part the world plodded on in its endless and thoughtless routines, ignorant that something of cosmic importance was taking place. The difference is that when Jesus returns, life as we know it on our planet will end. We'll either be saved or lost. It is absolutely necessary that we hear and follow the instruction in His last-day message proclaimed by the three angels of Revelation 14.

Years ago, shortly after noon on one November day, viewers of WFAA TV were watching the *Julie Bennell Variety Show,* at that time featuring a model demonstrating a fashionable coat. Accessories included a pair of sleek gloves equipped with nifty zippers to make their placement easy. Suddenly the blanched-faced program director, Jay Watson, interrupted the telecast with the announcement that President John F. Kennedy had been shot.[2] The coat modeled on the *Julie Bennell Show* didn't seem very important anymore. Whether the gloves had zippers or not didn't matter. The president had been shot! The content of the variety show now seemed incredibly hollow in the light of the dramatic event.

Someday soon Christ our Savior will return just as He promised. When He does, the things that have gripped the attention of so many people will appear of less significance than the zippered gloves on that TV show. They will seem hollow and empty. Jesus loves us dearly and wants us to be ready for that day, but the devil wants to distract us so that we're unprepared. The explicit goal of the messages of the three angels is to prepare us to welcome our coming King.

This study seeks to make them understandable and easy to comprehend. It is hoped that the reader will not only learn what the messages are about but also gladly follow the light given within them. Remember, the blessing pronounced in the opening verses of Revelation goes to those who read, hear, *and* keep those things written therein. If we don't apply to our lives what we learn from the Bible, it does us no good. Rejected light becomes darkness. May God give us wisdom as we seek Him and His truth!

----

[1] See, for example, http://en.wikipedia.org/wiki/Ultra.

[2] See http://www.wfaa.com/news/local/64518552.html.

CHAPTER 1

THE THREE ANGELS' MESSAGES

The apostle John wrote: "Then I saw another angel flying in the midst of heaven, having the everlasting gospel to preach to those who dwell on the earth—to every nation, tribe, tongue, and people—saying with a loud voice, 'Fear God and give glory to Him, for the hour of His judgment has come; and worship Him who made heaven and earth, the sea and springs of water.'

"And another angel followed, saying, 'Babylon is fallen, is fallen, that great city, because she has made all nations drink of the wine of the wrath of her fornication.'

"Then a third angel followed them, saying with a loud voice, 'If anyone worships the beast and his image, and receives his mark on his forehead or on his hand, he himself shall also drink of the wine of the wrath of God, which is poured out full strength into the cup of His indignation. And he shall be tormented with fire and brimstone in the presence of the holy angels and in the presence of the Lamb. And the smoke of their torment ascends forever and ever; and they have no rest day or night, who worship the beast and his image, and whoever receives the mark of his name.'

"Here is the patience of the saints; here are those who keep the commandments of God and the faith of Jesus" (Rev. 14:6-12).

To Whom Did God Direct Those Messages?

Notice that the messages precede the description of Jesus' return to earth. We know that, because just after the three angels delivered them, we read: "Then I looked, and behold, a white cloud, and on the cloud sat One like the Son of Man, having on His head a golden crown, and in His hand a sharp sickle. And another angel came out of the temple, crying with a loud voice to Him who sat on the cloud, 'Thrust in Your sickle and reap, for the time has come for You to reap, for the harvest of the earth is ripe.' So He who sat on the cloud thrust in His sickle on the earth, and the earth was reaped" (verses 14:14-16).

Without doubt it is a portrayal of Christ's second advent, because the Lord Himself said, "the harvest is the end of the age" (Matt. 13:39, NIV). Therefore the messages preceding it must constitute heaven's last warning, God's last call to Planet Earth. Could there possibly be anything of more importance than this? Since the "signs of the times" scream that His coming is near, the messages most certainly are meant for us!

Understanding them will lead us to a different way of thinking, of looking at life. Introducing our minds to a new reality, they make it clear that God has an agenda for our world. *He has a plan for Planet Earth*. We therefore have a choice. Either we can base our lives on the visible world and pack as much pleasure into them as we can, pursuing our own wants and aspirations without any regard to a divine design, or we can learn about and accept God's plan for our planet and choose to accept His will. Then we can focus on His agenda and make all of our plans subservient to His will. These two concepts for living are literally worlds apart.

Sometime for your own interest conduct a little test. While you're in the shopping mall or any other place where there's a crowd, pay attention to what people are saying around you. Ask yourself, Do any of them reflect the reality of God's plan for our planet? Or do they exhibit a mentality oblivious to the fact that God's plan will soon come to completion. What is the subject matter of most conversations? This world or the next? Are people aware at all that "all this" will come to an end soon? No wonder the three angels of Revelation need to cry with a "loud voice"!

The Christian who understands what God is about to unfold will have his eyes trained upward, looking for His cloud to break the sky. That mental outlook predominates the thinking of the true believer. Everything else is subordinate to God's agenda. And yet, how many give any thought to what God intends for the earth! Today's world is no different than when Noah preached that a flood would wipe out the earth of his time. Nearly everyone paid him no mind, but went about their lives as if things would continue indefinitely.

But it makes no sense, when you think about it, to live that way. Nothing here really lasts, anyway. Paint peels, lettuce wilts, cars break down, and health fails. Relationships can crumble. We all find ourselves on a path that leads only to the cemetery. Sooner or later, should the Lord tarry, we will all walk through the valley of the shadow of death. If we attain 70 years or even more, still it is not really very long. Our lifespan is like "a vapor" (James 4:14). And to live as if "this is all there is" is a pitiful thing.

A BMW Z4 zipped past me on the freeway the other day with the license plate "wurt zw8," which I interpreted as saying "worth the wait." For those who have faith and the perspective that the Bible provides, life takes on meaning and purpose. We may not have all the answers, but we can gain a sufficient understanding of what's going on. Heaven will be worth the wait! The three angels' messages alert us to the nearness of that event, the issues that will impact it, and the necessity of preparing for it.

God has a plan for this planet—of that we can be absolutely certain. Our thoughts and deeds must conform to what He intends to do here. To know what faces the earth at the end of time is crucial! And the three angels' messages focus on those very issues. Consider the following for a minute. Suppose you came up to Adam in the Garden of Eden before sin and asked, "Have you heard about the two trees, the tree of life and the tree of the knowledge of good and evil? Do you know what their significance is? Why are they important?" What if he responded, "No, I don't think I've ever heard about them. I've been very busy working on my house and doing some gardening. Aren't these grapes lovely?" Would God have left Adam in ignorance about the meaning of the two trees? That's unthinkable! Knowing about those two trees was life-and-death information!

But how many know about the messages of the three angels today? They are just as crucial in our time as was the message of the two trees in Adam's time! The fact that Adam failed because he ate the fruit from the forbidden tree, resulting in God revealing His wonderful plan of salvation, makes it even more important for us to know what issues face us in these last days. We can't afford to end up on the wrong side now! This is our "second chance." There won't be another after this!

My poor plum tree is mixed up. As I looked out my back window I saw it covered with blossoms, which should be good. But it's the middle of January. Because of some unusually warm weather we've enjoyed lately, the tree thinks it's spring. It's totally confused about the "times and seasons," something that we as Christians can't afford to be. We should be able to discern the "signs of the times" and know that Christ's coming is near. Soon—sooner than most realize—His plan will come to completion, and those who have committed their hearts to Him will enjoy the eternity that He has in store for those who love and follow Him. Life is not just going to continue indefinitely here on earth—the Lord has a design, and it *will* come to pass. Regrettably, despite all of God's gracious overtures, most of the world will register complete shock when it sees Him in the sky.

When He comes back, life here as we know it will come to an end. Human projects and enterprises, into which so many have invested time, money, sweat, and energy, will cease. It will all come to a climactic end. Oh, how differently things will look in the light of His return! The "zippered gloves" of this life will pale into insignificance. But God has graciously allowed us to know the basics of His plan and how we can fit into it. To live life without an interest in or knowledge of the divine design is to make the ultimate mistake—one that will lead to eternal death. God wants us to be saved! We must study the three angels' messages!

Method of Study

We will address their content in two ways: first, in an abbreviated overview, and then second, going into greater and greater detail. The reason for this is so that the reader can gain a general understanding of the overall picture rather quickly. From this perspective, the more detailed specifics will be easier to understand.

CHAPTER 2

A BRIEF OVERVIEW OF THE THREE ANGELS' MESSAGES

Remember that in this chapter we're taking only a "bird's-eye view" of their content, with further study to follow. The introduction of the first angel appears in verse 6 of Revelation 14 with its message contained in the next verse. "Then I saw another angel flying in the midst of heaven, having the everlasting gospel to preach to those who dwell on the earth—to every nation, tribe, tongue, and people—saying with a loud voice, 'Fear God and give glory to Him, for the hour of His judgment has come; and worship Him who made heaven and earth, the sea and springs of water.'"

We should understand the term *angel* as "one who bears a message." The original Greek is *angelos,* which forms the root for the word "evangelism." It describes one who is giving news, someone who has a message to share. Since the book of Revelation is filled with symbols, we needn't think that we should take this picture of three angels flying in the sky literally. It depicts three *messages* going to all the world.

The first component of the message is the "everlasting gospel"—the good news of salvation revealed throughout the Bible. It is the message of God's love that forms the basis for all the truths of Scripture. God loves us very much! The good news includes the forgiveness of past sins, the power to overcome temptation today, and the promise of a home in a future kingdom "where righteousness dwells" (2 Peter 3:13, NIV).

This message particularly seeks to alert those who "dwell" on the earth—those who make our world their home. In Scripture God's followers are not of those who "dwell" here. Called to be "pilgrims," "strangers," and "aliens" as we "sojourn" in this world, we recognize that this world is not our home. God summons us to look by faith, as did Abraham, to the kingdom above, the city "which has foundations, whose builder and maker is God" (Heb. 11:10).

A global message, the gospel is to go to every "nation, tribe, tongue, and people" and is to be proclaimed with a "loud voice." God wants everyone to know the content of all the messages before He comes back in glory. Just as Noah warned his world before the Flood, so these messages are designed to make the entire world aware of what will soon take place.

The angel cries out, "Fear God and give glory to Him." To "fear" God in the biblical sense does not mean to cringe in abject terror. God is our heavenly Father who seeks a relationship with His creatures based on appreciation, not dread. To "fear God" in this context means to respect, reverence, love, and obey Him. Said the wise man Solomon as he closed his sermon, "Fear God and keep His commandments, for this is man's all" (Eccl. 12:13).

This phrase encapsulates the basic issue that is the understructure of God's kingdom. Testifying to our relationship with our Creator, it is the issue that surfaced in the Garden of Eden and that will reappear at the end of time. Will we, as creatures from God's hand, render to Him the loyalty and allegiance He deserves as our Maker? Will we trust Him and heed His Word? Will we love and obey Him at all costs? The Bible tells us that Adam and Eve failed. They disregarded the Word of God in the garden and ate the forbidden fruit. Setting aside His commandment, they listened to the devil masquerading as the serpent. Loyalty to God expressed by loving obedience will be the prime issue of the last days.

What does the angel mean by declaring, "Give glory to Him"? We do that by our lips, but more important by our lives. The Bible is calling us to holy living in these last days. Yes, we should "continually offer to God a sacrifice of praise—the fruit of lips that openly profess his name" (Heb. 13:15, NIV). But giving "glory to Him" goes far beyond what we say. It impacts our whole lifestyle. We honor God when we live in a way that gives evidence that His Spirit is operating in our lives. Paul wrote, "Whether you eat or drink, or whatever you do, do all to the glory of God" (1 Cor. 10:31). Thus we glorify God when we obey the laws of health and don't poison and pollute our bodies but treat them as God's temple. "You were bought at a price; therefore glorify God in your body and in your spirit, which are God's" (1 Cor. 6:20). And we glorify Him when we think, act, and behave in ways in harmony with His principles. God will enable us to do this if we ask Him.

The angel proclaims that "the hour of His judgment has come." The Bible constantly teaches accountability, responsibility, and judgment. When the wise man King Solomon said, "Fear God and keep His commandments, for this is man's all," he immediately added, "For God will bring every deed into judgment, including every hidden thing, whether it is good or evil" (Eccl. 12:14, NIV). Notice, though, that when Solomon wrote, as well as did other Bible authors, he spoke of the judgment as being in the future. In contrast, the first angel of Revelation 14 clearly speaks of the hour of His judgment as having come and taking place—at least part of it—before Christ's return. This is a crucial point!

The prophecies of the book of Daniel reveal that since the year 1844 we have been living in the time of God's judgment. (We will go into the biblical basis for this date later.) The phase of judgment that involves the opening of the books and the investigation into who will be the heirs of His kingdom takes place prior to the Advent, for when He returns His reward is with Him (Rev. 22:12). Just as an earthly trial includes separate and distinct phases of investigation, decision-making, and execution, so also God's system of divine justice operates on similar principles.

As revealed in Scripture, it has been the consistent pattern of God to investigate before taking action, not because He needs to, but to inspire confidence in the minds of His creatures. Before He returns He will have completed the phase of the judgment that involves "investigation." Scripture promises that "at that time your people shall be delivered, everyone who is *found written* in the book" (Dan. 12:1). The text obviously contemplates a process of looking into "books" prior to the great deliverance. Daniel describes a heavenly judgment setting that takes place prior to the Advent, in which thrones are put in place with the Ancient of Days presiding and the numberless hosts of angels attending as the "court was seated and the books were opened" (Dan. 7:10).

The message that we are now living in the "hour of His judgment" gives impetus and momentum to the angel's cry. One of the very last items on God's agenda is being fulfilled right now! His coming is imminent!

The first angel continues with his proclamation. "Worship Him who made heaven and earth, the sea and the springs of waters." The central issue of the last days will focus on worship. We know that because the word "worship" appears no less than eight times in chapters 13 and 14 of Revelation. The call is to worship God and not worship the beast or his image.

The call to worship God has a specific aspect—to worship the God "who made." The creatorship of God is the fundamental platform on which rests His right to reign. It is the reason why He is to be revered and worshipped. "You are worthy, O Lord, to receive glory and honor and power; for You created all things, and by Your will they exist and were created" (Rev. 4:11). "Thus shall you say to them: 'The gods that have not made the heavens and the earth shall perish from the earth and from under these heavens.' He [the Lord] has made the earth by His power, He has established the world by His wisdom" (Jer. 10:11, 12).

The biblical summons to worship "Him who made," the Creator-God, must include a call to return to the keeping of the seventh-day Sabbath, the day that the Lord set aside as a reminder of His creation. Instituted at Creation, it is embedded in the Ten Commandments written by God's own finger. In an age that presents evolution as the explanation of how life began, there is to be a clear and decisive appeal to return to the understanding of God as Creator and to observe the only day that Scripture identifies as being sanctified and blessed—His memorial of creatorship, the seventh-day Sabbath.

The Second Angel's Message

"And another angel followed, saying 'Babylon is fallen, is fallen, that great city, because she has made all nations drink of the wine of the wrath of her fornication.'" Clearly we must understand Babylon here as being symbolic. It no longer existed in John's day, nor has there been a literal Babylon built at any time since.

Of what is apocalyptic Babylon a symbol? Built on the very ruins of the ancient tower of Babel, the ancient city came to represent unbelief, self-exaltation, confusion, defiance, rebellion, false teachings, and oppression. It stood as the "capital" of Satan's kingdom. As such, Scripture employs it to represent those who persist in such characteristics. God gave the Babylon of Nebuchadnezzar an opportunity to fulfill His purpose, even to serve as His tool to discipline Judah. But eventually it repelled His Spirit and apostatized.

Even before the book of Revelation was penned, the concept of a symbolic Babylon was already in place. Peter closed his first epistle by saying, "She who is in Babylon, chosen together with you, sends you her greetings" (1 Peter 5:13, NIV). No physical Babylon existed when the apostle composed his letter. Because pagan Rome at that time filled the role of Babylon with its arrogance and persecution, Peter felt free to apply the term to her. Finally, apocalyptic Babylon represents the enemies of God, with the ecclesiastical structure of the church of the Middle Ages taking a leading role in more recent times.

Here we must stress, right at the outset of our study, that prophecy is speaking against the system and structure of the Papacy and the way that it functions, and not individual members of that church or any other religious community. God has His followers among all churches and faith groups. He loves Catholics! Human beings cannot judge hearts and motives. Only God can do that. But He does require us to discern between truth and error as defined by Scripture. The devil seeks to deceive and destroy, and we must be on our guard to know what is truth. Because he induced people—perhaps well-meaning ones—to change how to approach and understand the Bible, it is the papal system and the way it operates that falls under prophecy's indictment. When we speak of the "church" in this context, we do not refer to its members, multitudes of them God-fearing people, but rather the ecclesiastical structure that shapes its belief system. We are speaking about *Catholicism* and not *Catholics*. Because it is so important to emphasize this distinction, we will again address it later in our study.

What does the "fall" of Babylon mean, and why does it get mentioned twice? What are the two "falls" of which the second angel speaks? The church established by Jesus began in purity and victory, but later "fell" from its sanctified position. The apostle Paul predicted its apostasy or "falling away" (2 Thess. 2:1-8). The first "fall" occurred when the church slid into apostasy during the Middle Ages.

In the period between Christ's first and second Advents, the era under the spotlight in the book of Revelation, the medieval church has predominately occupied the role of Babylon. As we shall see, it has cherished the very same attitudes and nourished the same practices of ancient Babylon, especially with its departure from Scripture and with its oppression of dissenters. The light of the gospel nearly vanished during those centuries. Yet a cry for reform began to ascend, reaching a crescendo pitch in the movement led by Martin Luther, John Knox, John Calvin, Ulrich Zwingli, and others who "protested" against the abuses of the ecclesiastical structure.

But Protestantism, which began with such lofty ideals, itself declined and departed from its original principles. It also has "fallen away" from the truths of Scripture. Thus we find the second angel identifying two "falls" or apostasies: "Babylon is fallen, is fallen." The condition of the Papacy of the Middle Ages was the first fall while the transformation of Protestantism in more recent centuries is the second. And yet there will be an even greater fall, as one day Babylon will "make," or coerce, all nations to abide by its dogmas on pain of persecution and death.

What is the "wine" that Babylon gives to all nations? It is the intoxicating false teachings that result in confusion and dependency. Just as there was "confusion" at the tower of Babel, just as the drinking of alcohol results in addiction and produces confusion of mind, so the teachings of Babylon induce dependency upon her and spiritual disorder. Having imbibed her cocktail of heresies, all nations "stumble" and "fall."

What does the imagery of "fornication" represent? In the literal sense it describes an illicit relationship between two partners. And in the spiritual sense it also depicts a wrong union between two entities. Revelation 17 gives us a clear picture of this improper alliance involving

Babylon, in that an impure woman, on whose forehead is written the name Babylon, representing apostate religion, rides upon (oppresses and/or is supported by) a beast, symbolizing a kingdom or state.

A "woman" riding a "beast" serves as a prophetic portrayal of the illicit union of church (a woman) and state (a beast)—spiritual fornication. Throughout the Middle Ages there existed such a dangerous connection between church and state. Great oppression and persecution resulted as the church relied on political power rather than the power of the Holy Spirit to accomplish its goals. Babylon's dissemination of unbiblical teachings and dependence on the power of secular agencies has resulted in her fall. A later angel's message, contained in chapter 18 of Revelation, summons all of God's true followers to "come out of Babylon."

The Third Angel's Message

The message of the third angel contains the most awesome warning in all of Scripture. "Then a third angel followed them, saying with a loud voice, 'If anyone worships the beast and his image, and receives his mark on his forehead or on his hand, he himself shall also drink of the wine of the wrath of God, which is poured out full strength into the cup of His indignation. He shall be tormented with fire and brimstone in the presence of the holy angels and in the presence of the Lamb. And the smoke of their torment ascends forever and ever; and they have no rest day or night, who worship the beast and his image, and whoever receives the mark of his name. Here is the patience of the saints; here are those who keep the commandments of God and the faith of Jesus'" (Rev. 14:9-12). Can anyone today take the risk of not knowing what it all means?

A "beast" in symbolic prophecy represents a kingdom or power. (For example, "The fourth beast shall be a fourth kingdom on earth" [Dan. 7:23].) Here in Revelation 14 the angel points back to the beast introduced in the first verses of chapter 13, the leopard-like beast that rose from the "sea" (a populated area), received great authority from the "dragon" (Satan working through pagan Rome), spoke "blasphemies" (made improper claims to being equal in with God), continued in an uninterrupted reign for 42 prophetic "months," or 1,260 literal years

(A.D. 538 to A.D. 1798), made war with the saints (persecuted God's people), received a mortal wound (when the pope was captured in 1798, jeopardizing the future of the Papacy), and experienced a remarkable resurgence resulting in all the world marveling at, following, and worshipping the beast. It has the code identity of "666," the "number of his name." (We'll discuss these points in greater detail later.) The first beast of Revelation 13 can be no other entity on earth than the organizational structure of the Roman Catholic Church.

The identification of the "beast" as being the Papacy rests upon at least seven different scriptural passages, an interpretation embraced and confessed by virtually all the Reformers, although their spiritual descendants have nearly all abandoned this position. That Protestantism today, as a whole, no longer accepts this view is a part of its remarkable and mysterious "fall."

What does the angel mean by the "image of the beast"? An image is a likeness—a replica or copy. This image of the beast, or image to the beast, receives life from a second prophetic animal in chapter 13, rising from the "earth" (a nonpopulated area) about the time the first beast (the Papacy) experiences its deadly wound (1798) and having two "Lamb-like" horns (having a Christian appearance). The second beast of Revelation 13 represents the United States, which at first exemplifies the principles of freedom, but which later "speaks like a dragon," or employs force, brought to bear by legislation, to compel the conscience.

The use of state power to enforce religious dogma was the method of operation of the first beast described in that chapter. The Papacy has through the centuries claimed the authority to dictate in spiritual matters on pain of persecution or death. In this respect the second beast copies or replicates the behavior of the first beast. It makes an "image" or likeness *of* it (because it is copying what the first beast did), and *to* it, since by so doing it compels worship in the manner directed by the Papacy. While this has not happened yet, it soon will, as unbelievable as it may seem.

What about the "mark" of the beast? We know that the beast represents the concept of power displayed by the Papacy. What has it claimed as a mark or indication of its authority? It is the change of the day of worship from the seventh to the first day of the week. That which God enjoined by placing in the very heart of the Ten Commandments, the seventh-day Sabbath—the commandment beginning with the word "remember"—the Papacy has claimed the authority to change without any scriptural backing. It even challenged modern Sundaykeeping Protestantism to find scriptural support for worshipping on the first day of the week. Thus it offers Sunday worship as evidence of its ecclesiastical authority to shape doctrine on earth. The shift of the day of worship from the seventh to the first is its "mark of authority."*

Since Revelation 13 and 14 repeat the word "worship" no less than eight times; since we are invited to worship "Him who made" in the first angel's message; since those described as being saints at His coming are those who "keep the commandments of God," does it not follow that the intentional disregard of God's commandment regarding the day of worship is a solemn and serious act of defiance?

Does anyone have the "mark of the beast" today? No. It is *only* when the second beast "speaks" as a dragon, which it does through its legislative body, that such a mark is implemented. When Sunday worship becomes law, then anyone who knowingly transgresses against the sacred Sabbath of Jehovah will be "marked" as being apostate. This rather brief synopsis summarizes the subjects to which we will now give greater and more detailed attention.

---

* All of these matters will be discussed in greater detail in subsequent chapters.

CHAPTER 3

THE MESSAGE OF THE FIRST ANGEL

As we have seen, the word "angel" in Greek *(angelos)* means "messenger." It is true that most often in Scripture the term refers to the hosts of heaven who minister to their king (the classic meaning of the word "angel"). But the Bible applies the word to others who do not belong to the heavenly company.

In fact, we find an apt illustration of the word "angel" in the Gospels. For example, did you know that the Scriptures call John the Baptist an "angel"? It's rather hidden, but such usage is very much in point, because John was the delegated messenger sent to herald the first coming of Jesus. God commissioned him "to make ready a people for the coming of the Lord" (Luke 1:17). It is precisely the objective of the messages found in Revelation 14. They precede and prepare for the coming of the Lord—not His first coming, as was the case for John the Baptist, but His glorious and climactic second coming.

Where does it say that John the Baptist was God's "angel"? Notice how Jesus Himself described him. When Christ spoke to the multitude concerning him, He asked, "What did you go out into the wilderness to see? A reed swayed by the wind? If not, what did you go out to see? A man dressed in fine clothes? No, those who wear fine clothes are in kings' houses. Then what did you go out to see? A prophet? Yes, I tell you, and more than a prophet. This is the one about whom it is written: 'I will send my messenger ahead of you, who will prepare your way before you'" (Matt. 11:7-10, NIV). Here Jesus quoted from the close of the Old Testament, Malachi 3:1.

If you were to read this passage in the Greek language, both from Matthew's account in the New Testament as well as from the Septuagint

(Greek) version of the Old Testament passage from Malachi, you would see that Jesus said, "Behold, I send My *angelos* [My "angel"] before Your face." In a sense then, John the Baptist was God's "angel" delivering the message that would announce the coming of Jesus and prepare for His arrival. Likewise, the "angels" of Revelation 14 occupy a similar role as did John the Baptist, in that they proclaim the second coming of Jesus with a message calculated to prepare the world for the momentous event. Last-day "John the Baptists" or "angels" who give to the world God's last warning message, they symbolize human beings doing a heavenly work.

And since Jesus is quoting from the Old Testament book of Malachi, we should note that the Hebrew word translated "messenger" in that text is *malak,* a word used scores of times to refer to the angels of heaven as well as being translated about an equal number of times as "messenger" and referring to humans in a role of bearing a message. The very title of that last book of the Old Testament comes from this root *malak* and can be rendered "My messenger."

In addition, we might also point out that Bible students have long regarded the letters of Christ to the seven churches (Rev. 2 and 3), each addressed to the "angel" of a church, as being directed to the pastors of those churches. And, because he conveyed the gospel to them, Paul in his letter to the Galatians mentions that they received him as an "angel of God" (Gal. 4:14).

In a literal sense "angels in the sky" sang their announcement of the first coming of Jesus to the shepherds of Bethlehem. But in a figurative sense the "angels in the sky" depicted in Revelation 14 are actually human beings, God's last-day messengers, who bear the final warning message to Planet Earth announcing His second coming. They are the spiritual descendants of John the Baptist whom God sent to "make ready a people prepared for the coming of the day of the Lord."

"Having the Everlasting Gospel"

Revelation 14 initially introduces the first angel as "having the everlasting gospel." It all begins with God's love—His patient, forbearing, and limitless love. And it has to. There's no other way. "We love Him because He first loved us" (1 John 4:19). The most famous verse of the Bible tells us that "God so loved the world" that He sent His Son to die, not for "saints," but for the "world," a word referring to the ungodly, the unlovable. He loved and treasured the children of His making, though they had fallen deep into the soil of sin. This is the good news that the Bible reveals, the message that the three angels herald.

In 1995 Lena Paahlsson lost her wedding ring, which she had designed herself, a white gold band with seven small diamonds. Busy with a baking project, she had set it on the kitchen counter but then couldn't find it. She and her family looked everywhere, even pulling appliances away from the walls. Later when undertaking a kitchen remodeling project, they ripped up the kitchen floorboards to search for the ring, but to no avail. Eventually she lost hope of ever seeing it again. To her amazement, while she was working in her garden in central Sweden 16 years later in October of 2011, she pulled up a carrot "wearing" her treasured ring! It was firmly embedded around a carrot, the carrot growing right through the middle of it. And it was a very small carrot that she had almost tossed away.

Her daughter Anna heard a terrific scream coming from the garden patch and feared that her mother had hurt herself. She found Lena sitting in a chair looking rather shocked, staring at the small carrot wearing her ring. The family believes that the ring must have been inadvertently swept among the vegetable peelings destined for the compost pile, and thence into the garden plot.[1]

In a similar way, something very precious to our God—something He personally designed—became lost long ago. Sin dumped humanity into the garbage heap of what our world became through transgression. But though lost, humanity was never forgotten, and our God has spared no effort to recover His missing children. The gospel tells the story of His relentless endeavor, His tireless effort to regain the human family.

One evening in March 2009 Robert Lemire was talking on his cell phone outside a pizza parlor in Lawrence, Massachusetts, about 25 miles north of Boston, when he noticed a toddler dangling from a third-story window 30 feet above the ground across the street. The

45-year-old-father of two dashed across the street, where he gained the attention of Alex Day, who had just come out from a home Bible study. Together they caught 18-month-old Caliah Clark before she hit the ground, saving her from serious injury or death.[2]

As incredible as that was, it's nothing compared to what God did for us! Let's take a careful look at His glorious good news, the gospel. It's vital to understand His great plan for our redemption. But knowing what the future holds makes no sense if we're not ready for what's coming. What good would it do to know all the facets of Christ's return if we're not prepared to meet Him in peace?

Scripture identifies the good news as the everlasting gospel. The adjective "everlasting" indicates that the gospel has never changed. It is the same from Genesis to Revelation. But, you might ask, didn't God save people in a different way in the Old Testament? No, the Bible describes only one way that His plan of salvation operates. By putting two simple texts together, we obtain the divine formula for redemption. Paul declared, "For by grace you have been saved through faith" (Eph. 2:8). To the Galatians he wrote, "For in Christ Jesus neither circumcision nor uncircumcision avails anything, but faith working through love" (Gal. 5:6).

Synthesizing the two passages, we arrive at the Bible formula for salvation, God's great news. How does salvation become ours? It is by grace through faith that works by love. That's simple, isn't it? Grace is God's wonderful gift of eternal life bestowed through the sacrifice of Christ. Faith is our appreciation of His great gift and of our laying hold of the promise and trusting Him to fulfill it. Having done so, we walk in the Spirit and live by His precepts. "Works" are the fruit of our relationship with Christ. They do not earn us salvation, but they attest that we are truly connected with Him, as the branch is to the vine. And all this takes place within the context of love. We don't obey Him for fear of being lost, but in wondrous admiration for His incomprehensible gift. Thus salvation comes to us by grace through faith which works by love.

Every word in the biblical formula has its place. If it is not of grace, it is worthless because humanity is helpless by itself to build a bridge to heaven. Should we fail to exercise faith, God's grace avails us nothing.

And if our faith is not genuine—bringing forth deeds reflective of godliness—we need to reexamine it. Above all, if we attempt to accomplish any of this without love, it profits nothing (1 Cor. 13:1-3).

Note carefully that Scripture doesn't talk about "faith and works." Rather, Paul speaks of "faith which works." It is a living, dynamic faith relationship that "naturally" results in the fruits of righteousness. We use the word "naturally," because Christ gives to us a new nature—in fact, we become partakers of the "divine nature" (2 Peter 1:4).

The New Testament makes it abundantly clear that God saved people in the Old Testament through the same formula. A brief examination of Romans 4 and 5 along with Hebrews 11 confirms that He delivered His people even then by grace through faith, and that their deeds testified of their righteousness in Christ. God saves in no other way. The people of the Old Testament did not save themselves through their own efforts. Old Testament religion is not one of legalism. Paul argues passionately against such a claim, demonstrating that Abraham was the father of faith: "What does the Scripture say? 'Abraham believed God [that is, he exercised faith in God], and it was credited to him as righteousness.' Now to the one who works, the wages are not credited as a gift but as an obligation. However, to the one who does not work [in order to obtain favor with God] but trusts God who justifies the ungodly, their faith is credited as righteousness" (Rom. 4:3-5, NIV). Nearly all of Romans, and indeed much of the rest of Paul's writings, clearly establish this teaching.

What passage did the apostle quote when developing his thesis of salvation by faith? Genesis 15:6, an Old Testament verse. This concept of salvation is embedded in Scripture from the very beginning. How did Adam and Eve become "covered" after the Fall? By God providing the tunic of skins to their nakedness (Gen. 3:21). Quite obviously, an animal had to die in order to have the coat of skins for the guilty pair. Clearly the Old Testament teaches salvation by grace. Pharisaical legalism is not the religion of the Old Testament—it is a corruption of God's plan. No one on earth can earn his or her salvation, whether before or after Calvary. Adam's salvation came by grace, as did Abraham's, David's, and that of all the other saints of the Old Testament period. Their deeds—works—didn't gain God's favor, but they did verify that their faith was real. The Lord saved them by the very same mechanism that we are today: by grace through faith that works by love. The everlasting gospel has never changed.

It is true that we in post-New Testament times no longer express our faith in a coming Redeemer by offering an animal sacrifice. The true Lamb of God, Jesus Christ, came and died on the cross for our sins. The Lord gave clear indication that the system of types and shadows of the ceremonial system is no longer necessary, by ripping the curtain of the Temple from top to bottom at the time of Jesus' death (Matt. 27:51). Scripture emphatically draws a line of distinction between the ceremonies that reached their end at the cross and the moral law, the Ten Commandments, that endures forever. Paul sums it up eloquently by stating, "Circumcision is nothing and uncircumcision is nothing, but keeping the commandments of God is what matters" (1 Cor. 7:19). The early Protestant churches recognized and taught the distinction between the ceremonial and moral laws, but it appears that in the past century it has become somewhat hazy and ill-defined.

Today it's getting so bad that you don't want to turn on the television, radio, or open a newspaper for fear of being overwhelmed by stories of global violence and unrest, floods, hurricanes, tornadoes, earthquakes, economic instability, job insecurity, murders, kidnappings, and shootings. Thank God that our joy and peace do not depend on external circumstances. Our hope rests on the sure footing of His plan: Christ's victorious mission in dying for our sins and the Holy Spirit's leading in our lives. "For God so loved the world, that He gave His only begotten Son, that whoever believes in Him should not perish but having everlasting life" (John 3:16). God has a plan both for our planet and your individual life The messages of the three angels are really a single message—one of God's love for a dying world.

---

[1] See http://www.thelocal.se/38248/20111230.

[2] See http://www.boston.com/news/local/breaking_news/2009/03/lawrence_men_pr.html.

CHAPTER 4

GOD'S THREE-PART GOSPEL

God's good news—the gospel—is a complete package. His salvation takes care of the mistakes of the past, the trials and temptations of today, and provides for a future that will forever banish sin. He forgives the transgressions of yesterday, gives power to overcome the temptations of today, and promises that He will take us to a place where all the effects of sin will be eternally absent. That's good news!

Part One of the Everlasting Gospel: Forgiveness for Past Sins

On March 26, 1942, the *Dixie Arrow*, an oil tanker carrying 96,000 barrels of crude oil, was traveling near Cape Hatteras, North Carolina. It was one of several tankers, including the *China Arrow*, the *India Arrow*, and the *Yankee Arrow*, built for the Socony-Vacuum Oil Company, also known as Mobil Oil.

The United States had just declared war against Japan after it attacked Pearl Harbor, Hawaii, a few months earlier. Germany declared war against the United States, and so America found itself engulfed in what became known as World War II. While the Pearl Harbor raid in the Pacific is known by almost all Americans, what is not as well known is the threat to American sea vessels posed by German U-boats, or submarines, lurking off the Atlantic coast. The German submarines sank or crippled virtually all of the Arrow tankers belonging to Mobil Oil.

On that morning of March 26, the *Dixie Arrow* was in route to Paulsboro, New Jersey, with her vital cargo of fuel. The German submarine U-71 had been lurking near Diamond Shoals, off Cape Hatteras, hoping to encounter American ships. As daylight

33

approached, Captain K. K. Walter Flascheenberg was about to give the order for his submarine to go to the bottom when he spied the masts of the *Dixie Arrow*. He skillfully guided his U-boat into position and at 8:58 a.m. fired three torpedoes into the starboard side of the tanker. Quickly flames engulfed it and its cargo of volatile crude oil.

The first torpedo hit at the midship deckhouse, killing most of the deck officers. Then about a minute later the second and third torpedoes struck, cutting the vessel in two. One can only imagine the scene as the oil poured from the ruptured vaults and ignited, turning the deck of the ship as well as the surrounding waters into an inferno. Because of the direction of the wind, the flames whipped from the bridge to the bow, trapping a group of men who now faced the terrible choice of remaining on board and being burned to death, or jumping into the sea, now a veritable lake of fire.

At that critical moment, seaman Oscar G. Chappell made a decision. Though he was injured, he remained at his post in the wheelhouse. Chappell banked the ship hard to the right and held the *Dixie Arrow* into the wind, which drove the waterborne flames away from the men trapped on deck and allowed them to jump into a portion of the sea clear of burning oil. However, by turning the ship in that direction, it drove the flames directly toward his station at the wheelhouse, and he soon perished. His conscious choice and sacrificial action resulted in the saving of his shipmates, who were rescued by the destroyer U.S.S. *Tarbell*.

After his death, Chappell was awarded the Merchant Marine Distinguished Service Medal, and a ship was later named in his honor. Today the Navy League annually awards the "Able Seaman Oscar Chappell Award for Outstanding Maritime Stewardship" to recognize "selfless dedication to shipmates."*

While this is an amazing and inspiring story, it doesn't come close to what Jesus did for us. His sacrifice goes far beyond that of any human being. Seeing our world in a desperate situation, He voluntarily put His life in danger, knowing that by so doing the "flames" would engulf Him. Leaving His throne of exquisite glory and honor, Christ, the world's Redeemer, paid an infinite price for our salvation, and having invested so much in it, will spare nothing to see that every opportunity for salvation is provided us. "For if when we were enemies we were reconciled to God through the death of His Son, much more, having been reconciled, we shall be saved by His life" (Rom. 5:10). "He who did not spare his own Son, but gave him up for us all—how will he not along with him, also, generously give us all things?" (Rom. 8:32, NIV).

God freely bestows His great mercy upon us. The word "mercy" suggests kindness toward the erring and presupposes need. The unfallen angels had no need for mercy before sin entered the picture. But mercy has always been a part of God's character. Although it did not become manifest until the necessity arose, that doesn't mean it wasn't part of His divine attributes before sin first manifested itself.

"The mercy of the Lord is from everlasting to everlasting" (Ps. 103:17). We can't conceive of an infinite past, but God's mercy was there. It is "from everlasting." Mercy has always been within God's great heart of love. Jesus was the Lamb slain "from the foundation of the world" (Rev. 13:8). The plan of salvation was not an afterthought, but has always been there in God's mind, but when the dark night of sin fell upon the earth, the shining star of God's mercy became visible. He first announced it to fallen humanity in Eden, when He promised that He would "put enmity between you [the serpent] and the woman" (Gen. 3:15).

The problem of sin began when a snake hung in a tree. The solution for sin came when a Savior hung on a tree. The cross of Christ is the divine response to the tragedy of sin. The Old Testament is filled with confirmations of His wonderful gift. God Himself covered the nakedness of Adam and Eve with garments He provided, made from skins of an animal, typifying the future atonement at Calvary to cover our inadequacies. The Lord gave to His children the sanctuary service in the wilderness tabernacle and later the Temple to foreshadow the sacrifice of Jesus on the cross for our sins.

The Godhead has extended mercy to us through the life, death, and ministry of Jesus Christ, the sin-bearer of Calvary. His blood is sufficient to cover all our faults and defects. How do we receive it? How is it that His righteousness can be imputed to us? It is by exercising what the Bible calls faith. In the Bible, "to have faith" is the same thing as "to believe" or "to trust: Faith itself is a gift from God: He has given to all "a measure of faith" (Rom. 12:3). Everyone receives a "mustard seed" of faith, for Christ is "the true Light which gives light to every [man and woman] coming into the world" (John 1:9).

But it is up to us to *exercise* that gift of faith: to choose to rest in the confidence of believing and trusting what He says and to surrender our wills to Him. Faith is not blind, but takes its stand based on the evidence provided in the fulfilled prophecies of God's Word, the testimony of God's love and power seen in nature, and the witness of God's presence and providence operating in our lives. "Faith is confidence in what we hope for and assurance about what we do not see." (Heb. 11:1, NIV).

Bible faith is active and takes steps forward, though "proof" is not yet visible, for now we "see in a mirror dimly" (1 Cor. 13:12). Before the children of Israel entered Canaan, the command of the Lord through Joshua was that the vast company should cross the Jordan River, which at that time was in flood stage. From all natural appearances that seemed impossible, and apart from the Word of the Lord, they had no physical reason to believe that they could ford the rampaging river. Yet they did have an abundance of evidence that His power would accompany His command and would somehow open a safe passage. Had not Israel walked through the Red Sea? Did they not breakfast that very morning on manna, the miracle bread that had sustained them during their wanderings? Had not the cloud, which had provided shade from the stifling desert heat, led them to this point? Had not God just given them remarkable victories over Sihon and Og, monarchs of mighty kingdoms east of Jordan (Num. 21:21-35)?

Yes, there was plenty of evidence—if one chose to focus on it. But it wasn't until the priests, bearing the ark, entered by faith into the swirling currents that God "separated the waters from the waters and created dry land," if you want to draw an analogy between this miracle and the Creation story of Genesis 1. That's Bible faith.

Exercising that gift (the measure of faith given to all), means putting obedience into action even when "proof" is absent, resting securely on the evidence already abundantly provided. By continuous growth in the faith experience, we become "full of faith," which leads to becoming faithful. We return obedience to God for the right reason—not to earn salvation (that has already been given to us as His free gift); not to impress others (what does it matter what others think?); but to bring joy to the heart of the Creator-God. Does He not deserve our loyalty and allegiance?

Being full of faith (being faithful) leads one to obey all His commandments and keep holy His Sabbath day, though it might jeopardize livelihood or even life. Bible faith leads us to return a faithful tithe and give generous offerings, though the budget numbers might not seem to add up. It produces acts of kindness, deeds of generosity given in love and appreciation for God's great gift of salvation. Such faith creates kind words in the home and gentle relationships within the family.

A story tells about a climber who set out to scale a certain peak. While ascending the mountain, a sudden storm caused visibility to shrink, temperatures to drop, and rocky surfaces to become slippery with moisture. For safety, the climber was careful to fasten his rope, tied around his waist, securely to trusty pitons hammered into the cracks of the rocks.

It happened, according to the story, that he lost his grip and began a precipitous fall, only to be suspended in midair as his rope reached its end. He could see nothing around him and prayed, "Lord, help me."

The Lord answered him and asked, "Do you trust Me?"

"Oh, yes," the climber said, "I trust You!"

God replied, "Cut the rope."

As the story goes, two or three days later a search party found the man, his frozen body dangling from his rope, two feet above the ground. Are you willing to "cut the rope" and trust God? Are you willing to place your confidence in Him completely and obey Him in all things, even if the future is not fully visible? That's Bible faith!

Through the grace of God He forgives our sins. The Bible uses several illustrations to help us understand His gracious act. It depicts our sins as "cast . . . into the depths of the sea" (Micah 7:19). They are "cast . . . behind Your back" (Isa. 38:17), "blotted out, like a thick cloud" (Isa. 44:22), "sealed up in a bag" (Job 14:17), and "[plastered] over" (verse 17, margin). What marvelous mercy is this! Though we don't deserve it, we are treated as royalty! It truly is good news!

Part Two of the Everlasting Gospel: Power to Overcome Today

God's great good news goes beyond the forgiving of our past sins. His program of salvation has three parts. It not only deals with the past, but with the present and the future. Thus Paul could say that God "delivered [past tense] us from so great a death, and does deliver [present tense] us; in whom we trust that He will still deliver us [in the future kingdom of glory]" (2 Cor. 1:10).

Many preachers and commentators tend to emphasize part one (the forgiveness from past sins) and part three (the future home in glory) and neglect or deemphasize part two, which involves righteous living today. Part two of God's plan is the "cross in the middle." We hear a lot about God's gracious act of forgiving past sins, which is part one. And we hear much about the future kingdom of glory, the third part of His plan. But we don't hear too much about the second part—overcoming sin through His grace today. Yet the Bible makes it clear that there is no crown without a cross. For that reason we desperately need His saving power to be active in our lives today.

The gospel summons us to put away sin, to think and live as did Christ, to pursue that "holiness, without which no one shall see the Lord" (Heb. 12:14). Human nature wants to cling to sin and to salvation at the same time. But that's not possible! Light and darkness cannot coexist. No one can serve two masters. It is very popular to preach a "gospel" that emphasizes forgiveness and future glory, but not the present battle against the flesh, which involves bearing a cross. And yet God is willing and able to overcome sin in us and for us, if we will let Him.

When we exercise faith and let Jesus come into our lives, He begins a work of restoration and change. Originally, the Creator made humanity "in the image of God" (Gen. 1:27), or as the book of Ecclesiastes put it, "upright" (Eccl. 7:29). The entrance of sin marred that image of godlikeness, godliness. Humanity lost its power of self-control, its majestic and noble character. It became self-centered, and its thoughts and actions reflected a selfish and sinful orientation.

One of the saddest verses in all the Bible is Genesis 5:3, which speaks of Adam who "begot a son in his own likeness, after his image, and named him Seth." Once the "image of God" created in Adam was lost though sin, Adam could only pass on to his children his own likeness, that of a fallen creature with a flawed character. Like vessels coming from a cracked mold, each one of us has inherited that same defective nature.

However, God sought to rectify the situation. Jesus came to save us from our sins (Matt. 1:21). A popular "gospel" would have the text read, "He came to save us *in* our sins," giving the impression that a present-day battle against temptation is not necessary—that we can coast along and neglect spiritual conflict. That it's just fine to be a "Christian" but never experience the saving power of Christ now, to know the "power of His resurrection" today (Phil. 3:10).

But that is not what the passage says. It says that He came to "save us *from* our sins." God is too wise and too kind to exclude victory in the warfare against sin today from being a part of His plan. According to the grand purpose of the gospel, He works within us to restore our characters to be like His, thus bringing us back to holiness in thought and deed. We can't do that on our own—it's impossible. But He can. In fact, it's His specialty. When we allow Him to change our way of thinking, overcoming becomes easy, natural. As He writes His laws within our minds, we become new creatures, or a new creation.

Why is that so important? Because it does us no good to know what's coming unless we're prepared for it. We can know all about the prophecies (the Jews in Jesus' day were quite skilled in their knowledge of Scripture), but without a new heart, without a godly character, we will find ourselves lost when Jesus returns. He's coming back to transform our bodies (Phil. 3:20, 21), not our minds or characters. When Jesus returns, there will be no mystical transformation in our thinking that will take place as we travel between the moon and Mars on our way to heaven. The work of changing the way we reason and behave must take place while we are here on earth. The present life is the "vineyard" in which God prunes the grapes of character.

One of the fascinating features of the building of Solomon's Temple was that all the shaping of the stones took place off-site. "In building the temple, only blocks dressed at the quarry were used, and no hammer, chisel, or any other iron tool was heard at the temple site while it was being built" (1 Kings 6:7, NIV). Do you see how the spiritual application of that passage echoes the goal of the gospel? The great and glorious purpose of our lives is for God to remake us now in His likeness. All of the shaping and polishing of our characters happens here, on this earth. This is the quarry, Jesus is the sculptor, and now is the time. Listen to the chisels in Solomon's quarry as they preach that truth!

Our house is more than 24 years old, and time has taken its toll on a few things. The sliding glass door that leads to the backyard was becoming increasingly difficult to open. Being a four-foot panel of dual-pane glass, it is quite heavy, probably weighing 75 pounds or more. Grit and grime, wear and tear had caused the track and rollers to deteriorate and lose all semblance of smoothness. It required great effort to open, and sometimes the rollers would jump off the track, requiring a pry bar to lift it back in place.

Since our dogs needed the door opened and closed several times a day, it was becoming more and more a source of frustration. Finally I went online and ordered new rollers and something called a "snap-cap," a stainless-steel horseshoe-shaped piece of metal that fits over the old track, effectively making it brand-new. What a difference! The first time I tried it, I almost lost my balance, my body being used to the great effort previously required to slide the door open. Now one finger is sufficient to operate it.

That was something like what Jesus does in our lives. He makes us brand-new. Things go more smoothly with Christ at the steering wheel. It doesn't mean there won't be trials, but nothing will come into your life for which He hasn't made provision. Most important of all, He has the capability of restructuring our priorities and goals so that we *want* to do what is pleasing to Him. The psalmist prayed, "Teach me, O Lord, the way of Your statutes, and I shall keep it to the end. Give me understanding, and I shall keep Your law; indeed I shall observe it with my whole heart. Make me walk in the path of Your commandments, for I delight in it. Incline my heart to Your testimonies, and not to covetousness. Turn away my eyes from looking at worthless things, and revive me in Your way" (Ps. 119:33-37). What is the "testimony" that David refers to? A careful study of the Old Testament will bear out the fact that it is God's Ten Commandments. As if in answer to David's prayer, the New Covenant promises that He will indeed write His laws in our heart and within our minds (Heb. 8:8-10).

The grace of Christ places us in an advantageous position. When sin entered, our predisposition and inclination became to do evil. If God had left us to remain in that situation we would have had no hope. But when Christ comes into our lives, we are reborn, and a new nature emerges within us. When we become "born of God," in a new and special way we partake of His nature.

It's a principle of life that children share the nature of their parents. When we become God's children by being born again, we receive His nature. "His divine power has given us everything we need for a godly life, through our knowledge of him who called us by his own glory and goodness. Through these he has given us his very great and precious promises, so that through them you may participate in the divine nature, having escaped the corruption in the world caused by evil desires" (2 Peter 1:3, 4, NIV).

God creates a new heart within us. New desires, new attitudes take shape in our minds. An inclination to do right and please God is planted inside us. "As many as received Him [we have to consent for this to happen], to them He gave the right to become children of God, to those who believe in His name: who were born, not of blood, nor of the will of the flesh, nor of the will of man, but of God" (John 1:12, 13).

Through His regenerative power God changes our wills, our thinking, our behavior, our habits, our characters, and our destinies. He inclines our hearts toward right thinking and right doing. Through the gospel He transforms us by the "renewing of [our] mind" (Rom. 12:2). The heavenly invitation is to "let this mind be in you which was also in Christ Jesus" (Phil. 2:5). "We know that the Son of man is come, and hath given us an understanding [or "mind"], that we may know him who is true" (1 John 5:20, KJV). Through the power of the Holy Spirit "Take captive every thought to make it obedient to Christ" (2 Cor. 10:5, NIV). Paul is describing a process by which our very way of thinking changes and new thought patterns develop. It follows that when thoughts and attitudes alter, behaviors and actions will follow, and therefore our habits, characters, and destiny. Along with His focusing our hearts toward His principles, He counteracts the force of our old nature. David prayed, "Do not incline my heart to any evil thing, to practice wicked works with men who work iniquity" (Ps. 141:4).

A while back while driving, I came up behind a Nissan Murano that had the license plate "TNT NRG." I interpreted it as meaning "dynamite energy." I don't know why the driver chose those letters for his license plate, but I can tell you that it correctly represents the power contained in the gospel. Paul testified, "I am not ashamed of the gospel of Christ, for it is the power of God to salvation for everyone who believes, for the Jew first and also for the Greek" (Rom. 1:16). The word he used for the term translated "power" is the Greek word *dynamis,* which is the source of "dynamite" as well as many other words. A new and active purpose becomes dynamic in the Christian's life, as each day God leads us further into the freedom of His will. A Christian's walk with Him becomes closer and closer until one day it will blend into the immortal life that He has always wanted for His children. Those changes will bring glory to God, delight to His angels, consternation to the devil, and amazement to ourselves. Is it your choice to have them take place in your life?

Part Three of the Everlasting Gospel: the Future Kingdom of Glory

I came upon a verse a few days ago that has something in it I hadn't seen before. The end of Isaiah 21:2 reads: "All its sighing I have made to cease." When I saw the word "cease," I was curious and looked the original Hebrew up. It is *shabbat,* which means literally "to cease, to keep a sabbath." (The primary meaning of the word "Sabbath" means "to stop, or cease.") Think of the implications of the passage. In heaven there will be complete rest, a thought reflected also in a psalm that declares, "That You may *silence* the enemy and the avenger" (Ps. 8:2). Here again, the word "silence" in Hebrew is *shabbat.* Sorrow, sighing, and the work of the enemy will be on permanent sabbatical! Has a trial or difficult experience brought forth from you a sigh lately? Today we live in a world filled with things that bring tears and sorrow, crying and sighing. But one day soon that will all end. All tears and sighing will vanish. The sighing will be "made to cease," and the enemy will be silenced.

Can you imagine such a life? To be free from all physical pain and emotional stress? It's hard for our minds to grasp such a perfect existence, because all we've ever known is pain, suffering, and death. But the day is coming soon when, living in His kingdom made new, in the glory of His gracious presence, we will struggle to recall to mind the trials and tribulations of this life. You'll try to remember what wrinkles were or what arthritis felt like. Although we might labor to remember our greatest hardship, our worst trial, in the end we will give up and with a shout of "Glory!" we'll praise God for His mercy for lost sinners. You want to be there, don't you? This good news, this everlasting gospel, was meant for you!

----

* See http://www.nc-wreckdiving.com/WRECKS/DIXIE.HTML.

CHAPTER 5

DON'T BE AN EARTH-DWELLER!

Something happened a short time ago that many found amusing. Maybe you saw it. A security camera caught a woman walking through a shopping mall, her head down as she concentrated on texting a message. Not watching where she was going, she failed to notice a large pool with a fountain gracing the courtyard of the mall, into which she directly walked. Apparently with nothing but her pride injured, she walked away in her wet clothes and with her soaked cell phone.[1]

It reminded me that many in the world are just like her. They go about life with their heads down, so absorbed in what they are doing that they have no clue as to what lies just ahead. Let us not be like them! Jesus is coming soon! Everything we've read or studied in the Bible is going to come to pass just as the Lord promised. Time is short—much more so than most people think.

God has a plan for our planet. Being unaware of that plan, or failing to comply with its qualifications, will be costly. Going about life with our collective heads down, ignoring the issues that face our world in the context of God's great plan, is a huge mistake. The Bible speaks of those who go about life this way as being earth "dwellers."

The warning messages of the three angels specifically target those who "dwell" on earth. It's true that in a sense all of earth's inhabitants "dwell" here, whether they are in tune with God's program or not. But the Scripture uses the word "dwell" to refer to those who have the mental outlook that "this life is all there is"—that God has no great and grand future in mind. Such shortsighted people have settled into an existence that pays no attention to the fabulous design that God has envisioned. They are like the woman walking through the mall with her head down.

The Greek word translated "dwell" here is *katoikeo,* which comes from the root *oikos,* meaning "house" or "home." Our English word "economy" (meaning "house law") derives from that root. We have other words in our language that incorporate that root, such as "ecology," "ecosphere," and "ecosystem." The word *katoikeo* has the added prefix *kata,* which has the effect of giving emphasis. Most often the prefixes in Greek compound words have this effect. Thus the verb means to "settle down, to abide, to thoroughly make that place your home, to inhabit." The Greek lexicon gives the meaning as to "live, dwell, settle (down)."[2] Used in a positive way, Paul gives us encouragement to allow Christ to "dwell" in our hearts by faith—to allow Him to make His permanent home in our hearts (Eph. 3:17).

But to "dwell" on the earth means to regard this life as being all there is. It is to look at the present world as being our permanent home. But it is a very shortsighted view, one of spiritual myopia. Jesus said that His coming would be a "snare on all those who dwell on the face of the whole earth" (Luke 21:35).

In the book of Revelation itself the word "dwell" is a familiar component. To the church of Philadelphia the True Witness writes, "Because you have kept My command to persevere, I also will keep you from the hour of trial which shall . . . test those who dwell on the earth" (Rev. 3:10). Just before the unleashing of the fifth trumpet, the first of the three awesome woes, John heard an angel cry out saying, "Woe, woe, woe to the inhabitants ["dwellers," from the same word] of the earth, because of the remaining blasts of the trumpet of the three angels who are about to sound" (Rev. 8:13). Revelation 11 tells us about those who defied and attempted to destroy the "two witnesses." Concerning these we read, "And those who dwell on the earth will rejoice over them, make merry, and send gifts to one another, because these two prophets tormented those who dwell on the earth" (Rev. 11:10).

A cluster of usages of this word appears in chapter 13, a section intrinsically linked with the messages of three angels and providing its immediate context. Such passages therefore deserve a very careful look. "All who dwell on the earth shall worship him [the first beast of this chapter], whose names have not been written in the Book of Life of the Lamb slain from the foundation of the world" (Rev. 13:8). "And he [the second beast of the chapter] exercises all the authority of the first beast in his presence, and causes the earth and those who dwell in it to worship the first beast, whose deadly wound was healed" (verse 12). "And he [the second beast] deceives those who dwell on the earth by those signs which he was granted to do in the sight of the [first] beast, telling those who dwell on the earth to make an image to the beast who was wounded by the sword and lived" (verse 14).

In Revelation 17 judgment falls on the impure woman who rides a beast, "with whom the kings of the earth committed fornication, and the inhabitants ["dwellers"] of the earth were made drunk with the wine of her fornication" (Rev. 17:2).

What do these passages tell us about those who "dwell" on the earth? We see that those who make this world their permanent home resist the influence of the Holy Scriptures, the Old and New Testaments, that witness to God and His ways. As the prophecy of Revelation 11 describes, they attempt to destroy them and put His warnings out of their consciences. Earth-dwellers are happy when the Scriptures get set aside, whether literally or figuratively. That is because they have adopted a lifeview contrary to that presented in the Bible.

Those who "dwell" on this earth will especially fall prey of Satan's delusions during the trial and test described in Revelation 3:10. In a special way they are the recipients of the final three "woes," as portrayed in Revelation 8. Revelation 13 tells us that those who "dwell" on the earth will be the subjects of Satan's kingdom and will perform his commands. Deceived by the miraculous wonders performed by satanic agencies, they will worship the beast and his image, receiving his mark.

From the very beginning, God has intended that His children look at this life as a short, temporary stay. He has always directed their gaze to a coming kingdom, a city that has foundations, a home that will last forever. Thus God called Abraham, the father of the faithful, as a spiritual prototype to leave his comfortable home in Ur of the Chaldees, with its conveniences such as indoor plumbing.[3] Pay careful attention to the words Scripture uses to describe his actions and his attitude. "By faith Abraham obeyed when he was called to go out to the place which he would receive as an inheritance. And he went out, not knowing where he was going. By faith he dwelt in the land of promise as in a foreign country, dwelling in tents with Isaac and Jacob, the heirs with him of the same promise; for he waited for the city which has foundations, whose builder and maker is God" (Heb. 11:8-10).

Abraham's pilgrimage, conducted in a literal way, living in tents and moving from place to place, was to be an allegory for all the faithful. In a lesser sense, he foreshadowed the Son of God who would come and have "nowhere to lay His head" (Luke 9:58). We find Abraham continuously shifting his tent from place to place, not settling down in a permanent structure. "Abram passed through the land" (Gen. 12:6). "He moved from there to the mountain east of Bethel" (verse 8). After returning from his sojourn in Egypt, "he went on his journey from the South as far as Bethel" (Gen. 13:3). God commanded him, "'Arise, walk in the land through its length and its width, for I give it to you.' Then Abram moved his tent" (verses 17, 18).

After the destruction of Sodom, "Abraham journeyed from there [Mamre] to the South, and dwelt between Kadesh and Shur, and stayed in Gerar" (Gen. 20:1). He explained to King Abimelech that God had "caused me to wander from my father's house" (verse 13). Later, "Abraham stayed in the land of the Philistines many days" (Gen. 21:34).

Not owning a place to bury his wife Sarah, Abraham told the sons of Heth, "I am a foreigner and a visitor among you. Give me property for a burial place among you" (Gen. 23:4). After leaving the advanced civilization of Ur, never do we find Abraham living in anything but a tent. Those who follow in his footsteps have a pilgrim's mind-set. Realizing that the present earth is not their permanent home, they are not "earth-dwellers." Rather, they lived here "as in a foreign country" (Heb. 11:8), confessing that they are "strangers and pilgrims on the earth" (verse 13).

The biblical author uses two different words for "lived" here. One indicates something short-lived and impermanent, while the other speaks of something long-lasting. As we've seen, the word "dwell" is *katoikeo*. The other Greek word is *paroikeo*, built from the same root *oikos* ("home") but with *para* (cf. parallel, paralegal, parable, etc.) as its prefix, thus with the meaning of "beside, along side of." It gives the nuance of being "tangent to, not firmly embedded in, not completely a part of." The lexicon definition is "to inhabit as a stranger."[4] To be a "sojourner" reflects the concept of being transitory and impermanent. Peter, as he addressed the "pilgrims" scattered through the Diaspora, or "dispersion"(1 Peter 1:1), wrote, "conduct yourselves throughout the time of your stay here in fear" (verse 17).

We are not of those who "dwell" on the earth. Abraham's true seed are those who look at life in a completely different way. Thus we embrace the attitude of David who prayed, "We are foreigners and strangers in your sight, as were all our ancestors. Our days on earth are like a shadow" (1 Chron. 29:15, NIV). The true Christian is one who has the same mental outlook on life as did his Master, who said, "My kingdom is not of this world" (John 18:36). Yes, we must deal with the mundane things of life as anyone else, but with a different viewpoint. Instead, we must view everything from the perspective of God's great plan for our planet, and with Him as the first object of our affections.

Paul spoke to this way of thinking when he said, "What I mean, brothers and sisters, is that time is short. From now on those who have wives should live as if they do not; those who mourn, as if they did not; those who are happy, as if they were not; those who buy something as if it were not theirs to keep; those who use the things of the world, as if not engrossed in them. For this world in its present form is passing away" (1 Cor. 7:29-31, NIV). As pilgrims on earth we are to live here as though it is not our permanent home.

We can see an interesting illustration of this frame of mind in the construction of the wilderness tabernacle, made up of gold-clad boards covered by a series of curtains. The first curtain—the one seen when the priest entered its chambers—was made of "fine woven linen and blue, purple, and scarlet thread; with artistic designs of cherubim" (Ex. 26:1). There were actually 10 curtains made coupled together with gold clasps to make them "one." Now here's the interesting part. Verse 2 says, "The length of each curtain shall be twenty-eight cubits." Let's do a little computation. The height of the walls of the tabernacle was 10 cubits, as was its width. That would mean that a curtain that would cover the entire sides and ceiling would need to be 30 cubits in length. Very intentionally, the inner curtain was not that long. It was 28 cubits, making it hang one cubit above the ground on the sides. The outer curtains were indeed 30 cubits in length, and therefore reached to the ground. But not the first, or inner one.

What was the message of such a design? Or was it just arbitrarily done that way? I believe that everything in that structure had meaning and purpose. But what was the significance of that first curtain being shorter? God gave the tabernacle to teach us about Christ. He was the one who "tabernacled" among us (see John 1:14; the word often translated "dwelt" in the Greek literally means "to live in a tent"). I suggest this part of the structure sought to convey the idea that in His inner being He was "not of this world." The inner curtain didn't embrace the ground. Yes, on the "outside" He lived here as a human being and in a literal sense His feet touched the ground. But in His inner self He was the one who came from above.

Paul used a verbal image worth noting, one describing the reality of what is now the unseen world and how it will completely take over and envelop the present visible existence. Quoting from the Old Testament, he said that when Jesus comes, "then shall be brought to pass the saying that is written, 'Death is swallowed up in victory'" (1 Cor. 15:54). In his second letter to the Corinthians he made use of the same imagery when he penned, "For we who are in this tent groan, being burdened, not because we want to be unclothed, but further clothed, that mortality may be swallowed up by life" (2 Cor. 5:4). When something is "swallowed up," it means that it is consumed and totally disappears.

When Moses went to Egypt to deliver God's people, as a sign he threw down his rod and it became a serpent. Pharaoh's magicians "did likewise," but the rod/serpent of Moses swallowed up the rod/serpents of the magicians. They were no more—gone. So it will be with the present mortal, visible life when Jesus returns. The eternal reality of Christ's coming will "swallow up" the current existence, and it will be no more. Instead of concentrating on the "here and now," which according to Scripture will soon pass away, we should be focusing our minds on the "then and there." Do our conversations reveal that our minds are trained on what is soon to happen? Or are we walking along in life like the woman texting in the mall, oblivious to what is just ahead?

Here's a question for you to consider. Is your name Gershom? Probably you are glad that it isn't. But you may wish to reconsider your answer when you read the following text, which tells about Moses who had fled from Egypt and married Zipporah, the daughter of the priest of Midian. "And she bore him a son. He called his name Gershom; for he said, 'I have been a stranger in a foreign land'" (Ex. 2:22). What an appropriate name for a Christian! Do you know that you are a "stranger in a foreign land"? Paul counseled us, "Set your mind on things above, not on things on the earth" (Col. 3:2).

The Lord brought His children from Egypt and set their feet on a path toward Canaan. Between Egypt and Canaan was the wilderness, in which they wandered as sojourners. "Egypt" represents the land of bondage, the life of sin in which we as Christians lived before the light of the gospel broke through the chains of darkness. "Canaan" represents that future home, our permanent abode in the heavens. Between these two we, like Israel of old, find ourselves as sojourners in the wilderness of this earth. We have renounced the slavery of Egypt, but we are not yet in the land of promise.

The children of Israel, as they left Egypt, made their first encampment at a place called Succoth. "Then the children of Israel journeyed from Rameses to Succoth" (literally, "booths") (Ex. 12:37). When Israel left Egypt and began their sojourn to the Land of Promise, it was fitting and prophetic that their first encampment would be in Succoth, the "place of booths." They would spend the next four decades as wanderers, living in temporary abodes.

During the next 15 centuries the Israelites would commemorate the experience each fall as the Feast of Tabernacles. After they entered Canaan and settled into life in the Promised Land, they would still spend one week of each year, in the autumn, reminding themselves of this part of their history. As the years rolled by, the children of Israel, scattered into distant lands by the Diaspora, would assemble in Jerusalem and for that week live in tents or makeshift booths. Those whose homes were in the city of Zion would participate by pitching a tent in their courtyard or erecting a booth on their rooftop. Thus they would keep fresh in their minds the lessons of the past.

But was it just to recall the twoscore years of desert pilgrimage? Or was it also to preserve the recognition that this world, even if you resided in Jerusalem, is only a temporary place. It would be well for us to enter the spirit of the Feast of Tabernacles and share in the pilgrim perspective.

The book of Jeremiah employs a colorful image used to illustrate the concept of becoming too comfortable in this life—in being an earth dweller. It comes from the context of grape juice that had been allowed to rest undisturbed to the point that the dregs had settled at the bottom. For this purpose, the Lord announced to Moab that He would allow the enemy to come in and "shake her up." " 'Moab has been at rest from youth, like wine left on its dregs, not poured from one jar to another—she has not gone into exile. So she tastes as she did, and her aroma is unchanged. But days are coming,' declares the Lord, 'when I will send men who pour from pitchers, and they will pour her out; they will empty her pitchers and smash her jars' " (Jer. 48:11, 12, NIV).

Back in their day, there were laborers whose job it was to shake or tilt (the KJV has the word "tilters" for "wine-workers") the vessels so as to prevent settlement. This lesson, of course, applies both to Israel of old—and to God's people today. If we become too complacent in this life, the Lord may allow trials to "shake" and "sift" us. Don't regret those trials! They are God's "wine-workers" to prevent us from becoming too settled in this life. He doesn't want us to become earth-dwellers!

I've enjoyed growing grapes the past couple of years. It's very rewarding to go out in the yard and enjoy freshly picked grapes. But it's even better to squeeze them and make your own homemade grape juice. When pruning the growth this year, I noticed that one of the vines had come off the main trunk quite close to the ground and had actually trailed along the earth for a short distance before climbing back on the fence. Now, a few months later, having lain on the moist ground, guess what I found when I came to trim it back? It had grown roots in the area where it had contact with the soil! I tried to pull it up, but found that it was securely attached. There was a sermon in what happened there for me. Don't let your roots extend into the soil of this earth!

Paul said that Christ would come as a "thief" to those not expecting Him. Then the apostle said, "But you, brethren, are not in darkness, so that this Day should overtake you as a thief" (1 Thess. 5:4). "Here we do not have an enduring city, but we are looking for the city that is to come" (Heb. 13:14, NIV). Be careful not to allow "this world" to become your home. It will soon pass away. You are an heir to a kingdom eternal, called to separate from those who "dwell" on this earth.

The three angel's message is to go to "every nation, tribe, tongue, and people" (Rev. 14:6). When God looks at our globe, He doesn't see the boundary demarcations that human beings have drawn. He doesn't notice the walls and fences that humanity has constructed by prejudice and pride. We are all His offspring, He having made the human race of "one blood" (Acts 17:26)—not only in the physical sense but also in the spiritual. The saving blood of Jesus who died for the whole world draws all humanity together.

In Christ we find "neither Jew nor Greek," but we are one in Him (Gal. 3:28). National origin is of no consequence to the one who is "no respecter of persons" (Acts 10:34, KJV). The ground is level at the foot of the cross, where all the supposed distinctions and sources of self-elevation disappear in the light of His good news. Differences of skin color, national heritage, education, material wealth, physical beauty, or anything used as rungs on the ladder of human importance go unrecognized by the one who is Father of all. Thus it is appropriate that the last-day message containing the everlasting gospel stretches from east to west, from north to south on a map without grids, a globe without lines. It is for everyone—and it is for you!

---

[1] http://www.youtube.com/watch?v=jPW8xmI4w6U.
[2] William F. Arndt and F. Wilbur Gingrich, *A Greek-English Lexicon of the New Testament*, p. 425.
[3] Walter C. Kaiser, *The Christian and the Old Testament*, p. 46.
[4] Arndt and Gingrich, p. 634.

CHAPTER 6

"FEAR GOD AND GIVE GLORY TO HIM"

To "fear God and give glory to Him" has to do with how we "think" ("fear God") and how we "do" ("give glory to Him"). It means to have a proper attitude and therefore an appropriate expression of that attitude in the way we live. There is the invisible part (what we think) plus the visible aspect (our actions). Both are important and play a role in our Christian walk. In a similar vein we find in the Bible numerous exhortations to amend our "ways and our doings," a phrase appearing 11 times in the NKJV, especially in the book of Jeremiah (see Jeremiah 4:18; 7:3, 5; 17:10; 26:13; add to it another eight occurrences of the phrase "ways and deeds"). It likewise describes the combination of our thoughts and feelings (our "ways") and our actions and behaviors (our "doings").

The order of the words is meaningful in that we must first have a proper mental framework with relation to God (to "fear" Him) which will then result in proper behaviors (giving "glory to Him"). Notice that in the above-mentioned phrase "ways" always precedes "doings" or "deeds." Of the two components, the former ("fear God") is the more important, because what we "think" has a direct influence on what we "do." The mistake many of the Jews made was to assume that the "outside" could be correct while the "inside" was corrupt. But that's impossible!

That's why Jesus wasn't nearly as concerned about the washing of hands, utensils, and food as He was about a clean heart. He explained to His disciples, "Those things which proceed out of the mouth come from the heart, and they defile a man. For out of the heart proceed evil thoughts, murders, adulteries, fornications, thefts, false witness, blasphemies. These are the things which defile a man, but to eat with unwashed hands does not defile a man" (Matt. 15:18-20). He also said: "A good man out of the good treasure of his heart brings forth good; and an evil man out of the evil treasure of his heart brings forth evil. For out of the abundance of the heart his mouth speaks" (Luke 6:45). The mental must precede the physical, the thoughts the behaviors. Paul challenged us to be renewed in the "inner man," and then appropriate works will follow. If we have the "ways" right, the "doings" will also be. Once the source of the river is pure, the water downstream will be clean.

This principle of "ways" and "doings" applies also to those who reject God. Scripture tells us that when the day comes that burns "like an oven," all the "proud" (those who have an improper mental attitude) and all that "do wickedly" (the resultant unacceptable behavior patterns) will find themselves cast in its flames (Mal. 4:1).

Revelation's invitation to "fear" God has biblical roots that penetrate deeply into the soil of Scripture. It is worthy of note that in all three languages relevant to our study (Hebrew, Greek, and English) the word "fear" has both a negative or a positive sense. In the Old Testament the noun *pachad* appears about 50 times. For example, speaking about the curses to fall on Israel if they disobeyed, Moses declares, "In the morning you shall say, 'Oh, that it were evening!' And at evening you shall say, 'Oh, that it were morning!' because of the fear *[pachad]* which terrifies your heart, and because of the sight which your eyes see" (Deut. 28:67). In the book of Proverbs King Solomon depicted Wisdom as saying, "When your terror (*pachad*) comes like a storm, and your destruction comes like a whirlwind, when distress and anguish come upon you, then they will call on me, but I will not answer" (Prov. 1:27, 28). Both passages are examples of "fear" in the negative sense.

On the other hand, the very same noun can have a positive connotation in the Old Testament. The biblical writer can use it to represent the Deity, as when Jacob said to Laban, "Unless the God of my father, the God of Abraham and the Fear of Isaac, had been with me, surely now you would have sent me away empty-handed" (Gen. 31:42). Later, after Jacob and his uncle had made their peace, Jacob "swore by the Fear of his father Isaac" (verse 53).

The same pattern appears in the verb form of this word. We find it used negatively in the promise, "Do not fear, nor be afraid; have I not told you from that time, and declared it? You are My witnesses. Is there a God beside Me?" (Isa. 44:8). However, Hosea testified, "Afterward the children of Israel shall return and seek the Lord their God and David their king. They shall fear the Lord and His goodness in the latter days" (Hosea 3:5).

Another Hebrew verb for "fear" is *yare*. Used negatively, the word reads, "After these things the word of the Lord came to Abram in a vision, saying, 'Do not be afraid, Abram. I am your shield, your very great reward'" (Gen. 15:1, NIV). When Moses discovered that word of his murderous act against the Hebrew taskmaster had begun to spread, he "feared and said, 'Surely this thing is known!'" (Ex. 2:14). As the Egyptian forces pursued Israel after the Exodus, "Moses said to the people, 'Do not be afraid. Stand still and see the salvation of the Lord, which He will accomplish for you today'" (Ex. 14:13).

But then only a few verses later, when the Egyptian forces were miraculously destroyed, we see *yare* used in the positive sense. "Thus Israel saw the great work which the Lord had done in Egypt; so the people feared the Lord, and believed the Lord and His servant Moses" (verse 31). Note also in the following passages the strong and frequent connection between godly fear and obedience to His law. In Moses' last speech to Israel he recited to them God's revealed law "that you may fear the Lord your God, to keep all His statutes and His commandments which I command you" (Deut. 6:2). "And the Lord commanded us to observe all these statutes, to fear the Lord our God, for our good always, that He might preserve us alive, as it is this day" (verse 24).

When considering what the phrase "fear God" means, we can find no clearer commentary than what Moses challenged the people in his farewell address. "And now, Israel, what does the Lord your God require of you, but to fear the Lord your God, to walk in all His ways and to love Him, to serve the Lord your God with all your heart and with all your soul, and to keep the commandments of the Lord and His statutes which I command you today for your good? . . . You shall fear the Lord your God; you shall serve Him, and to Him you shall hold fast" (Deut. 10:12-20).

Following the counsel to reject all apostate prophets, Moses counseled, "You shall walk after the Lord your God and fear Him, and keep His commandments and obey His voice; you shall serve Him and hold fast to Him" (Deut. 13:4). As a part of godly stewardship he advised them to be faithful in their tithing "that you may learn to fear the Lord your God always" (Deut. 14:23). Should Israel demand a king to be like their neighbors, the ruler should make ample usage of the written law. "It shall be with him, and he shall read it all the days of his life, that he may learn to fear the Lord his God and be careful to observe all the words of this law and these statutes, that his heart may not be lifted above his brethren, that he may not turn aside from the commandment to the right hand or to the left, and that he may prolong his days in his kingdom, he and his children in the midst of Israel" (Deut. 17:19, 20).

Concluding his magnificent speech, after recounting the blessings that would attend obedience, Moses said, "If you do not carefully observe all the words of this law that are written in this book, that you may fear this glorious and awesome name, THE LORD YOUR GOD, then the Lord will bring upon you and your descendants extraordinary plagues—great and prolonged plagues—and serious and prolonged sicknesses" (Deut. 28:58, 59). It is an interesting concept, proclaimed just before Israel entered the Promised Land, that it needed to "fear God" lest it receive "extraordinary plagues." Sixteen centuries after Moses spoke, a proclamation contained in the three angels' messages of Revelation, geared especially for those on the very borders of the heavenly Canaan, also invites us to "fear God" lest the seven last plagues, the most extraordinary plagues of all, come upon us.

Look at the following impressive list of attributes and blessings available to those who exercise this type of godly "fear" of the Lord. Why wouldn't anyone want to receive such benefits?

"The fear of the Lord is the beginning of knowledge" (Prov. 1:7).
"The secret of the Lord is with them that fear Him" (Ps. 25:14).
"The eye of the Lord is on those who fear Him" (Ps. 33:18).
"The angel of the Lord encamps all around those who fear Him" (Ps. 34:7).

"There is no want to those who fear Him" (Ps. 34:9).

"His salvation is near to those who fear Him" (Ps. 85:9).

"Great is His mercy toward those who fear Him" (Ps. 103:11; cf. 13, 17).

"He will bless those who fear the Lord" (Ps. 115:13).

"He fulfills the desires of those who fear Him" (Ps. 145:19, NIV).

"The Lord delights in those who fear Him" (Ps. 147:11, NIV).

"It will go better with those who fear God" (Eccl. 8:12, NIV).

"A book of remembrance was written before Him for those who fear His name" (Mal. 3:16).

"But to you who fear My name the Sun of righteousness shall arise" (Mal. 4:2).

So we see that in the Old Testament while the word "fear" can be either negative or positive, godly fear is something to greatly covet. The New Testament word shares the same dual aspect. The Greek *phobos* appears 39 times and is the source of the English word "phobia." It can have a negative sense, as when the disciples met for fear of the Jews (John 20:19). Paul writes, "For you did not receive the spirit of bondage again to fear, but you received the Spirit of adoption by whom we cry out, 'Abba, Father'" (Rom. 8:15). John comments that "there is no fear in love" (1 John 4:18).

On the other hand, godly "fear" fueled the early church. The book of Acts tells us that the churches were "walking in the fear of the Lord and in the comfort of the Holy Spirit" and increased in number (Acts 9:31). Cornelius is described as a "devout man and one who feared God with all his household" (Acts 10:2). Peter stated, "In truth I perceived that God shows no partiality. But in every nation whoever fears Him and works righteousness is accepted by Him" (verses 34, 35).

The Epistles address godly "fear." Paul exhorted the Corinthians, "Therefore, having these promises, beloved, let us cleanse ourselves from all filthiness of the flesh and spirit, perfecting holiness in the fear of God" (2 Cor. 7:1). He instructed the believers in Philippi to "work out your own salvation with fear and trembling" (Phil. 2:12). The book of Hebrews tells us that Jesus "offered up prayers and supplications, with vehement cries and tears to Him who was able to save Him from death, and was heard because of His godly fear" (Heb. 5:7). Peter writes, "Honor all people. Love the brotherhood. Fear God. Honor the king" (1 Peter 2:17).

The book of Revelation highlights godly "fear" several times. "The nations were angry, and Your wrath has come, and the time of the dead, that they should be judged, and that You should reward Your servants the prophets and the saints, and those who fear Your name, small and great" (Rev. 11:18). At the conclusion of the second "woe," we read: "In the same hour there was a great earthquake, and a tenth of the city fell. In the earthquake seven thousand people were killed, and the rest were afraid and gave glory to the God of heaven" (verse 13). The question is asked, "Who will not fear you, Lord, and bring glory to your name?" (Rev. 15:4, NIV). In praise to God after the fall of Babylon, as John listened, "a voice came from the throne, saying, 'Praise our God, all you His servants and those who fear Him, both small and great!'" (Rev. 19:5).

What then does it mean when the Bible, in the positive sense, speaks of "fearing God"? What is the angel addressing when he calls the world to "fear God"? To "fear God" in the biblical sense does not mean to cower in terror, but to have a proper appreciation of His awesome character and might. It is to have an attitude of respect toward the one who governs the universe, which leads to a relationship of love, worship, and willing obedience. As a result, the creature has an appropriate relationship with his or her Creator, fitting properly into His kingdom. The world today is in desperate need of such a way of thinking!

Looking over the multitude of counsels to give reverence to the Lord in godly fear, we can't help noticing the great number of occurrences that combine godly fear with obedience. As we will see, the messages of the three angels are not only a call to fear and worship, but also to obey our Creator-God.

The book of Deuteronomy literally breathes this concept. "Oh, that they had such a heart in them that they would fear Me and always keep all My commandments, that it might be well with them and with their children forever!" (Deut. 5:29). "That you may fear the Lord your God, to keep all His statutes and His commandments which I command you" (Deut. 6:2). "Therefore you shall keep the commandments of the

Lord your God, to walk in His ways and to fear Him" (Deut. 8:6). "And now, Israel, what does the Lord your God require of you, but to fear the Lord your God, to walk in all His ways and to love Him, to serve the Lord your God with all your heart and with all your soul, and to keep the commandments of the Lord and His statutes which I command you today for your good?" (Deut. 10:12, 13). "You shall walk after the Lord your God and fear Him, and keep His commandments and obey His voice; you shall serve Him and hold fast to Him" (Deut. 13:4). "That he [the ruler] may learn to fear the Lord his God and be careful to observe all the words of this law and these statutes" (Deut. 17:19).

On the inauguration of the new monarchy Samuel admonished, "If you fear the Lord and serve Him and obey His voice, and do not rebel against the commandment of the Lord, then both you and the king who reigns over you will continue following the Lord your God" (1 Sam. 12:14). David testified, "I am a friend to all who fear you, to all who follow your precepts" (Ps. 119:63, NIV). Solomon completed his sermon in the book of Ecclesiastes by saying, "Let us hear the conclusion of the whole matter: fear God and keep His commandments, for this is man's all" (Eccl. 12:13).

The "blameless and upright Job," who "feared God and shunned evil" (Job 1:1, 2), declared, "Behold, the fear of the Lord, that is wisdom, and to depart from evil is understanding" (Job 28:28).

We need more godly fear today than ever before. Our current world has a disrespect for God that is alarming! Society has a casualness, a lack of awe, that is foreign to the heavenly intelligences. At the name of Jehovah angels fold their wings. Commonly in our culture He is thought of as "the man upstairs." Even professed Christians speak the name of the Lord with informal indifference, and many who confess to know and respect the Creator of the universe employ the commonly abbreviated expression OMG. Such is not consistent with "fearing God" in the biblical sense.

Worship styles today often reflect a similar casualness, with worship teams dressing in attire more appropriate for the beach than for the house of the Lord. This attempt to "bring God down to us" does not reflect the honor and respect that the Sovereign of the universe is due. Worship does not bring Him *down* to us—it raises us *up* to Him. Should worshippers today confront the awesome majesty of the divine, they would make haste to cover their faces and repent of their cavalier demeanor. We need a healthy respect when approaching the Deity, and to this the angel calls when he cries out, "Fear God and give glory to Him."

The devil and his angels know the reality of the power of God, but they do not cherish His principles—they do not love and worship Him. Although Lucifer wanted to be like the Most High, he desired only God's authority, not His character. The appreciation of God's character lies at the root of Bible faith. "Without faith it is impossible to please Him, for he who comes to God must believe that He is, and that He is a rewarder of those who diligently seek Him" (Heb. 11:6).

Satan charged God with being restrictive and austere, saying that His law was impossible to keep. A proper relationship to our Creator leads us to recognize that such claims are false as we see that God is love and His law is "holy and just and good" (Rom. 7:12). We understand that true freedom and joy exist only in walking the safe path of His will. Not only He is (that is, there is a supreme being who exists and rules the universe) but He rewards those who diligently seek Him. The word "and" in that text is crucial, for it separates those such as the devil who confess His existence of God but reject His character of love. We must know *that* He is and *who* He is.

When Jesus was on earth, the devils acknowledged that He was the Son of God, but they refused to receive Him as a loving God worthy of worship. To "fear" God embraces both concepts. Today true Christians will not only believe that God exists, but will also cherish the wonderful and inspiring attributes of God's character that induce an attitude of worship and a walk worthy of their calling.

Coupled with the invitation to "fear God" is the command to "give glory to Him." How do we do that? Let's look through the Bible and see how it uses that phase. It most certainly has to do with how we express our praise to Him. There were "angels in the sky" when Christ came the first time, offering their praise. "Suddenly there was with the angel a multitude of the heavenly host praising God and saying, 'Glory to God in the highest, and on earth peace, goodwill toward men!' "

(Luke 2:13). We should see Revelation's picture of an angel in the sky inviting the giving of glory to God in connection with what took place at His first coming.

Here's a simple way that we can give glory to our Creator-God. We can eliminate from our vocabulary such words as "lucky" and "fortunate" and replace them with such words as "blessed" or "providential." Think of the difference even this small change will make! Instead of "I was fortunate in getting that promotion at work," say "I was blessed in getting that promotion." Your hearers will instantly know that you are ascribing glory to God for the good thing that happened. They will pick up on the idea that you believe that your life is ordered from above, that there is One whom you recognize as being in charge of your steps. Isn't that biblical? Of course it is! He's the giver of every good gift (James 1:17). Things don't "just happen." "The steps of a good man are ordered by the Lord" (Ps. 37:23).

On the other hand, when we deny God's involvement in our lives by just saying it was "lucky" or "fortunate" that something good happened, we might as well burn incense to the pagan god Meni, the deity of fortune against whose worship Isaiah protested (Isa. 65:11). It's a form of atheism—a denial of the Bible truth that reveals a loving God deeply involved in our everyday lives.

Some years ago, for a surprise gift, I presented my wife with a new Chrysler PT Cruiser, a car she had long admired. It's been a good car for us, providing reliable transportation through almost a decade. A short time ago we completed a 500-mile trip from northern to southern California, traveling along Interstate 5, passing through a somewhat barren region of about 200 miles, then over the "Grapevine" pass just north of Los Angeles. The next day after we returned, I heard a discomforting "slapping" sound, and, remembering the advice of my auto mechanic, surmised that the timing belt might be complaining of old age and fatigue. I drove it immediately to his shop, and he confirmed that the belt was crying desperately for replacement.

Later, with some degree of amazement, he showed it to me. Not only was the rubber belt split in a section of some 15 inches, but many of the molded teeth on the belt were missing or greatly diminished in size. One part of the belt had three teeth in a row completely gone.

The mechanic assured me that it could easily have caused the engine to cease functioning and led to catastrophic engine failure.

Was I merely "fortunate" that the timing belt didn't disintegrate while driving through that remote stretch of Interstate 5? Was I just "lucky" that the car engine didn't die and suffer serious damage while climbing the ascents of the Grapevine? The prospect of such things bring nothing but a shudder to one's spine. No, I was neither "fortunate" nor "lucky." I was blessed. As is our custom, we pray each time we begin a journey, be it for 500 or 5 miles. Believing that the hand of the Lord guides us and sustains us in life, whether during travel on Interstate 5 or the entire journey of life, we give God constant glory for all His goodness and protection. Though life is not free of bad things (the cost of the repair was more than $1,000) even for Christians, how often it is true that looking back we can praise Him that it wasn't as terrible as it could have been. In so many ways we can "give God glory." Saying "It was a blessing" instead of "I was fortunate" is just one.

We encourage all to use the word "blessing" instead of "luck," "providential" instead of "fortunate." In this way you will be giving God the glory. "Therefore by Him let us continually offer the sacrifice of praise to God, that is, the fruit of our lips, giving thanks to His name" (Heb. 13:15). "If anyone suffers as a Christian, let him not be ashamed, but let him glorify God in this matter" (1 Peter 4:16). Abraham "did not waver through unbelief regarding the promise of God, but was strengthened in his faith and gave glory to God" (Rom. 4:20, NIV).

But giving glory to God goes much deeper than merely what we say. Another way that Scripture tells that we can "glorify God" is in the manner in which we take care of our bodies. Our physical bodies are "fearfully and wonderfully made," the work of a Master Designer. Daily we learn more and more about their complexity and amazing capabilities. The Creator has lent them to us as a gift, entrusting us with the responsibility to care for them properly.

Paul wrote to the church at Corinth, "Do you not know that your body is the temple of the Holy Spirit who is in you, whom you have from God, and you are not your own? For you were bought at a price;

therefore glorify God in your body and in your spirit, which are God's" (1 Cor. 6:19, 20). In the same letter he counseled, "Therefore, whether you eat or drink, or whatever you do, do all to the glory of God" (1 Cor. 10:31).

The messages of the three angels brings into view the understanding of correct principles of temperance and self-control. We may define temperance as abstaining from things harmful and judiciously using those beneficial. This is vital because the Lord's Spirit communicates to us through our brains. It is through the impressions and convictions sent to us in our minds that God speaks to us. If intemperate habits weaken and befuddle our minds, it inhibits their ability to grasp and appreciate the lofty concepts He would like to share with us.

Why is this especially important in the last days? Because the test that looms ahead, as revealed in the messages of the three angels, will require the strongest faith ever. To survive the coming ordeal will demand that our physical and mental condition be optimum. Our connection with God will have to be unrestricted and unhindered for us to live through the times ahead. Satan's desire, of course, is to lead us into the path of indulgence whereby we disqualify ourselves from the race. It is his purpose to push us in the direction opposite of temperance and self-control so as to heighten his influence over our weakened selves.

A while back we were having trouble with our computer cable service. When I called the technician, one of the first things he asked me to do was to check the connection between the cable and the modem. He wanted to make sure that the coaxial cable was properly secured and that the "pin" was clean and straight, unhindered by corrosion.

Similarly, God wants to communicate with us through our brains. If we abuse our health through poor habits, we limit or retard the process. By upholding Bible temperance principles, we can ensure that we will hear the Lord's voice. Particularly in the last days, when it is of utmost importance that we have a clear understanding of God's will and when Satan will be exercising his powers of deception in ways we haven't seen before, we need sharp intellects and clear minds.

The prophet Daniel is an excellent example of how the correct application of temperance guidelines prepared him for the trials he would encounter and the service he would render. When the officials in charge at court assigned him and his Hebrew companions the royal diet, they opted instead for a simple plate of natural foods: "vegetables." And after being tested, they were found to be many times the superior of those who had eaten the king's fare (Dan. 1:18-20).

Today we need our brains to be operating at optimal efficiency, as well as having our bodies in the best condition possible to withstand the trials of the last days. The messages of the three angels includes a call to healthful living. By this we "give Him glory."

CHAPTER 7

"FOR THE HOUR OF HIS JUDGMENT HAS COME"

We will examine the subject of God's judgment, as revealed in the messages of the three angels, in three parts. First, we'll take a brief look at the fact and the phases of the judgment. Second, we'll study the necessity of this particular judgment brought to view in Revelation 14. And third, we'll give attention to its timing. As a result, we will see that a vital phase of God's judgment, one which must conclude before Christ's return, began in the year 1844. This adds incredible momentum to the messages of the angels. One of the last items on God's agenda has already started, bearing testimony that His Advent is very near.

The Fact of God's Judgment

Throughout Scripture we find the teaching of the judgment revealed. Accountability and responsibility are built into the fabric of God's system of governing. The opening saga of earth's story, contained in Genesis 1-3, includes a chapter on judgment and accountability. God's visit to Adam and Eve after their sin is a model and a prophecy of the judgment to be projected on a global screen.

Other references to the judgment include Solomon's parting exhortation as he concludes the book of Ecclesiastes. "Let us hear the conclusion of the whole matter: fear God and keep His commandments, for this is man's all. For God will bring every work into judgment, including every secret thing, whether it is good or whether it is evil" (Eccl. 12:13, 14). Previously we noted the similarity between this passage and the message of the first angel, who calls the earth to "fear God."

Jesus affirmed the reality of the judgment. He said, "You have heard that it was said to those of old, 'You shall not murder,' and whoever murders will be in danger of the judgment. But I say to you that whoever is angry with his brother without a cause shall be in danger of the judgment" (Matt. 5:21, 22). Jesus revealed that He, the Son of God who experienced life on this planet, will be the cosmic judge. "The Father judges no one, but has entrusted all judgment to the Son" (John 5:22, NIV).

Paul spoke of the judgment often. To the Areopagite philosophers on Mars Hill he said, "In the past God overlooked such ignorance, but now he commands all people everywhere to repent. For he has set a day when he will judge the world with justice by the man he has appointed" (Acts 17:30, 31, NIV). When Paul "reasoned about righteousness, self-control, and the judgment to come, Felix was afraid and answered, 'Go away for now; when I have a convenient time I will call for you'" (Acts 24:25, 26). The apostle wrote to the Corinthian believers, "For we must all appear before the judgment seat of Christ, that each one may receive the things done in the body, according to what he has done, whether good or bad" (2 Cor. 5:10). In the book of Hebrews we read, "As it is appointed to men to die once, but after this the judgment" (Heb. 9:27).

We'll discuss this in greater detail later, but note that the difference in Revelation's proclamation by the first angel is one of timing. Whereas other Bible references point to this event as being in the future, the angel of Revelation 14 speaks of the judgment as being a present reality as he loudly proclaims that the hour of His judgment "has come." Actually, the verb tense for "has come" is in the aorist form *(elthen)* and could be rendered simply, "The hour of His judgment came."

The word "for" is especially vital, as it connects the phrases "fear God and give glory to Him" and "the hour of His judgment has come." The word "for" in the original is *oti*, which often has a strong causal implication* and thus establishes a direct link between the phrases. It is because the hour of His judgment *has* come that we should fear God and give Him glory. Interestingly, Paul used the same line of reasoning and the very same word *oti* in his discourse on Mars Hill. There he preached, "Truly, these times of ignorance God overlooked, but now commands all men everywhere to repent, because *[oti]* He has appointed a day on which He will judge the world in righteousness" (Acts 17:30, 31).

Both Paul and the first angel call attention to the need of preparation in expectation of the judgment, but the difference between the apostle's sermon and the message of the first angel is that while Paul used the future tense in describing a coming judgment, the angel of Revelation states categorically, "The hour of His judgment has come." If, back then, Paul considered it necessary for "all men everywhere" to repent, in view of a coming judgment, can you imagine the sermon he would deliver if he were alive today and knew that we were presently living in the hour of His judgment! He would be preaching it not only from Mars Hill, but from every hill and everywhere.

The message of the first angel is of particular importance because an event, critical to the completion of God's plan, has begun. Impetus and urgency add strength to the voice of the angel because of the judgment. The phase of the judgment that must conclude before He returns has started.

Phases of God's Judicial Process

To gain a perspective on how God's system of judgment works, we may consider how people conduct judicial proceedings in our world. What happens in a typical court setting? We find that earthly trials include separate and distinct phases that pertain first to the investigation of the facts, next a decision is made based on the facts as the judge applies the law, and finally the disposition and execution of the sentence takes place.

First, there occurs the trial phase, which introduces evidence and questions witnesses. The investigative portion seeks to ascertain the facts in the matter at hand, as determined by the finder of facts, be it judge or jury. This "investigative phase" is a separate and distinct segment of the judicial process. At the conclusion of the process the court makes a determination as to whether the one charged is guilty or not. Following will come the announcement of the sentence and its implementation. Such phases of trial in an earthly court setting are similar to God's system of divine justice.

The Bible reveals that God has an investigative phase of His justice system. The prophet Daniel received a vision of the auspicious proceeding. "I watched till thrones were put in place, and the Ancient of Days was seated; His garment was white as snow, and the hair of His head was like pure wool. His throne was fiery flame, its wheels a burning fire; a fiery stream issued and came forth from before Him. A thousand thousands ministered to Him; ten thousand times ten thousand stood before Him. The court was seated, and the books were opened" (Dan. 7:9, 10).

The language couldn't be clearer. The opening of books speaks loudly to a process of investigation and inquiry. The close of Daniel's book contains the promise "At that time your people shall be delivered, everyone who is found written in the book" (Dan. 12:1). The phrase "found written" in the passage obviously contemplates an investigation that takes place prior to deliverance.

The phase of judgment addressed by the first angel in Revelation 14:7 concerns the process involving the opening of the books in heaven prior to Jesus' return. This is fitting, since a few verses later, in Revelation 14:14, we have a picture of Jesus' arriving in the clouds, a depiction of His second advent. The message of the three angels has preceded His return, including the announcement that the hour of His judgment has commenced. It also agrees with the picture Daniel saw in his vision, in that the setting of the heavenly court scene (Dan. 7:9, 10) takes place before the destruction of the beast/horn power (verse 11), which happens, according to Paul's analysis in 2 Thessalonians 2:1-10, at the return of Jesus.

In addition, it harmonizes with the close of the book of Revelation. An angel announces to John, "He who is unjust, let him be unjust still; he who is filthy, let him be filthy still; he who is righteous, let him be righteous still; he who is holy, let him be holy still" (Rev. 22:11). The declaration obviously indicates that decisions have been finalized, the determination of which is the function and purpose of the judgment. That this process has been completed prior to Christ's return is clear from the fact that the very next verse says, "And behold, I am coming quickly, and My reward is with Me, to give to everyone according to his work" (verse 12). According to the sequence of the verses then, the finalization of every decision for life or death, recognized by the heavenly court, will have come to its completion before Jesus returns.

Christ Himself said, "As it was in the days of Noah, so it will be at the coming of the Son of Man" (Matt. 24:37, NIV). The parallels between the two events include the violent and godless condition of society, the warning of the approaching event, the incredible and blind ignorance displayed by the population in general concerning the impending event, and the disproportionate number of those who reject the message. Of course, destruction in Noah's day occurred from flood while at the end it will result from fire. Salvation came to Noah by way of an ark, and at the end it will be by way of a cloud.

Still another parallel bears a direct application to our study. We have seen that prior to the salvation/destruction event at Christ's return, all decisions will have been made final, something brought to view in a striking manner in the story of Noah, in that seven days before the Flood struck, Noah and his family entered the ark "and the Lord shut him in" (Gen. 7:16). By that time, everyone had made his or her decision to be either in or out of the ark, choices recognized by heaven. We see the finality of those decisions demonstrated by the door of the ark being closed, but it would be a full week before the storms raged and the earth destroyed. There was a pre-event judgment in Noah's world, and there will be a pre-event judgment in ours.

God's hand wrote on Belshazzar's palace wall, "You have been weighed in the balances, and found wanting" (Dan. 5:27) before the ruler met his fate. Jesus said the time will come before His return that the "holy will remain holy, and the unholy will remain unholy." Before His second advent, that aspect of the judgment must have concluded.

The "Necessity" of a Pre-Advent Judgment

Some might ask, Why does God, the Omniscient One, need to look through records to see who will be saved? Doesn't He know already? The answer is yes, of course He knows. But there are actually at least two compelling reasons He does search the "books." First, the Bible reveals that it is God's desire that His administration be understood as absolutely fair—that it is transparent to the highest degree. Satan had charged God with being arbitrary and unjust. The prosecution of this inquiry concerning God's fairness lies at the very core of the controversy that has unfolded. God has deemed it appropriate that records be kept and accounts be tabulated so that the evidence is overwhelming as to His fairness and justice.

We must expand our view to see that the judgment isn't just about us. It's God's name that is on trial. In a very real sense it is the hour of "His" judgment. The outcome of the process will be the vindication of His holy name. Someday "every knee should bow" (Phil. 2:10) and the saints will erupt in a spontaneous anthem of praise singing, "Great and marvelous are Your works, Lord God Almighty! Just and true are Your ways, O King of the saints! Who shall not fear You, O Lord, and glorify Your name? For You alone are holy. For all nations shall come and worship before You, for Your judgments have been manifested" (Rev. 15:3, 4).

You and I have the privilege of playing an important part in this trial, in that as we allow His Spirit to work a miracle in our lives, it brings an answer to the charges that Satan brought: that God is unfair and that it is impossible to live in a way pleasing to Him. The lives of His saints constitute "exhibit A," recorded in the ledgers of heaven, to refute the allegations raised by the devil.

This phase of the judgment takes place prior to Jesus' coming in the clouds for yet a second reason. The court does not convene because God does not know the condition of the hearts of all humanity. He already has in mind who are to be saved. Rather the judgment's direct benefit is for His loyal angels who, although wiser than humans and excelling in strength, both physical and mental, are not omniscient. They can't read the heart and discern its motives, which is at the crux of the judgment. So before the Lord brings into the undefiled environment of heaven those from Planet Earth who were sinners, He graciously allows the angels the opportunity to see things as He does.

Because this is such a vital concept relating to the process and purpose of the judgment, let us give some attention to it. The judgment has to do with sin, and sin is a matter of the inmost nature. We often speak of sin as being an act, but it's much deeper than that. It touches the invisible aspects of thought, motive, and intent. Jesus alluded to this when He said that the one who harbors hatred has already committed murder and the one who lusts in his heart has already committed adultery. Acts of iniquity are simply the outgrowth of those principles cherished within the heart. They are the symptoms of what exists inside.

One day while riding in the back seat of our car as a youngster, my mom happened to look back at me and said, "Open your shirt!" I had no idea why she would say such a thing, but I did, revealing a chest speckled generously with the red splotches of measles. Having seen some suspicious markings on my face, she wanted further confirmation. What did my mother do then? When we got home, did she take a cloth and fill it with flour and blot it all over my chest and my face to cover the spots? Would that have taken care of my condition? No, the red blotches were merely the outward sign of something that existed much deeper.

So it is with sin. Sin is a matter of the mind and heart. It has to do with how we think. Outward deeds of wickedness only exhibit the problem. It reminds us of a sign attached to the face of a broken clock that read, "Don't blame my hands; the problem's on the inside."

Because sin involves the way we think, it's fair that God judges us according to our inner nature—that is, He judges us not only according to what we have done, but also according to what we would have done if the opportunity had arisen. That's why Jesus could say that the religious leaders of His day were "guilty" of the crimes of their ancestors. At the close of His ministry He issued a chilling indictment: "Therefore the wisdom of God also said, 'I will send them prophets and apostles, and some of them they will kill and persecute,' that the blood of all the prophets which was shed from the foundation of the world may be required of this generation, from the blood of Abel to the blood of Zechariah who perished between the altar and the temple. Yes, I say to you, it shall be required of this generation" (Luke 11:49-51).

Those to whom Christ spoke had not literally carried out the things He said. But it's fair nonetheless, because their hearts were in the same condition as those of their forefathers. Had they lived back then, their acts would have been the same. It is the inward heart and its condition that God is most concerned about. The acts are simply the outgrowth of the thought patterns that lurk inside.

Abel, of course, perished at the hand of his older brother Cain in the dawn of human history. Zechariah was murdered in the days of King Joash about eight centuries before Christ (2 Chron. 24:20-22). Apparently the heinous murder made an indelible impression on the Israelite nation and was long remembered. To get the "flavor" of Christ's statement, be aware that the book that we call 2 Chronicles occupied the last position in the order of the Scriptures used in Jesus' day. In other words, Christ's statement, with a large brush stroke, covered basically all the history recorded by the Old Testament. Today we'd say, "From Genesis to Malachi."

Here is a most interesting concept on how God views guilt and sin. How could the Jews of Jesus' day be guilty of Cain's sin, or the sin of those who murdered Zechariah? Is that fair? They weren't alive then. What Jesus was saying was that the Jewish leaders of His time were cherishing the same principles as did Cain, whose story appeared early in the Scriptures, as well as those who stoned the prophet Zechariah, whose account was part of the final book of the Bible of His time.

Because they nourished the same spirit as did their evil forefathers, it follows that *had they been alive* in the former times, their behaviors would have been exactly the same. Since sin is a matter of thought and mind, they were guilty of those same sins, because had they the opportunity, had they been alive during those events, they would have acted out the same behavior. Their hearts were beating in harmony with the rhythm of wickedness. It is the heart and its motives that God looks at. While it may be true that they weren't alive back then, because their hearts were just as wicked as the people who actually were, the religious leaders of Jesus' time were just as guilty. They would have participated in those same deeds.

Likewise, we should note, God looks with favor on those who, given the opportunity, would have rendered works of righteousness. Thus Jesus could say regarding a poor widow who dropped two mites into the offering chest that she had given more than the rest (Luke 21:3). It was the condition of her heart that God saw and evaluated. "Man looks at the outward appearance, but the Lord looks at the heart" (1 Sam. 16:7).

Sin is a matter of the heart, and only God can read its intents.

Angels, good or bad, cannot. But prior to Jesus' return to earth, God chooses to disclose to the loyal angels what He already knows. He opens the books in the presence of numberless hosts. Why does He do that? Can't He just ask the angels to "trust Him" that the humans coming to heaven are safe to save—that those redeemed from wicked Planet Earth won't pollute the sacred halls of heaven? Yes, He could, but God's character is in the direction of transparency and confidence-building. It is His supreme desire that His creatures—the loyal angels—be comfortable with the decisions made.

God of the "Second Mile"

The Lord is the "God of the second mile." During Christ's time on earth, Roman soldiers controlled Judea. By their rules of the occupation, a solder could conscript anyone to carry his duffel bag a distance of up to one mile. No matter how busy you were, no matter what you were doing, a legionnaire could interrupt you and compel you to shoulder his bag. It grated on the nationalistic minds of the Jews no end. Imagine their shock when Jesus said that if one asked you to go one mile, then go two (Matt. 5:41).

When Jesus spoke about the subjects of His kingdom being willing to "go the second mile," it was because that is His nature. The Sermon on the Mount is a revelation of His character, one that He invites us, through His grace, to copy. He, as we will see as we review a number of stories from the Bible, is the God of the second mile. No—He is the God of the third, the fourth, the thousandth mile. How is this relevant to our study of the judgment? Just this: it is true that He is not required to open the records to the view of the angels, but He does so anyway. So when we speak of the "necessity" of the investigative judgment that takes place before His coming, we confess that it really isn't necessary at least as far as what God must have to make the right decisions. He knows all and is the Sovereign God. No one can halt the arm of the Almighty and say, "What doest thou?" (Job 9:12, KJV).

And yet the Bible clearly reveals the fact of a pre-Advent judgment. We conclude that it is a part of His plan, because He goes beyond what is "required." He wishes to do things in a way that will inspire confidence that justice has been done. God desires that the heavenly hosts should know that the ones coming to heaven are free of the virus of sin and will not contaminate the celestial environment with iniquity. Daniel received a view of this very event, as he saw in vision that "the court was seated, and the books were opened" (Dan. 7:10). Prior to His return, in the presence of the myriads of heavenly hosts, the Lord opens the books and allows them to see what He already knows: that the hearts of all those coming to live in the purity of heaven have been cleansed from sin.

That this "second mile" characteristic of God's benevolent administration pertains to His system of justice is clearly shown by reviewing a number of stories recorded in Scripture. Though there are many, we'll look at just a few of them. They accurately reveal a picture of a loving God who inquires before He acts—conducts an investigation before sentencing. Again, it is not because the Lord doesn't know. He knows everything! Rather, He does it because it is His nature to demonstrate His absolute fairness and transparent justice. Thank God for His character of *agape* love and unimpeachable justice!

---

* W. F. Arndt and F. W. Gingrich, *A Greek-English Lexicon of the New Testament*, p. 593.

CHAPTER 8

BIBLE STORIES THAT ILLUSTRATE GOD'S SYSTEM OF JUSTICE

The very first episode dealing with sin recorded in Scripture sets the pattern for God's system of justice. The Lord had given clear instruction regarding the tree of the knowledge of good and evil, but the serpent deceived Eve and she ate from it, then gave the fruit to her husband Adam. Thus they sinned against the express command of the Lord. They believed the talking snake who had done nothing for them rather than the Creator-God who had done everything for them. As soon as they sinned, they became aware of their nakedness. "Then the eyes of both of them were opened, and they knew that they were naked; and they sewed fig leaves together and made themselves coverings" (Gen. 3:7). One of the first consequences of the Fall was the consciousness of shame, a feeling unknown to human beings before then.

When the Lord came to visit them in the "cool of the day," "Adam and his wife hid themselves from the presence of the Lord God among the trees of the garden. Then the Lord God called to Adam and said to him, 'Where are you?' So he said, 'I heard Your voice in the garden, and I was afraid because I was naked; and I hid myself'" (verses 8-10). Fear was the next consequence of sin.

"And He said, 'Who told you that you were naked? Have you eaten from the tree of which I commanded you that you should not eat?'" (verse 11). Notice this amazing portrayal of God's system of justice at work. It will serve as a model for all further dispositions, especially His final judicial process. In a matter of moments God would impose the sentence. The human couple would be expelled from their beautiful garden home and deprived of the life-perpetuating fruit from the tree of life.

Though devastating, that sentence was not as harsh as it could have been. God mingled it with mercy. The consequence of sin, as plainly declared by the Lord, was death. It was death that Adam and Eve deserved. By their transgression they had forfeited their opportunity to live. But the Lord put into operation His plan that had been in His mind from eternity. It pledged His life in the place of theirs. The "Lamb slain from the foundation of the world" (Rev. 13:8) would become their Savior. The curse would fall, as it must, but it would descend upon Him and not them.

But notice how God's system of justice worked. We might ask, Did God "need" to inquire if Adam had eaten the fruit? Did He in His omniscience not know that the man had disobeyed the divine command? Of course He knew! Yet He stooped to speak in a language that all could understand. He went about His work in a way that would inspire confidence that the sentence resulted from a position of knowledge. He inquired before taking action.

The manner in which He administered justice at the first occurrence of sin would become the model for later events. He says, "I am the Lord, I change not" (Mal. 3:6, KJV). It would become the pattern for the way He would deal with sin in its final disposition. What would give us the idea that His approach to sin at the end would be any different than the way He dealt with it at the beginning? The Bible reveals that before the gavel of justice fell in Eden, God conducted an investigation. Likewise at the end of time, before the verdicts of eternal life or eternal death—before the return of the Savior who comes "with His reward"—a phase of judgment involving investigation will have been completed.

One of the most striking examples of this aspect of God's gracious character is the story involving the destruction of Sodom and Gomorrah. If unchecked, the wickedness residing there would have spread and worsened. God had to do something. He had to take action. But before He did, He would conduct an investigation. The Lord would give the situation a second look, a final review. Now, aware as we are about God's all-knowing wisdom as revealed in the Bible, this doesn't seem to add up. Yet look carefully as to how He Himself described the purpose of His visit. See in this passage the heart of a deity who desires to be known as a God of justice, one who goes the second mile to demonstrate His fairness and equity. See in this text the one who inquires before He takes action. "Then the Lord said, 'The outcry against Sodom and Gomorrah is so great and their sin so grievous that I will go down and see if what they have done is as bad as the outcry that has reached me. If not, I will know'" (Gen. 18:20, 21, NIV).

When you think about it, it is one of the most remarkable statements in all of Scripture! The Almighty speaks as if He comes into the situation needing to investigate the sin of Sodom before executing judgment against it. No, it doesn't add up according to what the Bible teaches about God's omniscience. Of course He knew all about Sodom! Nothing is hidden from His eyes. Not only did He know about their wicked deeds, but He also discerned their hearts of rebellion and stubborn resistance. Thus He would have been entirely within His divine right to send the fire upon these cities without having made any formal inquiry into their iniquity, without making a personal visit through His emissaries the angels. Yet He chose to speak in a way that humans could understand. The Lord stooped to our level to inspire us that His justice would come from a position of knowledge. Such is the wondrous and gracious character of the one who rules the universe!

The third example we'll look at that illustrates the principle of investigation before action involves the city of Babylon. Historians identify the kingdom as "neo-Babylon," because of a previous kingdom of Babylon ruled by Hammurabi, a contemporary of Abraham, more than a millennium earlier. Nabopolassar, the father of Nebuchadnezzar, chiseled out the historical Babylon that the Bible talks about. God gave it mighty privileges and actually used it to discipline wayward Judah. The Lord Himself said of the Babylonians, "They worked for Me" (Eze. 29:20). The sudden rise of Babylon to power was the subject of a special prophecy revealed to Habakkuk (Hab. 1:5-11).

Though granted lofty privileges, Babylon in the end refused to comply with the divine plan and forfeited its privileged position. The "fall of Babylon," which occurred in a very literal sense, became the metaphor for Revelation's description of the fall of the church, both in the Middle Ages and in the post-Reformation period.

Babylon became the symbolic seat of Satan's kingdom and his counterfeit of God's capital, the New Jerusalem. Notice the biblical comparisons of ancient Babylon and God's city. If you look at an architectural layout of Nebuchadnezzar's capital, you will see that that it roughly comprises the shape of a square.* Not a perfect square, though, as it's a little skewed or distorted. Scripture describes God's eternal city as being four-square (Rev. 21:16). Babylon was known as the "golden city" (Isa. 14:4) while the Bible depicts the New Jerusalem as "pure gold, like clear glass" (Rev. 21:18). Its pavement is "pure gold, like transparent glass" (verse 21).

Ancient Babylon had a river running through it, the mighty Euphrates. God's city has the river of life flowing through it. Though now nothing but dusty ruins, ancient Babylon aspired to be eternal. "You said, 'I shall be a lady forever'" (Isa. 47:7). But God's city is the one that will never crumble into dust. Babylon ascribed to itself the position belonging to the omnipotent one, claiming, "I am, and there is no one else besides me" (Isa. 47:8), usurping the claim of the Lord who declares, "I, even I, am the Lord, and apart from me there is no savior (Isa. 43:11, NIV). "I am the First and I am the Last; besides Me there is no God" (Isa. 44:6). Babylon's king became the express image of Lucifer, as described in Isaiah 14.

Ancient Babylon grew in its wickedness and became ripe for punishment. On the eve of its destruction, as the armies of Cyrus approached the fortified capital, Belshazzar reveled in defiant mockery. He well knew of the dream of the metallic statue given to his grandfather, one that portrayed the march of the monarchies, the parade of nations. A "chest of silver" would follow the "head of gold." But the Babylonian ruler denied the prophecy and the God who spoke it. Furthermore, he made sport of the predictions of the Deity whose sanctuary furniture and utensils were on display in his temple museum, evidence in his mind that the Babylonian god Marduk was superior to Jehovah.

Hearing reports of the advances of Cyrus' troops, yet confident in his double-walled citadel with its multiyear supply of food calculated to withstand the hardest siege, Belshazzar summoned the articles from Solomon's Temple to use as his goblets while he held a feast to his gods.

In blasphemy beyond words he raised his cup, one taken from the Temple of God in Jerusalem, and gave a toast to his deities. Boisterous laughter and unrestrained boasting flowed freely with the royal wine.

Suddenly faces blanched and knees quaked as those at the banquet spotted letters of fire inscribed by a bloodless hand on the plastered wall. A strained, tense silence reigned where moments before had been hilarity. The Bible reports, "They brought the gold vessels that had been taken from the temple of the house of God which had been in Jerusalem; and the king and his lords, his wives, and his concubines drank from them. They drank wine, and praised the gods of gold and silver, bronze and iron, wood and stone. In the same hour the fingers of a man's hand appeared and wrote opposite the lampstand on the plaster of the wall of the king's palace; and the king saw the part of the hand that wrote. Then the king's countenance changed, and his thoughts troubled him, so that the joints of his hips were loosened and his knees knocked against each other" (Dan. 5:3-6).

No one could decipher the cryptic inscription: "MENE, MENE, TEKEL, UPHARSIN" (verse 25). Not even the royal advisors could interpret them. At last, they sent for the aged Daniel, now nearing 90. Politely waving aside the promised reward for unraveling the mystery, he proceeded to explain the coded message.

But before doing so, he had something to say to the haughty ruler. With words that must have chilled Belshazzar to the bone, Daniel reminded him of Nebuchadnezzar's experience when "his heart was lifted up, and his spirit was hardened in pride" (verse 20). The prophet recounted how Nebuchadnezzar had been "driven from the sons of men, his heart was made like the beasts, and his dwelling was with the wild donkeys" (verse 21). Bringing his brief sermon to a razor-sharp close, Daniel said, "But you his [grand]son, Belshazzar, have not humbled your heart, although you knew all this. And you have lifted yourself up against the Lord of heaven. . . . And the God who holds your breath in His hand and owns all your ways, you have not glorified" (verses 22, 23). The phrase "although you knew all this" reveals an important component to God's system of justice. The divine process of judgment takes into account the knowledge (or the opportunity to gain knowledge) that a person possesses.

Then Daniel turned to the fiery message on the wall and explained its meaning. "Mene: God has numbered your kingdom, and finished it. Tekel: You have been weighed in the balances, and found wanting. Peres: Your kingdom has been divided, and given to the Medes and Persians" (verses 27, 28).

The word translated "numbered" *(mene)* appears twice for emphasis. An accounting term, it implies that the moral ledger of Belshazzar and his kingdom had come under divine audit. Heaven had reviewed and double-checked it, reaching the conclusion of "spiritual bankruptcy."

The metaphor then shifts from an accounting image to one of testing metal. "Tekel: You have been weighed in the balances, and found wanting." The concept of scales as a symbol of the operation of justice is well known and documented. Figuratively speaking, the ore had been examined and found worthless. How accurately the words of the Lord through Jeremiah applied to the pagan despot: "The bellows blow fiercely to burn away the lead with fire; the refining goes on in vain: the wicked are not purged out. They are called rejected silver, because the Lord has rejected them" (Jer. 6:29, 30, NIV). The same grace that God exercised toward Nebuchadnezzar, resulting in his salvation, He also offered to his grandson Belshazzar, but with the opposite reaction and result.

Now, having announced that the inquiry and investigation have been accomplished ("God has numbered your kingdom. . . . You have been weighed in the balances") the sentence is pronounced. The kingdom will be shattered and given into the hands of the Medes and Persians. That very night Belshazzar perished, and the prophecy became fulfilled. Note that the incident clearly spells out the sequence of divine justice. The Lord specifically indicated that an investigation had been conducted before anything else happened. An inquiry took place before the sentencing. God already knew the wickedness of Babylon, as He had known the evil of Sodom and the sin of Eden, but true to His character of stooping to use language that humans understand, He gave a "second look" before issuing the sentence. If it was His approach toward ancient Babylon, why would we expect Him to deal any differently with apocalyptic Babylon?

Additional stories in Scripture bear the principle out, but these three satisfactorily emphasize the methodology of God's system of justice. An "investigative judgment" will conclude prior to His returning with His reward.

---

* http://www.bible-history.com/babylonia/BabyloniaHistory_of_Babylonia.htm.

CHAPTER 9

HOW CAN WE KNOW WHEN THE JUDGMENT BEGINS?

The Lord said through the psalmist, "When I choose the proper time, I will judge uprightly" (Ps. 75:2). Because, as has been established, the investigative phase of God's judgment must finish before He comes back, and because the cry of the first angel is "The hour of His judgment has come," we must ask, Can we determine in Scripture when it commences? The answer is yes. To do this we must spend some time studying the prophecies of Daniel.

It is not part of God's plan to give to us the "day and hour" of His return, but He has consistently provided "waymarks" by which we can know when it is near. Days before His death His disciples asked Him, "When will these things be? And what will be the sign of Your coming, and of the end of the age?" (Matt. 24:3). Jesus proceeded to outline several significant events that would serve as precursors to His return. He said, "When you see all these things, know that it is near— at the doors!" (verse 33).

In addition to the signs that Christ made known to His followers, the Scriptures have also provided us with a crucial date in God's timetable: the beginning of His investigative judgment in heaven. Though human eyes did not see the event (excepting the prophet Daniel in vision), we know by faith that it most certainly came to pass.

The Vision of Daniel 8 and the Cleansing of the Sanctuary

A most important prophecy in the book of Daniel helps us to know when the investigative judgment began. It is crucial to our understanding the relevance of the message of the first angel, "The hour of His judgment has come." Having seen the heavenly pre-

Advent judgment in vision during the "first year of Belshazzar king of Babylon" (Dan. 7:1), two years later the prophet received a second vision. Like the other "outline" prophecies in the book of Daniel, it ranged from "now" all the way to the "end." Thus the statue dream of Daniel 2 referred to the Babylon of Daniel's day and extended to the kingdom of the stone (Dan. 2:35), representing God's eternal kingdom. Then the vision featuring the wild animals of Daniel 7 began with Babylon and reached to God's kingdom, which "is an everlasting kingdom" (Dan. 7:27). In the same way, the vision of Daniel 8, which contains the prophecy that we're looking at, takes the prophet from the reign of Medo-Persia to the "end." Addressing this point, the angel said, "Understand, son of man, that the vision refers to the time of the end" (Dan. 8:17).

Our objective is to find the beginning point of God's pre-Advent judgment pictured in Daniel 7. We believe that we can do that on the basis of three "witnesses" found in Daniel 8:14. 1. The structural comparison between chapters 7 and 8 of Daniel shows that the "cleansing of the sanctuary" occupies the same place in its vision as the judgment scene does in chapter 7. 2. The legal connotation of the word "cleansed" which is *tsadaq*, as used in Daniel 8:14. 3. A study of the service of Yom Kippur is brought to view by the phrase "cleansing of the sanctuary."

A structural comparison between the contents of chapters 7 and 8 of Daniel, if you were to line up the component parts, reveals that the place taken by the heavenly court scene in the seventh chapter is occupied by something called the "cleansing of the sanctuary" in chapter 8. It is vital to recognize this parallel. In chapter 7 we find that the judgment scene is the hinge point of the prophecy. Up until that time, it appears that satanic agencies, led by worldly kingdoms represented by wild beasts and followed by a destructive horn power, have been in control.

Then something happens that changes everything. "But the court shall be seated, and they shall take away his dominion, to consume and destroy it forever" (Dan. 7:26). The seating of the heavenly court is crucial to the outcome of the events portrayed. If we reduce the content of the prophecy of chapter 7 to a simple outline, it could read: (1) reign of earthly kingdoms, including the horn power; (2) the inception of God's judgment; and (3) the destruction of earthly kingdoms and the establishment of God's eternal kingdom. In this analysis, the beginning of God's pre-Advent investigative judgment, when "the court was seated and the books were opened," is the turning point in the prophecy. As you read Daniel 7, you will see that a significant transition occurs three different times (Dan. 7:9, 22, 26). The horn power goes about its lethal activity, but then "a judgment" takes place (verse 22).

In the parallel prophecy of Daniel 8 we again see animals that represent earthly kingdoms, but this time they are not predators but "clean" ones, such as would be suitable for sacrifice in the sanctuary. A heavenly representative explains to the prophet that the ram in the vision represents "the kings of Media and Persia" (Dan. 8:20). By the way, pay particular attention to the fact that the word "kings" is plural. The ram doesn't represent just one king or individual but the kingdom of Medo-Persia, ruled by various monarchs. It is a vital distinction.

Following the conquest by the goat (specifically identified as the kingdom of Greece), a horn power emerges that wields great power and causes much devastation, just as did the horn power of the vision in chapter 7. In the vision of chapter 8 Daniel again witnesses earthly powers, led by Satan, that seem to be in total command.

Next, in the vision a supernatural being asks a question that anticipates the "turning point" in the prophecy: "How long will the vision be, concerning the daily sacrifices and the transgression of desolation, the giving of both the sanctuary and the host to be trampled under foot?" (Dan. 8:13). This question is the same as inquiring, "How long will it be that evil triumphs? How long will it be that the powers of wickedness prevail? How long will it be that God's truth and His saints get trodden underfoot?" Human beings have pled "How long, O Lord?" ever since sin entered.

In the next verse we find an answer: "For two thousand three hundred days; then the sanctuary shall be cleansed" (verse 14). This must be something of critical importance to be the answer to the momentous question, "How long?" Obviously, it plays a vital role in turning the tide from the onslaught of evil to the triumph of righteousness. From a structural point of view, as we line up the component parts of the vision, we can see that the cleansing of the sanctuary in Daniel 8 occupies the same place as the judgment in the vision of Daniel 7. The cleansing of the sanctuary represents the hinge point in the prophecy, as did the judgment scene in the previous chapter. Before this evil has been victorious while afterward God's justice takes over and the horn power will be "broken without [human] hand" (Dan. 8:25, KJV).

The Sanctuary Cleansing a Hinge Point

The question "How long?" and the answer, "the cleansing of the sanctuary," are the pivot points of the prophecy in Daniel 8. It has to do with the final victory of God, His truth, and His saints. Thus it represents the turning of the tide from evil to good. Sports analysts are always looking to identify the key play that made the difference in a game. Market analysts study trends to pinpoint the moment when the financial momentum shifts. Political analysts attempt to highlight the exact time when a candidate for office makes the turn from defeat to victory. What was it that "changed everything"? The "cleansing of the sanctuary" represents a radical shift in direction of the prophecy, the hinge at which everything changes and leads to the victorious conclusion. Ultimately we know that the answer to "How long?" pertains to the coming of Jesus. That is when Satan and his followers will be overthrown. But since we realize that it is not God's policy to reveal the "day and hour" of Jesus' return, what would be an appropriate answer to the question of "How long?"

Sometimes the Lord answers questions in an indirect way, but one that still provides helpful information. When He was about to ascend to heaven, the disciples asked, "'Lord, will You at this time restore the kingdom to Israel?' And He said to them, 'It is not for you to know times or seasons which the Father has put in His own authority. But you shall receive power when the Holy Spirit has come upon you; and you shall be witnesses to Me in Jerusalem, and in all Judea and Samaria, and to the end of the earth'" (Acts 1:6-8).

Notice that the questions that the 11 posed are not unrelated to the one in Daniel 8:13. The disciples wanted to know about the end of all things. Jesus didn't give them the date when He would restore the kingdom, but He did speak about something that must necessarily take place before that event. It is similar to the question and answer given in Daniel 8. "How long?" anticipates the end of the age. In God's wisdom He chooses not to give us a specific date. However, should the Lord choose to reveal the beginning of His pre-Advent judgment, an event that must happen before His return, that would be very helpful.

If we could know that this important phase of His agenda has started, it would give great encouragement that we are truly living in the last days—indeed, that "the hour of His judgment has come." Can we see in the phrase "the cleansing of the sanctuary" the concept of the pre-Advent judgment? Does it refer to the same event? Yes. Our study will indicate that it is indeed the case. Beside the fact that cleansing of the sanctuary in Daniel 8 lines up with "the court was seated and the books were opened" as reported in Daniel 7, we will see that the phrase "cleansing of the sanctuary" leads us back to a specific service in the Old Testament that typified God's judgment: the Day of Atonement. And we will discover that the word translated "cleansed" actually has a very strong legal nuance.

As we begin this part of our study, we should note that not all Bibles translate Daniel 8:14 with the word "cleansed" (Hebrew: *tsadaq*). This variation then becomes something on which we should spend a few minutes, because it is crucial in understanding when God's pre-Advent judgment begins. It involves what the text means when it says that the sanctuary was to be "cleansed." Newer Bible translations differ in the way they render the verb. You will find, for example, words such as "reconsecrated," "put right," "restored to its proper place," and "justified," to mention a few. It brings up the question: "Is the word 'cleansed' a bad translation?"

Let's briefly examine how Scripture uses *tsadaq*, the word translated "cleansed." We'll look specifically at two things concerning the word: the close connection between it and other words meaning "clean," and its strong legal implications. *Tsadaq* appears 41 times in the Old Testament. Lexicons give it the meanings "be just," "be justified," "be righteous," or "be vindicated."[1] While knowing such meanings is helpful, sometimes a better way to catch the flavor of a word is to see how it gets used in various contexts.

Why did the King James translators translate it as "cleansed"? For one thing, five times we find *tsadaq* employed in close association with words such as "clean" and "pure." One example is Job 4:17: "Can a mortal be more righteous *(tsadaq)* than God? Can a man be more pure than His Maker?" In this passage of poetry we find that the author has skillfully used words to construct a rhyme of concept between the two stanzas, what scholars call "synonymous parallelism." "A mortal" in the first line is echoed by "a man" in the second. "Be more righteous" in the first is repeated by "be more pure" in the second. "God" in the first line is equivalent to "Maker" in the second. "Pure" thus corresponds to "righteous" *(tsadaq).* Such close association in Hebrew poetry reveals a kinship between the word *tsadaq* and "clean."

In Psalm 19:9 we read: "The fear of the Lord is clean, enduring forever; the judgments of the Lord are true and righteous *(tsadaq)* altogether." Here the biblical author places "clean" *(tahor)* in parallel with "righteous" *(tsadaq).* As a result, we see that the idea of "clean," or "pure," is not unrelated or foreign to *tsadaq.* They are synonyms. When the translators of the KJV and NKJV used the word "cleansed," they were not inaccurate. Actually, it is a good rendering.

But there's more. As we shall soon see, the flavor of the word has to do with more than "clean" in a physical sense. In many occurrences we notice a distinct legal aspect associated with it. It suggests the concept of "cleansed" in a forensic context—that is, having one's record purged or cleansed, and consequently a word appropriate in a legal setting. Thus it would fit well as we think of the pre-Advent judgment and what it accomplishes. The result of that tribunal will be to forever "blot out" or "cleanse" the record of the saints by the blood of Jesus. In addition, it will purge and vindicate the name of the Lord from the smudges of Satan's insinuation against Him.

Notice carefully the following passages. Job 13:18 reads: "See now, I have prepared my case, I know I shall be vindicated *(tsadaq)*." That's courtroom language, isn't it? Deuteronomy 25:1 declares: "If there is a dispute between men, and they come to court, that the judges may judge them, and they justify *(tsadaq)* the righteous and condemn the wicked." This also presumes a legal setting. When the sons of Israel discovered Joseph's drinking cup in the sack of Benjamin, Judah lamented, "What shall we say to my lord? What shall we speak? Or how shall we clear ourselves *(tsadaq)?*" (Gen. 44:16). Such usages of *tsadaq,* the word translated "cleansed" in Daniel 8:14, speak volumes! They show clearly that the word is immersed in a courtroom atmosphere.

When Absalom attempted to wrest the kingdom from his father he "would rise early and stand beside the way to the gate [the "gate" in Old Testament times was where court business took place]. So it was, whenever anyone who had a lawsuit came to the king for a decision, Absalom would call to him and say, 'What city are you from?' And he would say, 'Your servant is from such and such a tribe of Israel.' Then Absalom would say to him, 'Look, your case is good and right; but there is no deputy of the king to hear you.' Moreover Absalom would say, 'Oh, that I were made judge in the land, and everyone who has any suit or cause would come to me; then I would give him justice *(tsadaq)'* " (2 Sam. 15:2-4).

Again, such examples make it obvious that the word in question often appears in a judicial context. Notice the things it presumes. It anticipates a court setting that examines evidence and renders a decision. Furthermore, it looks forward to the "clearing" of charges imposed, the "vindication" of a person's record. Isn't that exactly what the pre-Advent judgment is about? And isn't that what Daniel 7:9, 10 pictures? The judgment scene of Daniel 7 shifts to the vision of Daniel 8, but is embedded in the sanctuary motif. Merely seeing the word *tsadaq* in Daniel 8:14 would bring to mind the concepts of judicial review and administration. A reader of Daniel, familiar with the word and how Scripture uses it, would naturally associate judicial process with *tsadaq.* The translation "cleansed" is therefore most appropriate, especially if seen as a matter of legal vindication.

We saw that from a structural point of view the cleansing of the sanctuary occupies the same position in the vision of Daniel 8 as did the seating of the heavenly court in Daniel 7. Second, we noted also that the very word *tsadaq* breathes a legal connotation. But do we have additional evidence that cleansing of the sanctuary refers to a judgment process? Yes! In the book of Leviticus we find that on one day of the year there was a special ceremony by which the sanctuary was "cleansed." We will see that this cleansing of the sanctuary refers to an event in the Hebrew calendar that typified the process of the investigative judgment: Yom Kippur, the Day of Atonement.

The Sanctuary Cleansed on Yom Kippur

The sanctuary service was God's "show and tell" illustration of salvation. It presented the story of Christ's provision for redemption. Jesus is the tabernacle, the door, the high priest, and the Lamb. Only by Him can we be saved. His blood atones for our sins, as depicted in the offering of animal sacrifices whose blood typified that of Jesus. But why would the sanctuary need cleansing? Because the impurity of the sins of the people had been transferred from them to the sanctuary.

Every day sinners came with their offerings and laid (the Hebrew indicates "lean" or "pressed down") their hands on the head of the sacrificial victim, and then a priest slew the animal. In type, the sin was transferred from the sinner to the sanctuary by means either of the blood of the sacrifice being sprinkled on the veil separating the holy from the Most Holy place, or in some cases the flesh of the animal being eaten by the priests who served in the tabernacle (see, for example, Lev. 4:6; 6:29; 7:6). Thus the sanctuary became defiled by the "reminder of sins," and thus required cleansing from those sins that had accumulated through the year (Heb. 10:3). The annual cleansing took place on Yom Kippur.

Each year the "tenth day of the seventh month" was a most solemn occasion. Its name, Yom Kippur, meant "day of covering (in a special sense)." Notice how the concept of "cleansing" enters the discussion of the procedures and purposes of that annual event. "So he [the high priest] shall make atonement for the Holy Place, because of the uncleanness of the children of Israel, and because of their transgressions, for all their sins; and so he shall do for the tabernacle of meeting which remains among them in the midst of their uncleanness" (Lev. 16:16).

A number of animals were sacrificed that day, and as a part of his ministry, the high priest was to "sprinkle some of the blood on it [the horns of the altar] with his finger seven times, cleanse it, and consecrate it from the uncleanness of the children of Israel" (verse 19). Something in the sanctuary clearly required cleansing. Later we read, "This shall be a statute forever for you: in the seventh month, on the tenth day of the month, you shall afflict your souls, and do no work at all, whether a native of your own country or a stranger who dwells among you. For on that day the priest shall make atonement for you, to cleanse you, that you may be clean from all your sins before the Lord" (verses 29, 30). It is obvious that "cleansing" was a vital part of the service of the Day of Atonement. We learn from this passage that it wasn't just the physical structure of the tabernacle that was the object of the cleansing—it was the hearts of the people: "That you may be clean from all your sins."

While the word in Leviticus 16 *(taher)* isn't the same Hebrew word for "cleansing" as appears in Daniel 8:14 *(tsadaq),* it is a close synonym, as demonstrated in such passages as Job 25:4: "How then can man be justified *(tsadaq)* with God? Or how can he be pure *(taher)* that is born of a woman?" As we've noted previously, according to the rules of Hebrew poetry two words used in synonymous parallelism mean essentially the same thing.

Yom Kippur was a most solemn day on which the people were required to "afflict [their] souls," meaning that they engaged in deep contrition and repentance (Lev. 16:29). Israelites understood that God was reviewing their records and removing their sins from the camp in totality. It was a time of sacred judgment. All of this symbolized the final removal of sin from the records of heaven, a process described both by Daniel 7 in the depiction of the heavenly court and by Daniel 8 through its reference to Yom Kippur.

Just to review: given the parallel nature of the prophecies of Daniel 7 and 8, we would expect that something having to do with judgment would occupy this slot in the sequence. In chapter 7 we had earthly kingdoms, the horn, the judgment, and the end. Then in chapter 8 we've seen earthly kingdoms, the horn, and now we would expect something in keeping with judgment to be the next component of the series. The phrase that is put into the spotlight as being the critical hinge point of the prophecy, something vital to the answering of the question "How long?" is the "cleansing of the sanctuary."

Did ancient Israel recognize something in the sanctuary service that was distinctly related to judgment and cleansing? Yes! To this very day Orthodox Jews look upon Yom Kippur as the "Day of Judgment."

For those interested in how Jews today look at Yom Kippur, consider the following quotes: "The name 'Yom Kippur' means 'Day of Atonement,' and that pretty much explains what the holiday is. It is a day set aside to 'afflict the soul,' to atone for the sins of the past year. In *Days of Awe,* I mentioned the 'books' in which G-d inscribes all of our names. On *Yom Kippur,* the judgment entered in these books is sealed. This day is, essentially, your last appeal, your last chance to change the judgment, to demonstrate your repentance and make amends."[2]

"By *Yom Kippur* the 40 days of repentance, that begin with the first of Elul, have passed. On *Rosh Hashanah* God judged most of mankind and has recorded his judgment in the Book of Life. But he has given a 10-day reprieve. On *Yom Kippur* the Book of Life is closed and sealed. Those that have repented for their sins are granted a good and happy New Year."[3]

So even today observant Jews view the service of Yom Kippur, the Day of Atonement, as functioning as God's final judgment! That is most interesting, especially when we take into consideration that it was on that day that the sanctuary was "cleansed." As part of the service, the high priest "shall sprinkle some of the blood on it [the altar] with his finger seven times, cleanse it, and consecrate it from the uncleanness of the children of Israel" (Lev. 16:19). The purpose of the cleansing was to remove the record of sins deposited there throughout the year as the people confessed their sins day by day.

But where is the sanctuary to be cleansed in the "time of the end" referred to by Gabriel. It couldn't be an earthly one, because the Roman general Titus destroyed the Jerusalem Temple in A.D. 70. Is there another sanctuary beside the one on earth? Going back to the original instruction given to Moses, we find that God told him, "According to all that I show you, that is, the pattern of the tabernacle and the pattern of all its furnishings, just so you shall make it" (Ex. 25:9). The Lord revealed to him an original or pattern sanctuary in heaven, of which he made an earthly copy.

The writer of Hebrews comments: "Now this is the main point of the things we are saying: We have such a High Priest, who is seated at the right hand of the throne of the Majesty in the heavens, a Minister of the sanctuary and of the true tabernacle which the Lord erected, and not man" (Heb. 8:1, 2). It stands to reason then, that because a sanctuary no longer existed on earth when this prophecy came to its terminus (in "the time of the end"), it must be speaking about the sanctuary in heaven, the true and original, of which all earthly sanctuaries were only copies.

This once-a-year ceremony in the ancient earthly sanctuary illustrated God's final accounting with sin that takes place before Jesus' return, when the sanctuary in heaven, the "true tabernacle," gets cleansed from the record of the sins of the saints. It is in keeping with what we see in Daniel 7, in that the judgment scene given to Daniel tales place in heaven, not on earth.

So when the angelic being in the vision asks how long the "trampling" will be, we know that it cannot be a direct answer, because it is not God's policy to reveal the "day and hour." But, as Jesus did before He ascended to heaven, it is a response that while not direct, nevertheless reveals an important fact concerning a necessary prerequisite to His return. The vision announces the beginning date of the pre-Advent judgment, a vital part of God's plan.

Think of it this way. Let's say that your child is restless as you travel to visit a friend whose whereabouts are unfamiliar to you. You've scribbled some notes on a scrap of paper and you are doing your best to make all the correct turns. When the child asks, "When will we get there?" you reply, "I can't say exactly, but when we get to the Arco station on Edmonds Street, we'll be close, because they live in the next block." No, you don't know the exact time, but being able to identify something that is a last marker is helpful. That's the message of Daniel 8:13, 14. The question: "How long will the sanctuary be 'trampled underfoot'" (which comes to its end when Jesus returns)? The answer: "At the conclusion of the 2300-year time period the cleansing of the heavenly sanctuary (the pre-Advent investigative judgment) will begin."

That aspect of the judgment, brought to view in Daniel 7 when the Ancient of Days presides and the books are opened, illustrated by one of the festivals of the Jewish sanctuary service, Yom Kippur, will commence at the conclusion of the 2300-year prophecy. Remember, the vision of Daniel 8 has a sanctuary setting, with its animals being those employed in sacrifice, not the wild and unclean beasts of Daniel 7. While not a direct answer to the question "How long?" it is still a good one. Knowing the date of the beginning of heaven's final tribunal (which must conclude before Jesus can return) is something that will cheer the hearts of all those who cherish the fulfillment of God's great plan.

Some electronic gadgets today have an interesting feature that allows users, when spreading their fingers, to widen the screen and view more of an image. Before we leave the subject of the sanctuary being "cleansed" or "vindicated," we need to stress something very important. Keep in mind that it's not just about books being examined or furniture cleansed. And it's not just about the records of humans being reviewed to see who is going to be saved or lost, as important as that might be. Referring to the cleansing of the sanctuary is merely a verbal illustration trying to open our eyes to the real issues at stake. The screen is much wider than our earthly concerns. Remember that no trial has a basis for existing unless some prosecutor files charges. In his rebellion Satan accused the Lord of being unfit to rule the universe. He brought charges against God's government—His throne and His law. The devil said that divine law was too restrictive, and that society would be better off with no restraints.

As a result, God's name and character are on trial. It is in a very real sense, the "hour of *His* (God's) judgment." What part do we have to play in this? It is God's purpose to illustrate His justice and power in the transformation of the lives of those who yield to Him. He wants to build His case upon the evidence of changed characters. Thus He seeks to answer Satan's charges by the exhibits of the lives of those who say yes to Him. His proposition is, "I will make a mortal more rare ["precious," KJV] than fine gold" (Isa. 13:12). Notice that it's His promise—"I will make"—not something that we do.

In times past, through techniques known as "alchemy," human beings tried to find a way to make gold out of other substances. They never found out how to do it in the physical realm, but God says He can in the spiritual realm! The Lord can make our characters as gold. He has the creative power to render weak sinful human beings (notice the passage in Isaiah just quoted is talking about "mortal" humans) victorious through the merits of Christ. It is not legalism but grace at work—the gospel. But that process of refinement and purification can take place only if we say yes. The gospel, illustrated in the lives of His saints, is His answer to Satan's allegations. The heavenly investigation will clear God's name and vindicate Him of all accusations.

---

[1] See, for example, Francis Brown, *The New Brown-Driver-Briggs-Gesenius Hebrew and English Lexicon*, pp. 841ff.

[2] http://www.jewfaq.org/holiday4.htm.

[3] http://holidays.net/highholydays/yom.htm.

CHAPTER 10

THE CONCLUSION OF THE 2300 YEARS

Can we determine when the 2300-day prophecy of the cleansing of the sanctuary would reach its terminus? Can we know when the pre-Advent judgment began? Yes. By employing the day for a year in symbolic prophecy rule (see Num. 14:34; Eze. 4:6), we find that we are actually working with a period of 2,300 years, making it the longest time prophecy in Scripture. Such an approach makes sense, because the angel Gabriel forewarned Daniel, "The vision refers to the time of the end" (Dan. 8:17). Only with a "day for a year" yardstick could we have a prophecy extending from just after Daniel's day to modern times.

To know when it ends, we must determine when it begins. Although Daniel 8 does not establish any starting point, Daniel 9 does bring one to view. Although it may seem as if we're taking a detour, we must spend some time studying the prophecy of Daniel 9 and its vital relationship to the prophecy of the 2300 years in order to confirm the starting point of the prophecy of the "hour of His judgment." Establishing the beginning date for this crucial prophecy is indispensable.

A Vital Link Between Daniel 8 and 9

Before we go any further, we need to analyze the return of Gabriel and the message of explanation he brought, with particular emphasis on the relationship between what the angel said in chapter 9 and the vision of chapter 8, which had challenged Daniel's thinking (Dan. 8:27). Let me suggest to you that the two chapters are directly connected and cannot be correctly understood apart from each other.

H.M.S. Richards, beloved founder of the Voice of Prophecy radio program, used to tell the story of a driver of a car at a stop sign waiting for the evening traffic to break. Finally it looked as if things were going to clear when a pickup went across before him, followed by what he adjudged was adequate space. The driver started out into the intersection only to encounter a strange impediment. It seems the pickup was pulling another vehicle, attached by a chain that the driver of the car couldn't see in the dusk. Disaster! So it is with Daniel 8 and 9. They are linked by a chain of logic, which if unseen by the casual reader, will result in misunderstanding. Here are some of the links in the chain that tie the two chapters together.

1. It is the same Gabriel in chapter 9 who appeared to Daniel in chapter 8. The name "Gabriel" is composed of the Hebrew verb *gabar* ("to have strength, to prevail") plus the letter "*i*," which means "my," and the last part, "*el*," an abbreviated form of the name *Elohim*, or God. You see the same "*iel*" ending in the name Daniel. Thus we could translate the angel's whole name as "God is my strength," "Mighty one of God." Later Gabriel informed Zacharias, the father of John the Baptist, that he "stands in the presence of God" (Luke 1:19). That would make him one of God's most highly positioned angels. Daniel said that "the man Gabriel, whom I had seen in the vision at the beginning" (Dan. 9:21), was the one who returned to give additional understanding. Gabriel's presence in chapter 9 is a clear link to his visiting Daniel in chapter 8.

2. In chapter 8 God gives a command: "Gabriel, make this man understand the vision" (Dan. 8:16), but when Gabriel left, Daniel said that "no one understood it" (verse 27), leaving the impression that a return visit would be necessary to complete the assignment. When he came back, Gabriel said, "I have now come forth to give you skill to understand" (Dan. 9:22).

3. During his previous visit Gabriel had explained all of the symbols in the vision of chapter 8 (the ram, the goat, and the horn). The only thing left to clarify was the matter of the time period. Daniel had been particularly confused about the 2300 days, expressing his cherished hope that they would not be a lengthening of Israel's captivity in Babylon by the phrase, "Do not delay" (Dan. 9:19). Thinking that

perhaps the time period of 2300 days represented an extension of the captivity (foretold by Daniel's contemporary Jeremiah to be 70 years), in chapter 9 Daniel prayed a most eloquent prayer, asking the Lord not to delay the fulfillment of the covenant promise to restore Israel after the 70 years of captivity. At that point, Gabriel returned to give further explanation to the prophet concerning the time aspect of "the vision" (verse 21). Much of Gabriel's exposition in chapter 9 bears directly on the matter of time.

4. Although the vision of chapter 8 does present a time period (the 2300 days), we find no indication of when it starts. How could the time-related vision have meaning and relevance if you didn't know when it commenced? On the other hand, Gabriel does establish a very definite beginning point in chapter 9 when he declares, "Know therefore and understand, that from the going forth of the command to restore and build Jerusalem until Messiah the Prince, there shall be seven weeks and sixty-two weeks" (Dan. 9:25).

5. When Gabriel returns to Daniel, he tells him, "Therefore consider the matter, and understand the vision" (verse 23). Since we find no intervening vision requiring explanation, the only reasonable conclusion is that he was referring to "the vision" of chapter 8, which Daniel confessed he didn't comprehend. The definite article is significant.

6. The Hebrew word for "vision" used in the book of Daniel through chapter 7 has been *chezev*. The only exception is the very general statement found in Daniel 1 that states: "Daniel had understanding in all visions (*chazon*) and dreams" (Dan. 1:17). Chapters 8, 9, and thereafter employ two words for "vision": *chazon* (Dan. 8:1, 2, 13, 15, 17, 26; 9:21, 24) and *mareh* (Dan. 8:15, 26, 27; 9:23). Some scholars make the distinction that *chazon* indicates the entirety of a vision, while *mareh* refers to a part of the larger whole. It does seem to make sense when we note how the narrative employs the two words.

The bottom line is that up through the end of chapter 7, with the one exception noted, the text employs *chezev*, but beginning in chapter 8 *chezev* vanishes while *chazon* and *mareh* make their appearance, words absent before chapter 8. So when the angel says, "understand the vision" *(mareh)* in Daniel 9:23, and that word has not been used before chapter 8, and it is the word employed in chapter 8 when Gabriel is told to "make this man understand the vision" (Dan. 8:16), it is most reasonable to conclude that he is pointing Daniel to the vision of chapter 8 and none other.

It follows logically then that Daniel 8 and 9 are inseparably linked and that the explanation Gabriel gives in chapter 9 relates directly to the vision of chapter 8. Furthermore, whereas the vision of chapter 8 has no referenced starting point while one is in chapter 9, it follows that the beginning point Gabriel establishes in chapter 9 is also the starting one for the vision of chapter 8 and that the shorter period of time (the 70 weeks of chapter 9) is a part of it and in fact the initial segment of the larger period of chapter 8.

Gabriel Explains the 70 Weeks

In his address to Daniel the angel linked this visit with his former one by saying, "O Daniel, I have now come forth to give you skill to understand. At the beginning of your supplications the command went out, and I have come to tell you, for you are greatly beloved; therefore consider the matter, and understand the vision" (Dan. 9:23). Since we find no intervening vision, Gabriel must be referring to that of chapter 8, concerning which Daniel had unresolved issues.

During his second visit the angel focuses on the subject of time. Gabriel provides many details to Daniel, including the fact that the first part of the period of time is allocated in a special way to "your people," that is, the Jews. "Seventy weeks are determined for your people and for your holy city" (verse 24). So confident were some Bible translators that the 70 weeks should be understood by the day for a year in symbolic prophecy rule that they even translated the phrase as "seventy weeks of years."[1] Without question we should understand the 490 "days" as 490 literal years, in that the scope of material presented, including the restoration of Jerusalem and reaching to "Messiah the Prince," could not possibly have its fulfillment within 70 literal weeks.

Seventy weeks, or 490 literal years, are "cut off" (a meaning of the Hebrew word translated "determined")[2] and applied especially to "your people" to see if they will indeed live up to the covenant stipulations. Because two time periods are now under discussion (the

2300 days and the 70 weeks, or 490 days), and since there is only one beginning point mentioned, and because the verb "cut off" implies the shorter period being taken from the larger, it makes sense to see the two time periods as having the same starting date. And if it is true that the day for a year in symbolic prophecy rule applies to the first part, the 490 "days," a point widely accepted among commentators and Bible students, why would we think that it would not be equally relevant to the larger prophecy of 2,300 "days," of which the 70 weeks form a part? Therefore, we must understand the 2,300 "days" as 2,300 years.

The period of the 490 days/years pertained especially to the Jews and represented a period of probation, to see if they would indeed live up to the terms of the covenant. As history sadly records, its religious leadership not only didn't accept Jesus, they crucified Him. John the Baptist had preached that if the nation didn't comply with the divine template, the ax would be laid to the tree (Matt. 3:7-10). Jesus' parable of the vineyard describing the mistreatment of the servants and the son of the owner and its shocking conclusion that the "kingdom" would be taken from them and given to "another nation," became reality (Matt. 21:33-44). When the 490-year period of probation ended, the Jews were no longer the primary torchbearers of God's truth. The gospel went to the Gentiles, as demonstrated clearly in the book of Acts.

Gabriel then provides critical information by which we can ascertain the beginning of the time period involved here. "Know therefore and understand, that from the going forth of the command to restore and build Jerusalem until Messiah the Prince, there shall be seven weeks; the street shall be built again, and the wall, even in troublesome times" (Dan. 9:25). It must have encouraged the prophet to know that his beloved city of Jerusalem would again be rebuilt.

When Do the 70 "Weeks" Begin?

Can we know the date of the "command to restore and build Jerusalem"? Yes! Actually three different rulers (Cyrus, Darius, and Artaxerxes) each issued an edict involving Jerusalem. The last and most complete of the three is the one that initiated the time prophecy. Notice that Ezra 6:14 combines the three commands into one. "So the elders of the Jews built, and they prospered through the prophesying of Haggai the prophet and Zechariah the son of Iddo. And they built and finished it, according to the commandments of the God of Israel, and according to the command of Cyrus, Darius, and Artaxerxes king of Persia." The singular usage of the noun "command" is significant.

The edict of Cyrus went out shortly after the fall of Babylon in 539 B.C. and allowed the Jews to return to Jerusalem and rebuild. Second Chronicles 36:22, 23 and Ezra 1:1-4 refer to it. However, many discouragements hindered their progress. Darius I issued a second decree shortly before 515 B.C., a document found in Ezra 6:1-12. It concerns the rebuilding of the Temple.

A third edict, appearing in Ezra 7:12-26, became necessary. Proclaimed by Artaxerxes I, it provided funds from the king's coffers for the Temple services and sacrifices, and allowed the reconstruction of the city wall, a story chronicled by the prophet Nehemiah. It put the finishing touches on the Temple edifice. Ezra alludes to this latter component in his prayer: "Blessed be the Lord God of our fathers, who has put such a thing as this in the king's heart, to beautify the house of the Lord which is in Jerusalem" (Ezra 7:27). Thus the third decree, the one given by Artaxerxes I in his seventh year (457 B.C.)[3] and authorizing full restoration of Jewish life, Temple services, and the teaching of the Law of God, is the one that finalized all aspects of the rebuilding and is thus the one whose date is the subject of Gabriel's explanation. The date of 457 B.C. will be the anchor for the beginning of both the 70 "weeks" or 490 years and the 2300 days/years of prophecy.

It is noteworthy that the rebuilding of the wall under the leadership of Nehemiah, within the scope of the first part of the prophecy, took place under the most strenuous circumstances, including opposition from those who did not wish to see the work progress. Gabriel alluded to this very matter, as we shall see. The repair and rebuilding concluded by 444 B.C., well within the time allowed by the first segment of Gabriel's explanation of the 70 weeks (Neh. 6:15).

The Three Divisions of the 70 Weeks

The material presented by the angel appears in a careful literary structure, with the latter part of Daniel 9:24 comprising three couplets discussing goals to be accomplished within the 70 weeks. Then Gabriel subdivides the period of 70 weeks, or 490 literal years, into three parts, with specific fulfillments attached to each segment. They consist of a period of seven weeks (49 literal years) followed by another section of 62 weeks (434 literal years) ending with one prophetic week, or seven years, making a total of 490 years. The respective dates attached to the segments, based on the inception date of 457 B.C., are 408 B.C. for the first seven weeks, A.D. 27 for the 69 weeks, and A.D. 34 for the entire whole of 70 weeks. Gabriel's explanation is highly poetic, utilizing an "envelope" device, beginning with the restoration of Jerusalem at the beginning of the 70 "weeks" and ending with its destruction after the 490 years.

The conclusion of the first section (the seven weeks) would see the rebuilding process finished. "Know therefore and understand, that from the going forth of the command to restore and build Jerusalem until Messiah the Prince, there shall be seven weeks and sixty-two weeks; the street shall be built again, and the wall, even in troublesome times" (Dan. 9:25). As mentioned before, Nehemiah's able leadership completed the wall-building project well within the allotted time, as the seven "weeks" or 49 literal years would reach to 408 B.C.

At the conclusion of the 69 weeks (seven weeks plus 62 weeks), "Messiah the Prince" would appear, an obvious reference to Jesus the Christ. "Messiah" comes from the Hebrew word signifying "anointed one" and designates those commissioned for a specific work, including prophets, priests, and kings. Jesus is the consummate expression of all three of those offices. Since the Greek word for "anointed one" is the root for the word "Christ," therefore to say "Jesus Christ" is the same as "Jesus the anointed one," or "Jesus the Messiah."

It's important to note that anointing occurred as a person was about to begin their work. Thus the date mentioned by Gabriel on the prophetic calendar refers not to the birth of Jesus, but to the beginning of His ministry when the Holy Spirit anointed Him. Right on schedule, in the "fifteenth year of Tiberius Caesar," Jesus was baptized by John in the year A.D. 27 (Luke 3:1). Note that the B.C. era goes directly from 1 B.C. to A.D. 1 without an intervening zero year. Therefore we must add one more year to compensate for the lack, and so the 69 weeks, or 483 years brings us from 457 B.C. to A.D. 27, and not A.D. 26. When He was baptized, the Holy Spirit came upon Him in the form of a dove, signifying His being anointed for His task (Matt. 3:16). Peter referred to it in his sermon to Cornelius, saying, "God anointed Jesus of Nazareth with the Holy Spirit and with power, who went about doing good and healing all who were oppressed by the devil, for God was with Him" (Acts 10:38).

In Nazareth, as He started His work, Jesus quoted from Isaiah's prophecy: "The Spirit of the Lord God is upon Me, because the Lord has anointed Me to preach good tidings to the poor; He has sent Me to heal the brokenhearted, to proclaim liberty to the captives, and the opening of the prison to those who are bound" (Isa. 61:1). After reading from the scroll, Jesus said to His astonished audience, "Today this Scripture is fulfilled in your hearing" (Luke 4:21). Remember, the anointing of Christ signaled the beginning of His work in A.D. 27, not His birth. It occurred right on schedule, in perfect timing with the prophetic clock.

"And after the sixty-two weeks Messiah shall be cut off, but not for Himself" (Dan. 9:26). In the poetry structure employed (ABab), the explanation shifts between different subjects. Two examples appear in verses 24-27. Verse 25 and the first part of verse 26 focus on one subject, and verses 26 and 27 deal with another. The first part of verse 26 ("After sixty-two weeks Messiah shall be cut off, but not for Himself") comprises the final component of the first set while the rest of the verse is the first part of the second unit.

We see this format followed in the presentation of the time of the seven weeks (A), then the 62 weeks (B), followed in turn by the explanation of what happens at the conclusion of the seven weeks (a), and finally what takes place after the 62 weeks (b). That analysis explains the order presented in verse 25 and the first part of 26. We find that it exhibits perfect harmony when we see it this way.

Notice how verses 26 and 27 employ the same formulation as they contrast the mission and purpose of Messiah the Prince, Jesus Christ, with "the people of the prince," that is, the Roman leader who destroyed Jerusalem because of its failure to live up to the covenant obligations. In each verse the first part refers to Messiah the Prince (that is, Jesus Christ), and the second part of each verse points to the destruction of Jerusalem by Roman armies after the conclusion of the 490 years. In the middle of that last week He, the Messiah, would be "cut off, but not for Himself" (verse 26).

The language unmistakably points to the atonement made by Jesus on the cross of Calvary, which took place three and a half years after He began His ministry. It was not for His sins that He died, but for ours. Thus He was "cut off, but not for Himself." By the way, the expression "cut off" signifies much more than merely dying. In the language of the Old Testament the verb meant "to be disinherited, disenfranchised, abandoned, and rejected." Jesus experienced all of these things as He died for our sins, and cried out, "My God, My God, why have You forsaken Me?" (Matt. 27:46). Since these 70 weeks pertained to the Jewish people in a special way, at the close of the 70-week period the probation of the Jewish nation would come to a close.

All of this is important because the historical events terminating each section are visible events that took place on earth and provide helpful waymarkers to engender confidence that the prophecy in its entirety is trustworthy, because the event at the conclusion of the larger 2300-year prophecy has to do with something that does not occur on earth but in heaven, and therefore is unseen by humanity. The first angel cries out, "The hour of His judgment has come." Since the event portrayed in the book of Daniel takes place in heaven and is unseen by the human eye, how are we to know that it has commenced? The accurate fulfillment of the events foretold within the three segments will confirm the veracity of the larger vision and the event toward which it points, though it is invisible to us.

One of the specified purposes of the shorter 490-year period was to "seal up vision and prophecy" (Dan. 9:24). The force of the verb translated "seal up" means to "confirm or authenticate."[4] Graciously, God provided visible and measurable evidence to testify to the truth of the event (foretold by the larger vision) that happens in heaven: the beginning of the cleansing of the sanctuary. The completion of the rebuilding of Jerusalem, the appearance of the Messiah and His sacrificial death, and the close of the 490 years leading to the destruction of Jerusalem in A.D. 70 are all events verified by history, giving us confidence that the event at the terminus of the larger 2300-year period likewise met its fulfillment, though unseen by humanity.

Satan Attacks the Prophecy of Daniel 9

Such an important prophecy serves both to anchor the date of the beginning of the 2300 day/year prophecy as well as provide valuable signposts along the pathway of time, including insightful information concerning the mission of the Messiah. Naturally, you would not expect Satan to ignore it. No indeed! The 70-week prophecy provided far too much insight for God's people. Because of that, Satan attacked the 490-year prophecy not once but twice.

First, we must consider the fact that it provided a timeline to ascertain the coming of the Messiah. And so it was that John the Baptist preached, "The time is fulfilled" (Mark 1:15). The New Testament era had a general expectancy that the Messiah's approach was near. The Bible tells us that Simeon, who saw the Baby Jesus at His dedication, was one "waiting for the Consolation of Israel. . . . And it had been revealed to him by the Holy Spirit that he would not see death before he had seen the Lord's Christ" (Luke 2:25, 26). Because of Daniel's prophecy, believers knew that the time of the Messiah's coming was near.

Shortly after Christ's ministry on earth, questioning Jews quizzed their rabbis about the prophecy of Daniel 9. Frustrated by the clarity of the prophecy and the evidences of Jesus' divinity, the priests pronounced a curse on anyone who tried to identify the date of the Messiah's through Daniel 9.[5]

In "Has Messiah Come?" Avram Yehoshua says, "A most amazing thing occurs in the ninth chapter of Daniel: we're told when Messiah would come. But instead of explaining it to us, our Rabbis curse anyone wanting to find it out: 'Rabbi Samuel b. Nachmani said in the name (of) Rabbi Jonathan: "Blasted be the bones of those who calculate the end."' Some of our Rabbis, in a further attempt to keep us from Daniel, even state that Daniel was wrong."[6]

Alfred Edersheim was a noted scholar in both Judaism and the Talmud who later accepted Jesus as the Messiah and authored several books. He wrote that "later Rabbinism, which, naturally enough, could not find its way through the Messianic prophecies of the book, declared that even Daniel was mistaken."[7]

Satan was at work to hinder the work of God by obscuring what He had clearly revealed in the prophetic Word. Those who claimed to be skillful in the Scriptures and qualified to teach them began to make the prayer of Daniel and the explanations of Gabriel of none effect, obscuring the identity of the Messiah and His mission to die. But equally incredible is that it would happen again not only to the mission of Christ's death, but His high-priestly ministry as well!

The second attack on Daniel 9 has gained traction only in the past century or so. Before that, the beautiful, harmonious, and symmetrical understanding of the scope of the 70 "weeks" of Daniel was the standard interpretation accepted by virtually all the Protestant Reformers. But in recent times another radically different view has emerged to explain the 70 "weeks." The interpretation has taken such deep root that now much of Christianity embraces it, especially in North America among evangelicals. The devil's second attack against Daniel 9 has been even more effective than his first one!

While the Scriptures present a picture of the 70 weeks as one unit of time highlighting the mission of the Messiah in His sacrificial death and the tragic departure from the position of favor held by the Jewish nation, all of which nail down the certainty of the larger 2300-year prophecy, today a different analysis radically shifts its contents and meaning. Many theologians and large groups of conservative Christians assume that the last week of the 70 is separated from the other 69 weeks and shoved off until the end of time. However, we have absolutely no biblical justification for such a view!

Because he knows that we are now living since 1844 in "the hour of His judgment," a truth made certain by the prophecies of Daniel 8 and 9, Satan's special assault has been against those Scriptures that draw attention to this momentous event. By distorting the prophecy of the 70 weeks, he seeks to erode the foundation for the 2300-year prophecy.

Notice the pernicious errors that the new concept introduces. First, if you separate the last week from the others, you no longer have "70 weeks." You have whatever would be the sum of the 69 weeks, plus those intervening weeks during the "gap," followed by the last week at the end of the age. But it compromises and destroys the integrity and wholeness of the 70-week period.

Separating the last week from the other 69 demolishes the purpose of the 70 weeks as being allocated to the Jews in a special way (Gabriel said they were "determined for your people"). It was to be a period of probation for the Jewish nation; a time for them to live up to the terms of the covenant. The parable of the vineyard recorded in Matthew 21:33-45 brings this into sobering reality. After abusing the prophets that God gave to them, "last of all" He sent to them His Son. That phrase "last of all" is profound. According to the parable, the "stone" they rejected was to become the chief Cornerstone and the "kingdom" would go to another "nation."

History tells us that the Jewish leadership did indeed kill "the Son" who was sent to them "last of all." How could God expect them to proclaim the truth of Jesus as the risen Messiah when they were the ones who demanded His death on the cross? Or how could they proclaim the reality of His resurrection when they had bribed the soldiers to tell a lie about the empty tomb (Matt. 28:11-15). God had to inaugurate another entity, the Christian church, to herald the news of Jesus' death and resurrection—an entity that would incorporate individual Jews.

The apostle Peter alluded to the parable spoken by Jesus and said, "'The stone which the builders rejected has become the chief cornerstone,' and 'A stone of stumbling and a rock of offense.' They stumble, being disobedient to the word, to which they also were appointed. But you are a chosen generation, a royal priesthood, a holy nation, His own special people, that you may proclaim the praises of Him who called you out of darkness into His marvelous light; who once were not a people but are now the people of God" (1 Peter 2:7-10).

Here Peter quotes from the Septuagint (the Greek translation of the Old Testament done before the time of Christ) version of Exodus 19:5, 6 and puts the Christian church figuratively at the foot of Mount Sinai, receiving the covenant promise that places it in the position of privilege once occupied by the nation of Israel.

Did other prophets speak to this transference? Yes! Did not John the Baptist warn the Jews, "Do not think to say to yourselves, 'We have Abraham as our father.' For I say to you that God is able to raise up children to Abraham from these stones. And even now the ax is laid to the root of the trees. Therefore every tree which does not bear good fruit is cut down and thrown into the fire" (Matt. 3:9, 10).

In anticipation of this removal of privilege Jesus uttered those solemn words, "Your house is left to you desolate" (Matt. 23:38). Just the day before He had referred to the Temple as "My house," saying, "It is written, 'My house shall be called a house of prayer,' but you have made it a 'den of thieves'" (Matt. 21:13). What an awesome transition, from the Temple being "My house" on Monday of Passion Week to "Your house" which is left "desolate" on Tuesday! But the eye of Jesus could see the cross being raised, and His ear could hear the tramp of the Roman armies coming to demolish Jerusalem.

Paul spoke to this passing of the baton from Judah to the Christian church. "He is not a Jew who is one outwardly, nor is circumcision that which is outward in the flesh; but he is a Jew who is one inwardly; and circumcision is that of the heart" (Rom. 2:28, 29; see also Rom. 9:6-8). "If you belong to Christ, then you are Abraham's seed, and heirs according to the promise" (Gal. 3:29, NIV). Thus the Bible teaches the probationary nature of Israel's favored position and confirms the Christian church as "spiritual Israel," the entity to which heaven looks to carry the torch of truth to the world.

Removing the last week from the other 69 destroys the incredibly important feature of the Jewish nation being on probation and obliterates the historical evidence corroborating the prophecy provided by the transference of privilege from the Jewish leadership to the Christian church so well illustrated in the New Testament. It shatters one of the clearest waymarkers testifying to the truthfulness of the larger vision.

And it uproots another major signpost: the death of the Messiah in the middle of that last week. Prophecy said that in the middle of the week "he shall bring an end to sacrifice and offering" (Dan. 9:27). The pronoun "he" in that verse points to Jesus. All the animal sacrifices offered throughout the Old Testament period, beginning with the first one when in Eden God "made tunics of skin, and clothed" the shamed

Adam and Eve (Gen. 3:21), found their fulfillment in the death of the "Lamb of God," Jesus the Messiah. For thousands of years the blood of bulls and goats had typified the blood that Jesus shed for our sins. To say that Calvary was one of the most important events in history and deserving a position of honor in the prophetic spotlight, would be a huge understatement. Christ's death was the focus of the sanctuary service and was indispensable to the plan of redemption! We would fully expect that it would be the subject of a major time prophecy.

When Christ died on Calvary, the Lord Himself tore the curtain of the Temple from top to bottom (Matt. 27:51), signifying thereby that no longer were animal sacrifices necessary. History records that precisely on time Christ died on the cross for our sins in the spring of A.D. 31, three and a half years after He began His ministry and in the middle of that last prophetic week of Daniel 9. Paul stated that "when the fullness of the time had come, God sent forth His Son, born of a woman" (Gal. 4:4) and "for when we were still without strength, in due time Christ died for the ungodly" (Rom. 5:6). Jesus was born on time and He died on time, according to God's time clock.

The force of the phrase "due time" in the passage from the book of Romans translates the Greek *kairos*, which means "appropriate, precise or fixed time."[8] There is nothing uncertain about the date of Christ's death at all. Paul is saying, "At precisely the right time Christ died," doubtless knowing the content of Daniel's prophecy. The cross is planted securely in the middle of the seventieth week of prophecy. But the new view removes this important waymarker on the prophetic time line.

Jesus' role as the sacrifice for sin is the centerpiece of the last week, occurring in the spring of A.D. 31, but the new interpretations rob Him of the spotlight. The greatest event in the history of the world, the miraculous and magnificent accomplishment of Christ's death as given in the prophecy, fades into the background. Another—an antichrist—takes His place. How ironic! Satan would do anything to remove Jesus from the prophetic focus and diminish the spectacular achievement of the cross. On the Mount of Transfiguration Moses and Elijah spoke to Jesus about "His decease which He was about to accomplish" (Luke 9:31). The death of Jesus was just that—an accomplishment. Prophecy focused on this momentous event in the time line, but modern interpretations shift the spotlight to another—a usurper—instead.

This interpretation has introduced still other errors, including the teaching of a secret rapture at the beginning of the final prophetic week of the 70. The Bible, however, makes it abundantly plain that Jesus' coming will not be secret, but accompanied by the trumpet blast and the raising of the dead.

The only time that Scripture uses the word "rapture" (coming from the Greek 'arpazo) in conjunction with the Second Coming is 1 Thessalonians 4:17, where it is translated "caught up," clearly placing it in the context of the resurrection of the dead. Whatever anyone teaches regarding a "rapture" must be in harmony with Paul's instruction in this passage. We can see that there will be nothing secret about it! His coming is an event that is visible, audible, and most important, climactic! The Bible does not say anything about a seven-year period following the "rapture." When Jesus comes in the clouds and we are "caught up" to meet Him, human life on this planet ends. It's over. Those thinking that humanity will have an additional period of time to make decisions for God will be sadly mistaken. But the false concept has emerged as part of the devil's attack against Daniel 9.

The End of the 2300-Year Prophecy

Having established when the prophecy began (in 457 B.C.), and by having observed the confirmation of the prophecy by the events within and concluding the 70 weeks, we are now prepared to determine the closing of the 2300-year prophecy. It is a simple matter at this point, since the 490 year portion of its beginning concluded in A.D. 34. We add to that the remaining 1810 years (2300 – 490) and arrive at the date of 1844.

It makes sense that Yom Kippur, held in the fall of the year, would be the appropriate time when the 2300-day prophecy would be fulfilled, since it was that festival that highlighted God's final judgment. The date that conservative Karaite Jews observed Yom Kippur in that year was October 22.[9] It was on that date that Jesus entered upon the investigative phase of the judgment. The prophecy of Daniel 7 became reality, when the seer beheld "till thrones were put in place, and the Ancient of Days was seated. . . . Ten thousand times ten thousand stood before Him. The court was seated, and the books were opened" (Dan. 7:9, 10). That means that today this judgment is in process. Even now God is reviewing the names of those who have professed allegiance to Him, to see if their names may be retained in the book of life, or if they must be removed.

Everyone who has ever entered the service of Christ has had his or her name inscribed in the book of life. Jesus said to His disciples, following their successful missionary tour, "Do not rejoice in this, that the spirits are subject to you, but rather rejoice because your names are written in heaven" (Luke 10:20). The Lord had spoken through Jeremiah: "Those who depart from Me shall be written in the earth, because they have forsaken the Lord, the fountain of living waters" (Jer. 17:13).

But there is a review of those names "written in heaven" before the final makeup of Christ's kingdom. The Bible tells of a census conducted among Israel when it left Egypt, enumerating all those who began the journey (Num. 1:1-46). But not all completed it successfully because of unbelief, so a second census took place just before God's people entered Canaan (Num. 26:2-51).

Christ's parable of the wedding feast contained a review of the guests before the wedding feast was served. "When the king came in to see the guests, he saw a man there who did not have on a wedding garment" (Matt. 22:11). This process of "seeing" who is qualified (by grace) is what is now taking place in the investigative judgment. We don't have to understand that people will be physically in heaven and then found to be unworthy and removed. Rather, we are speaking figuratively that their cases are reviewed or examined. It is saying the same thing as Daniel 7's judgment scene, but now expressed in the parabolic language of a wedding. The names of all who have professed to follow Christ are examined to see if the "wedding garment"—the righteousness of Christ—is present in their lives. Though the language might be symbolic, the end result will be experienced in stark reality. Tragically, as in the case of the parable, those who are found lacking will be excluded.

What of those who have never professed faith in Christ? Jesus said, "He who does not believe [the same thing as having faith] is condemned already, because he has not believed in the name of the only begotten Son of God" (John 3:18). We are born "in sin." If we never take advantage of the gracious gift of salvation offered by God, our "natural condition" of sin leaves us in a position unworthy for heaven. The judgment that takes place before Jesus' return involves or concerns those who have claimed to be followers. "For it is time for judgment to begin with God's household; and if it begins with us, what will the outcome be for those who do not obey the gospel of God?" (1 Peter 4:17, NIV).

The purpose of this judgment is to "blot out" the sins of the righteous. But notice carefully that there are two types of "blotting out." Either, by His grace and through faith, our sins are blotted out, our records cleaned, and our names retained in the Lamb's book of life, or because of our refusal to cooperate with His Spirit, our names will be erased from it. Those are the only two choices. One or the other will happen. Either our sins or our names will be "blotted out"—completely removed forever. Peter said, "Repent therefore and be converted, that your sins may be blotted out" (Acts 3:19). The Lord speaks of Himself with the following words of reassurance: "I, even I, am he who blots out your transgressions for my own sake, and remembers your sins no more" (Isa. 43:25, NIV).

This "blotting out" of sins represents the final disposition of iniquity from the hearts and records of God's saints. Their minds are cleansed and the record of their transgressions is forever banished, represented by what took place on the festival of Yom Kippur. The purpose of that service was "that you may be clean from all your sins before the Lord" (Lev. 16:30). Those who refused to participate in the event were "cut off" from the congregation of the Lord (Lev. 23:29).

On the other hand, there will take place a "blotting out" of the names of those who refuse to comply with the divine plan, a subject that came up when Moses interceded on Israel's behalf following the sin of the golden calf below Mount Sinai. He said, "'Yet now, if You will forgive their sin—but if not, I pray blot me out of Your book which You have written.' And the Lord said to Moses, 'whoever has sinned against Me, I will blot him out of My book'" (Ex. 32:32, 33). Jesus' promise is "He who overcomes shall be clothed in white garments, and I will not blot out his name from the Book of Life; but I will confess his name before My Father and before His angels" (Rev. 3:5). Because of this, the angel cries with fervency and urgency, "Fear God and give glory to Him, for the hour of His judgment has come." With what awe, reverence, humility, and penitence we should relate to our God in this solemn hour of His judgment!

---

[1] See, for example, the *Good News Bible* ("seven times seventy years") and the *New Century Version* ("four hundred ninety years").

[2] F. Brown, *The New Brown-Driver-Briggs-Gesenius Hebrew and English Lexicon*, p. 367.

[3] For a full discussion of 457 B.C. being the "seventh year of Artaxerxes," see Seigfried H. Horn and Lynn H. Wood, *The Chronology of Ezra 7*, 2nd ed. (Washington, D.C.: Review and Herald Pub. Assn., 1970).

[4] F. Brown.

[5] Talmud Sanhedrin 97b, Soncino ed., p. 659.

[6] http://www.seedofabraham.net/nltr33.html.

[7] Alfred Edersheim, *The Life and Times of Jesus the Messiah*, p. 957.

[8] W. F. Arndt and F. W Gingrich, *A Greek-English Lexicon of the New Testament*, pp. 395f.

[9] http://en.wikipedia.org/wiki/Millerism.

CHAPTER 11

"WORSHIP HIM WHO MADE"

The final part of the first angel's message is "worship Him who made heaven and earth, the sea and the springs of water" (Rev. 14:7). It is clearly a call to worship God as the Creator. Yet what does it mean to "worship" Him? That might seem like a simple question, but on further inquiry, we discover a vital principle that many miss. Of course worship involves praise and the expression of gratitude. It requires devotion and homage.

But it's possible that such things can seem to be present, but the worship still be empty and without value! Didn't Cain "worship" in the offering of his fruit, and yet God had to reject his worship (Gen. 4:3-5)? Didn't the Jewish leaders of Jesus' day "worship" in the wearing of scripture boxes on their foreheads and Bible verses inscribed on the phylacteries on their forearms as well as the recitation of long prayers? Yet what did Jesus say about their worship? Quoting from Isaiah 29:13, Jesus said, "In vain they worship Me" (Matt. 15:9). What was missing? Why was their worship in "vain"? Reading on in Jesus' quotation of Isaiah, we find the answer clearly given. They were "teaching as doctrines the commandments of men" (verse 9).

The vital principle missing from the worship of the Jewish leaders and that of Cain is that of obedience. When we examine the Scriptures, it becomes clear that obedience is the highest form of worship, and that without it all worship is meaningless. What did Samuel tell Saul, when he had disobeyed and presumed to offer sacrifice in violation of the God's command? "Does the Lord delight in burnt offerings and sacrifices as much as in obeying the Lord? To obey is better than sacrifice, and to heed than the fat of rams" (1 Sam. 15:22, NIV).

This explains why God rejected Cain's offering. He gave it from an attitude of disobedience. God had requested a blood sacrifice, which is what Abel offered. But Cain presumed to think that it didn't matter what the Lord said, and that his substitute for God's express requirement would be acceptable. However, no fire fell from heaven to consume his rejected offering of fruit, and thus his worship was empty, or "in vain."

In a similar manner, the Jewish leadership of Jesus' day had figured out a way to get around God's commandment that said, "Honor your father and your mother" (Ex. 20:12). If a person's parents had a financial need that the son or daughter could alleviate, but chose instead to give it to the Temple as an act of "worship," Christ declared that their violation of the commandment rendered their worship vain (see Matt. 15:3-9). This raises a question: if Christ said that disobeying one of God's Ten Commandments, in this case the fifth commandment, resulted in one's worship being meaningless, would it be any different if it were the fourth commandment, the one that specifies God's holy Sabbath?

Obedience to God's will is an indispensable component of worship. David testified, "If I cherished sin in my heart, the Lord would not have listened" (Ps. 66:18, NIV). Solomon advised, "One who turns away his ear from hearing the law, even his prayer is an abomination" (Prov. 28:9). It's important to obey God! While our obedience is not what saves us, it is by it that we demonstrate our love and appreciation for Him and what He's done for us. The Bible teaches that genuine faith always expresses itself in obedience (James 2:18-24). John, the "apostle of love," puts it this way: "Now by this we know that we know Him, if we keep His commandments. He who says, 'I know Him,' and does not keep His commandments, is a liar, and the truth is not in him" (1 John 2:3, 4).

Though most of the world today is ignorant of the importance of obeying God by worshipping Him on His Sabbath, the seventh day, the time will come when all the world will become aware of the issue. Humanity will see that the decision between the two days symbolizes the choice between God's way and humanity's way; God's Word and humanity's word—God's commandments and humanity's commandments. By choosing the day of God's appointment, men and women will demonstrate their loyalty and faith in God. Jesus said, "If you love Me, keep My commandments" (John 14:15). But by ignoring or rejecting it people will in effect say, "I don't believe it matters whether you obey God or not. He's not that particular. It makes no difference."

I had one pastor say to me not long ago, "You don't really think that God is going to keep me out of heaven because of the day on which I worship, do you?" But could this be true? Is this sound reasoning? Let me suggest a comparison between the command that God gave in Eden regarding the forbidden tree and the commands that He proclaimed from the top of Mount Sinai, the Ten Commandments recorded in Exodus 20. Do you remember how the Bible describes the awesome splendor surrounding the presentation of the Ten Commandments? Now think back again to the story of Eden. Without question the Lord gave a commandment to our first parents and told them explicitly, "You shall not eat of the fruit of the forbidden tree" (see Gen. 2:17).

But where in Genesis 2 do we read that God descended in flames and set the whole garden on fire with His presence, as it says He did on Mount Sinai? When did the earth shake as He uttered His command? Did the sound of a trumpet, fire, darkness, and tempest make Adam, as did Moses at the foot of Mount Horeb, stand "trembling with fear" as God presented His command? (Heb. 12:21, NIV). Or where do we read in Eden that He inscribed His will on stone? Nowhere in Genesis 2 do we read any of this. All of these things pertain to the giving of the Ten Commandments at Mount Sinai, which was the most visible exhibition of God's power and glory since Creation and has never been equaled to this day.

And yet, without the demonstrations of glory and power that accompanied the proclamation of the Decalogue at Sinai, the violation of God's command respecting the forbidden fruit resulted in Adam and Eve's expulsion from the Garden. Considering the fact that God punished Adam and Eve for disobedience of His command in Eden, yet one given without the pyrotechnics manifested at Mount Sinai, how do you think He looks upon those who willfully trample on His law that He presented in such splendor? Will we be held less responsible for disobeying the Ten Commandments than was Adam for his disobedience in the garden?

Linguistic evidence suggests our present English "worship" is an abbreviated form of what was at one time the word "worthship."[1] The suffix "ship" has the sense of "state of," as in fellowship, friendship, companionship, etc. Worthship (worship) becomes that which we recognize has having the highest value, that which is worth the most. It is true then that whatever we place our highest value is what we worship, be it money, things, earthly relationships, or God.

Everyone worships—make no mistake about that. For everyone there is that "top spot," that "first place." It might even be themselves. But Jesus made it clear that to put anything ahead of devotion to God constitutes a violation of the first of the Ten Commandments, which declares, "You shall have no other gods before Me" (Ex. 20:3). God should occupy the first place in our hearts. He should be first, last, and everything to us. It is to Him that we should assign the highest value, the greatest worth. We should "worthship" Him. Of course, the consonants in that word are difficult to put together, and so through the course of time "worthship" became shortened to the word "worship."

It is because He is Creator that we worship Him. In heaven the 24 elders declare, "You are worthy, O Lord, to receive glory and honor and power; for You created all things, and by Your will they exist and were created" (Rev. 4:11). "For all the gods of the nations are idols, but the Lord made the heavens" (Ps. 96:5, NIV). It is His creatorship that separates Him from the worship of all false deities. After pointing out the futility of worshipping an idol made by human hands, the prophet Jeremiah proclaimed, "The Lord is the true God; He is the living God and the everlasting King. . . . Thus you shall say to them: 'The gods that have not made the heavens and the earth shall perish from the earth and from under these heavens.' He has made the earth by His power, He has established the world by His wisdom, and has stretched out the heavens at His discretion" (Jer. 10:10-12).

The Old Testament uses a word to describe the unique creatorship of God. In the very first verse of Scripture we read, "In the beginning God created the heavens and the earth" (Gen. 1:1). The word translated "created" is from the Hebrew *bara,* which in its active voice appears more than 30 times, but never once describes what a human being does. Humans "make" or "work," but they never "create." In our present parlance, we use the word "create" in a much broader sense. We speak of an artist "creating" a painting; a composer "creating" a symphony; a housewife "creating" a recipe. It would be technically inappropriate to speak of such things within the biblical sense of the word *bara*. Human beings always have to have something to start with. But God is not dependent on preexisting matter. He creates out of that which does not previously exist. Thus He can bring into being matter derived solely from His divine energy. "By faith we understand that the worlds were framed by the word of God, so that the things which are seen were not made of things which are visible" (Heb. 11:3).

Within the past century a physicist named Einstein proposed a bold theory that became the basis of a new comprehension of the physical world. On a chalkboard the fuzzy-haired scientist scribbled the formula $E = mc^2$. It completely changed our understanding of the world, becoming the description of what takes place in nuclear fission, the splitting of the atom. "E" stands for the energy that is released, which is immense. "M" indicates the mass that is converted (not technically destroyed) to energy and is a very small number, relatively speaking. And "C" represents the speed of light (roughly 186,000 miles a second), which is then squared, becoming a huge number. Thus even though the amount of matter converted to energy is relatively minute, the energy released is prodigious, as witnessed in the explosions of atomic bombs.

The same formula might well express what happens at Creation when God, through His divine energy, brings matter into being—an atomic bomb in reverse, if you please. The lesson to learn from what we now know about nuclear fission is that it would require huge amounts of energy to produce a small amount of matter. What can we then say about the vastness of God's divine energy when we see the matter represented in worlds, solar systems, galaxies, and the entire universe? How awesome is our God! No wonder that we are called to "worship Him who made"! He speaks and planets spring into existence. Should not the recognition of His immeasurable power and majesty invoke our deepest admiration and sincerest homage?

It is no coincidence that about the same time that the first angel began to sound his warning and invite humanity to "worship Him who made" in the mid-nineteenth century, different ideas began to surface regarding the origins of life. Charles Darwin and others began to propose an alternate view that left the Creator out of the picture. Many scientists began to question the teaching of creation as expressed by the first chapter of Genesis. Sadly, in the past century and a half the doctrines of Darwin have been the ones to take traction in our schools and textbooks. Jokes ridicule those who "actually believe" the Genesis account. But could we not also argue that we have never lived in an age when we find so much evidence that points to the origin of life by a Master Designer?

Some scientists today are becoming convinced that creationism makes more and more sense, because of two compelling reasons: design and irreducible complexity. Whichever paradigm one chooses—creationism or evolutionism—each of them requires faith. It requires faith to believe in the Creator-God, and equally it requires faith to believe that life evolved. Which has the stronger support based on the evidence? That is the question!

Design as an Evidence of a Creator

Would anyone believe that a common wristwatch resulted from an explosion in a gear factory? Or would anyone believe that a camera "just happened"? Does not the design of a watch or a camera testify to a designer? A short time ago the television game show *Jeopardy* featured a computer given the name "Watson" that competed with human contestants to give the correct answers first. Did that "just happen"? Those individuals who spent considerable time in programming those devices would feel insulted if they did not receive appropriate credit (which they did) for their skill in designing the computer. Yet it was a relatively simple machine compared to the complexities of any living organism. Indeed, where is the wristwatch or camera that has the capacity to "procreate" another in its likeness? One could argue that it takes more faith to believe in evolution than creation! The concept of "design" bears testimony to a "Designer."

Nature teaches us that the concept of design applies not only to function but also to aesthetics. About eight centuries ago an Italian mathematician by the name of Leonardo of Pisa, also known as Fibonacci (a contraction of *filius Bonacci*, or "son of Bonaccio"), explored a proportion often called the "golden mean," or the "golden ratio." Though discovered many centuries earlier, the name "Fibonacci" seems to be the one we associate most often with it.

Mathematically, it represents the number 1.618, obtained by beginning with the equation 1 + 1 = 2. If you add the last two numbers of the sequence together (1 + 1 = 2; 1 + 2 = 3; 2 + 3 = 5; 3 + 5 = 8; 5 + 8 = 13, etc.), you will obtain this ratio. The human brain perceives objects employing the ratio as the most pleasing to the eye. If you take a "golden rectangle," one built on the Fibonacci ratio, and block off a square within it, you will be left with a smaller rectangle, but one that displays the same ratio of 1.618. Remove from this smaller rectangle a square and a smaller rectangle will remain, which also will contain the same proportions, and so on. Should you continue doing this and connect the corners of the squares, you'll see something like the cross section of a nautilus shell.

Long before Fibonacci, people knew about it and incorporated it into architectural design. In the fifth century B.C. the Greek sculptor Phidias used the golden ratio extensively in the making of the Parthenon, reputed to be one of the world's most aesthetically drafted buildings. The ratio of its width to its height is a perfect golden rectangle. So familiar was Phidias with this ratio that the numeric value 1.618 was assigned the first letter of his name, "phi," in his honor, similar to "pi," which stands for the ratio of 3.14. Scholars have done extensive study of the golden ratio in Greek art. Other research has shown that the Egyptians incorporated the ratio in the construction of the great pyramids that pre-dated the Greeks by centuries.

The musical scale is also an example of Fibonacci numbers. There are 13 notes, including both ends of the octave. Looking at these notes on a piano, you will see that there are eight white notes and five black notes, all of which are numbers in the Fibonacci sequence. The fifth and third notes combine to form the basic chord. We find this scale and chords pleasant to our ears.

Is this something that human beings invented on their own, or do we see the golden ratio appearing in God's handiwork, nature? Scholars and researchers have written numerous books demonstrating that this ratio of 1.618 dominates the natural world about us. Just put the words "Fibonacci nature" into your computer search engine, and you will find a multitude of Web sites that feature pictures and diagrams showing this ratio in nature. Flowers exhibit it, the number of petals on many varieties being Fibonacci numbers, such as the 13 petals on a black-eyed Susan and the 34 petals on an ordinary field daisy.

The profile of a dolphin reveals it. The cross section of a nautilus shell is a magnificent example of a golden rectangle. The spirals on pinecones, pineapples, and sunflowers reflect it. The human body and face abound in illustrations of the golden ratio. Those faces that are blessed to conform closest to the golden ratio are perceived to be the most beautiful.[2]

Fibonacci discovered that many things in nature exhibit this "golden ratio." Does not the testimony of the harmony of aesthetics and design in nature bear witness to the existence and majesty of a great and powerful God, who is both an intelligent engineer as well as a lover of beauty? Today we have abundant reasons for worshipping "Him who made."

Irreducible Complexity Bears Witness to Fiat Creation

"Irreducible complexity" is a concept describing a machine or system from which you cannot remove any component without destroying its functionality. A mousetrap, for example, has only a few parts: the piece of wood on which the parts are mounted, the clamps to hold things in place, the spring, the bait tray, and the release bar. The point is that all of its elements must be in place for the trap to operate successfully. You cannot eliminate any one of them without destroying its ability to work. If you take away the clamps that hold the spring in place, the trap will not snap shut. Nor will it operate without the spring. This is "irreducible complexity."[3]

Scientists are beginning to see that in life, beginning at the "simple" (a great misnomer!) cell, all component parts must be present and working properly for the system as a whole to function. The logical deductions from this line of reasoning are astounding. It clearly refutes the entire concept of life evolving through eons of time, slowly adding new attributes bit by bit. It just couldn't happen that way. "Irreducible complexity" challenges Darwinian evolution. But there is a way of thinking that makes much more sense: "In the beginning God created." Because He is the awesome God who creates out of His divine energy, He deserves first place in our lives—He deserves our worship. It is a duty and privilege to respond to the first angel's call to "worship Him who made."

The Scriptural Time Line

When God created, He made all things intact and whole. They came forth from His hand complete and mature. If you had been able to see Adam in Eden the following Tuesday after God made him, for example, and someone asked you how old he was, you might have guessed him to be about 30 or so. Wrong! He's only days old! "How can that be?" you protest. The evidence doesn't suggest an origin that recent. No, it doesn't. The visible "evidence" is misleading in that it doesn't take into account the manner of his origin. He does appear to be about 30, no question about it. But he's not. Although he came into being only a few days before, God made him complete, fully mature. Adam came forth from the Creator as an adult in every aspect: thinking, speaking, and living.

Likewise the trees in the Garden of Eden might have appeared to be years old, laden with their bounty of fruit, but your eyes would have fooled you if you attempted to guess their age based on what they looked like. They were only a couple days older than Adam. But they, like him, originated complete and mature. What would have otherwise taken years to happen (the ripe fruit weighing down the branches) occurred instantly by the fiat creation of God.

Do not be misled by the claims of many as to the origin of life. The Bible record is perfectly reliable. To the modern atheistic scientist of today Jesus, the Creator-God, sadly shakes His head, saying, "You are mistaken, not knowing the Scriptures nor the power of God" (Matt. 22:29). God left much of the Bible to be written by the prophets, but His own hand inscribed the Ten Commandments that contain the truth "In six days the Lord made the heavens and the earth" (Ex. 20:11).

Nor do we need to assign large measures of time to the days of Creation week. The Hebrew grammar does not allow any such distortion. People misuse the text "with the Lord one day is as a thousand years, and a thousand years as one day" (2 Peter 3:8) when they try to connect it with Genesis 1. The expression "evening and morning" employed to describe the days of Creation week consistently means a literal 24-hour period of time.

Second, according to the rules of Hebrew grammar, the attachment of the ordinal to the word "day," as in "first day," "second day," etc., makes it certain that a literal day is meant. It is true that "day" (Hebrew *yom*) can sometimes refer to an indefinite period of time, as in the phrase "day of the Lord." That would be analogous to our usage "the day of computers." But never, when an ordinal is coupled with the word "day," does it mean anything but a regular 24-hour segment of time.

Scripture is clear that "by the word of the Lord the heavens were made, and all the host of them by the breath of His mouth. . . . For He spoke, and it was done; He commanded, and it stood fast" (Ps. 33:6-9; the word "done," appearing in many versions in verse 9, is supplied). Yes, in this age when many have left God out of the picture, the call to "worship Him who made" is of particular relevance.

This phrase derives from two ancient and important sources, each of which we should note. The angel quoted from the Ten Commandments when he cried out, "worship Him who made heaven and earth, the sea." The fourth commandment reads, "Remember the Sabbath day, to keep it holy. Six days you shall labor and do all your work, but the seventh day is the Sabbath of the Lord your God. In it you shall do no work: you, nor your son, nor your daughter, nor your male servant, nor your female servant, nor your cattle, nor your stranger who is within your gates. For in six days the *Lord made the heavens and the earth, the sea* and all that is in them, and rested the seventh day. Therefore the Lord blessed the Sabbath day and hallowed it" (Ex. 20:8-11).

The language employed by the first angel unquestioningly draws our attention to the memorial of God's creative act, the Sabbath. When the angel cries out, "worship Him who made," it logically directs our minds to the memorial of God's Creation, the Sabbath. God established it as the sacred reminder of how our earth and atmosphere came to be. "Thus the heavens and the earth, and all the host of them, were finished. And on the seventh day God ended His work which He had done, and He rested on the seventh day from all His work which He had done. Then God blessed the seventh day and sanctified it, because in it He rested from all His work which God had created and made" (Gen. 2:1-3).

This divine reminder has been under attack from the very beginning, for Satan saw how great a blessing the Sabbath can be when faithfully observed. The devil hates the Sabbath, because it identifies God as the Creator; because by taking time off and spending it with Him it builds our relationship with God; because it outlines salvation as a system of grace (we rest in His work); and because it demonstrates God's ability to bring His work to completion. The Sabbath is a statement that the same God who took a glob of matter "without form and void" and worked on it day by day through the power of His Word and made it "good" can likewise take my life, which spiritually is "without form and void," and through His creative Word re-create me day by day into something "good." The Sabbath is a teaching tool for the gospel.

Satan inspired God's children in Old Testament times to forget the Sabbath, leading to the discipline of captivity (Jer. 17:27). When they returned from Babylon, he induced them to heap mounds of unnecessary regulations and requirements upon the day of God's blessing, making it cumbersome and burdensome, obscuring its beauty. Thus when Christ came to earth the first time, many saw Him as a lawbreaker because He didn't countenance their useless and distracting rules of Sabbath observance. It was the devil's "setup" for the Jewish leadership to reject Jesus.

But Christ was not a lawbreaker, at least regarding divine law. Instead, He restored the Sabbath to its original magnificence, stating, "It is lawful to do good on the Sabbath" (Matt. 12:12). He had no intention to change or remove the Sabbath. "Do not think that I came to destroy the Law or the Prophets. I did not come to destroy but to fulfill. For assuredly, I say to you, till heaven and earth pass away, one jot or one tittle will by no means pass from the law till all is fulfilled" (Matt. 5:17, 18).

What was a "jot" and what was a "tittle"? They were parts of Hebrew letters. Today we might speak of the "dotting of an 'i' or the crossing of a 't.'" What Jesus said was "I have not come to destroy the commandments. I have not come to remove a paragraph, a sentence, a phrase, a word, a letter, or even a fragment of a letter from the law." How much plainer could it be? Contrary to the teaching of some, He didn't abolish the Sabbath. Rather, He lifted from the Sabbath those human-made impediments that dimmed its true luster.

During the centuries following Christ's ascension, Satan attacked the Sabbath again, inspiring the church to substitute God's day of appointment, the seventh day, with the first day, a common working day according to Scripture. "Six days you shall labor and do all your work." According to the Word of God, Sunday is an ordinary working day. In these last days the angel calls us to return to the simple obedience of the Ten Commandments, including the fourth, which specifies the day of worship to be the seventh day.

Someone might wonder, "What is the angel speaking about when he says, 'Worship Him who made heaven and earth'"? When Scripture speaks of the creation of "heaven and earth," it does not require us to understand that the entire universe came into existence during the seven days of Genesis 1 and 2. The Bible alludes to "three heavens"; the first being the atmosphere where the birds fly; the second being the area of space occupied by the stars, and the third being the dwelling of God Himself. Thus in vision Paul found himself caught up to the "third heaven" (2 Cor. 12:2, 3).

When Genesis states that "in the beginning God created the heavens and the earth" or when the fourth commandment declares, "For in six days the Lord made the heavens and the earth," it is not speaking of the universe in its entirety, but of that "heaven" that became the "firmament" or atmosphere of our planet (and perhaps the solar system). Thus the "new heaven and a new earth" of which John the revelator speaks will be not a complete revision of the universe, but a cleansing of our atmosphere that has become polluted with sin (see Rev. 21:1).

As we saw, the angel draws his command to "worship Him who made" from the language of the fourth commandment, inviting a return to the worship of the Creator-God on the day He set apart and hallowed. But a careful reading of the first angel's message reveals that it contains something beyond a quotation of the Sabbath commandment. The angel cries out, "Worship Him that made heaven, and earth, and the sea, and the fountains of water" (KJV). Nearly every word of that instruction is from the fourth commandment, except the phrase "fountains of water." Nowhere in the Ten Commandments do we find that wording. Where does it come from, and why is that significant?

We find that phrase derives from the Flood story. At that time the "fountains" of the deep were broken up, yielding a deluge of water (Gen. 7:11; 8:2). (The Greek word in Revelation 14:7, *pege,* "fountain or spring," is the same as in the Greek Septuagint translation of Genesis 7:11 and 8:2.) The angel is directing our attention to the two great geological events of Genesis, the Creation and the Flood, both denied by modern science. The Sabbath as a reminder of Creation is of primary importance, because the return to obedience to the Ten Commandments is vital. Thus we are directed to "worship Him who made."

But the angel also points us to the other cosmic event of antiquity: the Flood. He alludes to the "fountains" of water broken up at the Deluge. It's relevant because the Flood testifies to God's system of justice and His plan for our planet. When human iniquity passed the point of divine tolerance, God took action and destroyed the earth, although providing salvation through the preaching of Noah. That is the lesson the angel wants us to see in his warning message recorded in Revelation 14! Earth today is fast approaching the limits of divine forgiveness and is slated for destruction, not by water but by fire. "But as the days of Noah were, so also will the coming of the Son of Man be" (Matt. 24:37). There is utmost urgency in the voice of the angel! Remember Noah's ark!

Today scoffers roam the earth disputing the biblical record of the Flood. They question the concept of a worldwide deluge carving the earth into its present topography. Yet we find much to corroborate the scriptural record of a worldwide flood. When Edmund Hillary climbed Mount Everest in 1953, he encountered seashells at the 26,000-foot level.[4] How did they get there? If viewed with an open mind, we can find more than sufficient evidence to support the Flood story of the Bible.

The Flood, Scripture tells us forcefully, would be specifically mocked in the last days. "Knowing this first: that scoffers will come in the last days, walking according to their own lusts, and saying, 'Where is the promise of His coming? For since the fathers fell asleep, all things continue as they were from the beginning of creation.' For this they willfully forget: that by the word of God the heavens were of old, and the earth standing out of water and in the water, by which the world that then existed perished, being flooded with water" (2 Peter 3:3-6).

Peter said that the denial of the Flood by modern skeptics would be a characteristic of the "last days." Interestingly, it was in 1785 that Scottish geologist James Hutton presented some new ideas at the Royal Society of Edinburgh. He postulated that the earth was much older than the timeline represented by Scripture and that what we see in the earth's topography was not carved by a worldwide flood, as the Genesis story reveals, but instead he suggested that earth's formations were the result of long periods of slow geological changes.[5] Later in 1832 William Whewell coined the word "uniformitarianism."[6] Peter's phrase "all things continue as they were" could be a working definition for that term. In fulfillment of Peter's prophecy the concept was birthed in the "last days." However, his radical ideas didn't gain much support until Sir Charles Lyell, a lawyer, wrote the three-volume work *Principles of Geology*, in which he affirmed the concepts of Hutton, rejecting the Bible's information concerning the Flood.[7]

The God whom we are called to worship is the God of Genesis 1 and 2, who created the "heavens and the earth" by His divine word in six literal 24-hour days. Because He is Creator, He deserves our worship and homage. And because He is our Master, He merits our obedience by worshipping Him on the only day specified as holy in Scripture, the seventh day of the week. If God took the time personally to visit our planet in splendor and glory (such that even Moses said he feared greatly), lighting Sinai on fire with His presence and both speaking His holy law and inscribing it with His own finger in stone, should we not abide by His edict? As someone pointed out, they are correctly called the Ten Commandments, not Ten Suggestions.

God is not to be trifled with. He means what He says, and He has a plan for our planet. Sin, the unwanted intruder, has been confined in time and space. But the Lord will deal with sin, once and for all. He will destroy it and those who cling to it, not by water this time as during the Deluge, but by fire. Just as He provided deliverance in Noah's ark, He offers us salvation in Christ. The first angel calls us to worship this loving and caring God who, for the sake of the safety and serenity of the universe, will not allow sin to continue indefinitely.

---

[1] http://en.wikipedia.org/wiki/Worship.
[2] Check out such Web sites as http://www.goldennumber.net/ for more information and visuals.
[3] See, for example, http://www.ideacenter.org/contentmgr/showdetails.php/id/840.
[4] http://ianjuby.org/tour3.html.
[5] See, for example, http://www.marathon.uwc.edu/geography/Hutton/Hutton.htm.
[6] http://en.wikipedia.org/wiki/Uniformitarianism.
[7] http://en.wikipedia.org/wiki/Principles_of_Geology.

CHAPTER 12

"BABYLON" AND THE SECOND ANGEL'S MESSAGE

The message of the second angel reads, "Babylon is fallen, is fallen, that great city, because she has made all nations drink of the wine of the wrath of her fornication" (Rev. 14:8). The first question that comes to mind is What does He mean by "Babylon"? A recognized rule of Bible study is to take the Scripture as it reads, understanding its words and terms literally, unless compelled by context or reason to do otherwise. We find that the book of Revelation uses symbols and signs generously to convey its information. The book's very first verse informs us that the message would be embedded in "signs." Thus we may expect that the word "Babylon" might be used in a figurative sense. Second, since it was destroyed and lay in ruins for more than a century before Christ, a literal or physical Babylon no longer existed. Therefore we should understand the term in a symbolic sense. But what does "Babylon" mean? Are there clues to understand what the symbol signifies? And what does its "fall" represent?

Studying the Babylon of the past will give us insights as to how we should interpret it in its symbolic sense. In fact, as we noted previously, there are a number of "Babylons" to which we should give our attention, six of them altogether. First was the "Babylon" of the Tower of Babel, shortly after the Flood. The great Hammurabi ruled a Babylon during Abraham's lifetime. Nebuchadnezzar made "neo-Babylon" famous. The apostle Peter alluded to the "Babylon" of Rome. Then we have the "Babylon" to which Revelation refers, which appears in two separate manifestations. We need to study the "Babylons" of history in order to digest and distill the components that identify it and establish its character.

The "Babylon" of Babel

The roots of many of the symbols of Revelation trace back to the book of Genesis, and Babylon is certainly one of them. The first verses of Genesis 11 record the Tower of Babel, the first "Babylon": "Now the whole earth had one language and one speech. And it came to pass, as they journeyed from the east, that they found a plain in the land of Shinar, and they dwelt there. Then they said to one another, 'Come, let us make bricks and bake them thoroughly.' They had brick for stone, and they had asphalt for mortar. And they said, 'Come let us build ourselves a city, and a tower whose top is in the heavens; let us make a name for ourselves, lest we be scattered abroad over the face of the whole earth'" (Gen. 11:1-4).

The tower builders acted in defiance of the will of God. It had been His purpose to have people spread out across the land and repopulate it, not to congregate in great cities. Cities were the product of the descendants of Cain (Gen. 4:17), the children of Nimrod, the great hunter who arose in insubordination to the Lord. "And the beginning of his kingdom was Babel" (Gen. 10:10). From there he went and originated many of the great cities of antiquity, including Nineveh, the future capital of Assyria.

The builders of Babel disbelieved the divine promise whispered in the rainbow: that He would never again flood the entire world with water. They placed their tower on the foundation of unbelief and constructed it with the bricks of self-attainment. It was based on a system of "salvation by works," not faith. In stark colors we may paint these ideas on the canvas of "Babylon": unbelief, defiance, and salvation by works.

The name "Babel" meant literally "gate of the gods."[1] Designed to be the connection between the "here" and the "hereafter," it was their attempt to sidestep the revealed will of God and come to knowledge by another way, one of their own making. A well-known music group of the 1960s styled themselves in a similar role, thinking themselves as being the nexus between the now and the future. With that in mind, they called themselves the Doors.

The great deceiver, Satan, has always put forth other avenues and ways to penetrate the curtain of tomorrow. Through astrology and false science, through witchcraft and necromancy, Lucifer has peddled his version of the story. The Bible makes it clear that all such attempts to learn the secrets of the future are futile and dangerous, and therefore off-limits to the child of God. "The secret things belong to the Lord our God, but those things which are revealed belong to us and to our children forever, that we may do all the words of this law" (Deut. 29:29).

There is only one Way, only one Ladder, only one Mediator, and only one Door, and His name is Jesus. He was the ladder of Jacob's dream (see John 1:51). "I am the way, the truth, and the life. No one comes to the Father except through Me" (John 14:6). Jesus is the one mediator between God and humanity (1 Tim. 2:5). The tower builders missed, ignored, or outright rejected this truth in their construction of the "gate of the gods." Their project met with disaster, as have more recent attempts, such as the ill-fated Heaven's Gate movement. Such attempts to become the link between heaven and earth—a blasphemous and boastful claim to take the position that only our Savior Jesus can occupy—become a fundamental brick in the foundation of biblical Babylon.

The ancient priests of Babylon promoted themselves as being the connecting link between earth and heaven. They were the "bridge" across the chasm separating the visible from the invisible. To express their supposed role, they chose the title "bridgemaker." Later the concept migrated from Babylon to the emperors of ancient Rome and then filtered into the church of Rome. Today the head of the Catholic Church is called the "pontiff," which is an abbreviation of the title "Pontifex (from *pont*, "bridge," and *fex*, "to build") Maximus ("the greatest")," meaning "the greatest bridgebuilder."

The name "Babel" is similar to the Hebrew *balal,* "the confused." Through the use of wordplay it became identified with the concept of confusion. "Therefore its name is called Babel, because there the Lord confused the language of all the earth" (Gen. 11:9). The concept of "confusion" as a component in the fabric of Babylon is one that we will encounter later in our study. Defiant obstinacy, unbelief, salvation by works, blasphemous claims to divine wisdom, and confusion: these are the components of the "Babylon" of Genesis 11.

The Babylon of Hammurabi

Of the Babylon ruled by Hammurabi the Bible says little. When Scripture tells us that God called Abram to leave "Ur of the Chaldees," we may assume that he could have known of, or perhaps even been acquainted with, Hammurabi. They lived at roughly the same time. When we hear the name of Hammurabi, we often think of the seven-foot-plus diorite stele displayed in the Louvre in Paris, on which he had inscribed the laws of his kingdom. I've been privileged to see it firsthand. It's inspiring to stand in front of it and realize that you're in the presence of nearly 4,000 years of history. As I try to imagine the workers who chiseled the precepts and statues into its surface, I wonder if they could have ever dreamed that someone would one day fly in a jet across the ocean to view their work four millennia later!

Comparing the laws of Hammurabi with those given to Moses is interesting. Both sets of laws are quite thorough and in many respects quite similar. Overall, one can argue that the code of Hammurabi is a bit harsher in its punishments than the Mosaic law. From a wider perspective, we note that the Babylon of Hammurabi had a law, and that law was written in stone. That law was the foundation of its government.

Likewise, God's kingdom, the antithesis of scriptural Babylon, also has a law, and it too was written in stone. It wasn't chiseled by a mason's tool but rather traced by the finger of the Lord. Though the original of His law is not displayed in a museum as is the Code of Hammurabi, its tenets are most certainly valid and applicable to us today. It will be the law by which we will be judged (James 2:10-12). As long as heaven and earth exist, so will God's law (Matt. 5:17-19). When we consider the Babylon of Hammurabi, we think of its law—similar, but not really identical to the law of God.

The Babylon of Nebuchadnezzar

The third "Babylon" was the one established by Nabopolassar, the father of Nebuchadnezzar. He came to power in 626 B.C. and accomplished an astonishing amalgamation of what had before been some loosely held and disorganized communities.[2] What he achieved was so remarkable that God told the prophet Habakkuk in 630 B.C.:

"Look among the nations and watch—be utterly astounded! For I will work a work in your days which you would not believe, though it were told you. For indeed, I am raising up the Chaldeans, a bitter and hasty nation" (Hab. 1:5, 6).

Historians refer to his kingdom as "neo-Babylon," or "new-Babylon." The Babylon that Nabopolassar and his successors built was amazing. It featured the magnificent hanging gardens constructed by Nebuchadnezzar for his wife in case she might miss the forests and glades of her native Media. Nurtured by an intricate internal irrigation system that tapped the waters of the Euphrates, the river which ran through the city, it was touted as one of the Seven Wonders of the Ancient World.[3]

Babylon was a city of gold, with tons of it stored in a Fort Knox penthouse on the top of the temple of Marduk in the Esaglia, reputed to have been built on the very foundation of the ancient Tower of Babel. The historian Herodotus reported that it housed 800 talents of gold within its walls, including the gold that shimmered on the colossal statue of Marduk.[4] If an ancient talent were 75 pounds, you can multiply 800 (talents) times 75 (pounds) times 14.58 (ounces troy per pound) times the value of gold per ounce in today's market to come up with a dollar value. It would be sure to be a big number! Scripture declares, "Take up this proverb against the king of Babylon, and say: 'How the oppressor has ceased, the golden city ceased!'" (Isa. 14:4). "Babylon was a golden cup in the Lord's hand" (Jer. 51:7). Fittingly, in the statue dream of Daniel 2, the head of gold represented the kingdom of Babylon.

The parallels and lessons concerning ancient and apocalyptic Babylon are numerous and would require an in-depth study of Isaiah 14; 40-50, and Jeremiah 50 and 51, as well as some other portions of Scripture. That would be too broad for our scope here. We will limit ourselves to some of the highlights. Babylon of old conceived itself as being an "eternal city," aspiring to "be a lady forever" (Isa. 47:7). Its defense systems gave it a sense of impregnability. Surrounded by a wall thick enough to allow a four-horse chariot to make a U-turn on its top,[5] together with a moat that could be filled with water from the Euphrates, the security it felt inspired Belshazzar to call for a banquet when the forces of Cyrus prepared to attack. Babylon considered itself irreplaceable and indestructible. It said in its heart, "I am, and there is no one else besides me" (Isa. 47:8).

Yet prophecy had pronounced its doom a century and a half before, even identifying Cyrus by name as being the instrument that God would use to accomplish His purpose, as well as the means by which he would gain entrance into the city (Isa. 45:1, 2). Precisely fulfilling the prophecy, the engineers of Cyrus found a way to divert the waters of the mighty Euphrates that ran through the city.[6] When they approached the iron gates guarding the entrance, the troops were shocked to find them unlocked. Cyrus marched his army in and took the unsuspecting city without conflict. Belshazzar, who had raised his cup (one that came originally from the Temple of Yahweh) in defiant blasphemy against the word of the Lord, was slain that very night. The judgment inscribed by the bloodless hand in letters of fire on the palace wall, interpreted by God's prophet Daniel, was executed without delay.

Babylon had been God's tool for reform for Judah—God's "hammer" to effect discipline against Jerusalem (Jer. 50:23). It was He who gave Judah into the hand of Babylon's monarch (Dan. 1:2). The Lord offered the nation prestigious opportunities, and if it had complied with the divine plan, who can say what its future might have been. Yet, despite the conversion of Nebuchadnezzar, as a whole it denied the Holy One of Israel and scoffed at God's prophets. Refusing to recognize the authority of Yahweh, it credited the success of its victories to its lifeless deities (Hab. 1:11). Thus its day of opportunity came to a close. Instead of being something that God could use, it became fated to destruction. We must keep these ideas in mind when we consider what apocalyptic Babylon is all about.

God had to let ancient Babylon go because of its insolence and pride. Indeed, its hubris so closely mirrored that of the one who first fell in heaven that Scripture uses the story of the king of Babylon as a backdrop to describe the fall of Lucifer. When you read Isaiah 14, you will see that it begins by addressing the "king of Babylon," but then passes quickly and seamlessly to discuss the one who stood behind him, the entity who inspired him with the spirit of pride and self-seeking. "How you are fallen from heaven, O Lucifer, son of the morning!" (Isa. 14:12). The king of Babylon reflected the image of Satan, in whose character pride is a notable flaw.

The passage addresses the real monarch of "Babylon" as if seeking an explanation of his fall from glory. How could it be that sin would originate in the heart of a being created perfect (Eze. 28:15)? Of course, there is no satisfactory answer as to the origin of sin. The existence of iniquity has no reasonable explanation. When we discuss the fall of Babylon later in the second angel's message, let us not forget the fall of the original king of "Babylon," the one who was the "anointed covering cherub" but became the archenemy of God, the one who was the "light bearer" (the meaning of "Lucifer") who became the prince of darkness. Lucifer's mysterious fall is the prototype of the later fall of apocalyptic Babylon.

Another characteristic of ancient Babylon was its ruthless treatment of God's people. While it is true that God employed Babylon as a rod of discipline against backsliding Judah, the nation overreached, and the Lord took notice. "You were glad, . . . you rejoiced, you destroyers of My heritage" (Jer. 50:11). "The children of Israel were oppressed, along with the children of Judah; all who took them captive have held them fast; they have refused to let them go" (verse 33). God would hold them accountable for the ill treatment of His children. The horror of ancient wartime techniques brings a chill to the spine. "O daughter of Babylon, who are to be destroyed, happy the one who repays you as you have served us! Happy the one who takes and dashes your little ones against the rock" (Ps. 137:8, 9). For its pride, arrogance, cruelty, and attempt to take the place of God and to become "God"—for all of these things, ancient Babylon became the template for apocalyptic Babylon.

The "Babylon" of Civil Rome

The fourth "Babylon" is the city to which Peter referred when he closed his first epistle with the words "She who is in Babylon, elect together with, greets you" (1 Peter 5:13). It is obvious that the apostle could not have been speaking of a literal Babylon, since that no longer existed. Since we know that Peter was taken to Rome, it makes sense that he is alluding to that city in a figurative way. Why would he do so? No doubt he was thinking of the persecutions and oppressions brought about by ancient Babylon and drawing a similarity between Nebuchadnezzar's kingdom and Rome, the world empire of Peter's day.

Rome exercised an iron rule, both in severity and longevity. Among the components of Nebuchadnezzar's statue dream, the legs of iron, representing Rome, outlived the combined span of the three other kingdoms before it. Iron, as employed by the symbol of the statue dream, was an appropriate designation for the empire of Rome. "And the fourth kingdom shall be as strong as iron, inasmuch as iron breaks in pieces and shatters everything; and like iron that crushes, that kingdom will break in pieces and crush all the others" (Dan. 2:40). That's exactly what pagan Rome did.

God's people, both as the God-fearing Jews and the soon-to-be-born Christian church, felt the tread of the iron boot of Rome. A Roman governor gave the nod to crucify Jesus. Roman soldiers nailed Roman spikes that held the Savior to a Roman cross.

Roman authority brought about the persecution of early Christians when they refused to bow the knee to Nero. They became the food of lions in the Colosseum and the fuel for Roman torches to light their parties. Roman swords brought an end to the lives of many of Christ's followers, including the apostles James and Paul. It was in Rome that Peter met a martyr's end. Through the first centuries the wrath of Rome made it dangerous to be a believer in Christ. The persecution of Diocletian, the last convulsion of civil Rome's attempt to eradicate the new faith, was furious in its intensity. Well might the apostle Peter have used the word "Babylon" as a code term for the capitol of Rome.

The "Babylon" of Papal Rome

The fifth expression of "Babylon" is the church of the Middle Ages, the administrative organization known as the Papacy. Again, remember that we're speaking of the system and structure of the Papacy, not the church's individual members. We're addressing *Catholicism*, not *Catholics*. God-fearing followers of Christ exist within it and all other communities of faith. When we speak of the church of the Middle Ages, we are addressing not its individual members, but its ecclesiastical framework. Revelation 18 tells us that God has His people in Babylon, and that He loves them so much that He is calling them into His truth.

When the apostle John was invited to see the "judgment of the great harlot who sits on many waters" (Rev. 17:1) on which the title "MYSTERY, BABYLON THE GREAT" (verse 5) was inscribed, the clues leave little doubt that this picture includes the church that ruled with an iron fist for centuries. Often the Bible symbolically employs a woman to represent a church or other religious body (Jer. 3:14; 6:2, etc.). The image of the impure woman of Revelation 17 is one of the seven representations in Scripture we will study that depict ecclesiastical Rome. Under its medieval leadership, countless numbers faced martyrdom. Some estimate the toll as somewhere between 50 and 100 million.[7]

By the flame, by the rack, by the sword, and by countless other instruments of torture, the saints of God endured the intolerance of the religious leadership during the Middle Ages. Indeed, as prophesied through Daniel, the "power of the holy people" was "completely shattered" during this time period, the most frequently mentioned time prophecy in Scripture (seven times). Note that Scripture presents the theme of religious apostasy in seven "pictures," and its time span also seven times.

The persecutions of the Dark Ages lasted for 1260 years, a time span couched in three different symbolic ways. It is portrayed as 1260 "days" (a day standing for a year in symbolic prophecy; see Num. 14:34; Eze. 4:6), 42 "months," and 3½ "times" (years). We find these phrases in Daniel 7:25 and 12:7, and Revelation 11:2, 3; 12:6, 14; 13:5. A comparison of the passages makes it clear that they all refer to the same time period of 1260 literal years.

When did the time period begin? The transition from civil to ecclesiastical Rome did not happen overnight, but the third, fourth, and fifth centuries saw a general ascendancy of the papal administrative structure and a corresponding decline of pagan Rome. When the empire moved its seat of operation from Rome to Constantinople, the bishop of Rome filled the power vacuum left behind with his leadership.

In the year A.D. 533 the Emperor Justinian issued his famous code, the law of the empire, in which he specified the bishop of Rome as being the head of the Christian church and the "corrector of heretics."[8] By such language the emperor elevated the bishop of Rome to a status of unequaled authority and power. However, because of the threat of some of the tribes opposed to the new arrangement (particularly the Ostrogoths), the Papacy could not completely fulfill its new position of supremacy. The battles between the forces of the Papacy and Ostrogoths went back and forth for a time. When the Papacy regained the control of Rome, the Ostrogoths mounted an attack against it, but the forces of Emperor Justinian's General Belisarius aided it. The Ostrogoths abandoned their siege in A.D. 538, leaving the church leadership free to pursue its agenda.[9] This date marks the beginning of the Papacy's full reign.

The following centuries would witness increasing power and position, peaking in the eleventh-thirteenth centuries. The impact of the Protestant Reformation would etch into papal authority, and finally in 1798, General Louis Alexandre Berthier, under orders from Emperor Napoleon Bonaparte, took Pope Pius VI captive.[10] Many thought the Papacy was dead and would never revive. The time between these two dates, the 1260 years between A.D. 538 and A.D. 1798, comprises the prophetic time span of 1260 "days" mentioned seven times in Scripture.

Apocalyptic "Babylon"

While the historical Papacy is certainly part of the picture in Revelation 17's depiction of "Babylon," it is also true that the symbol reveals "Babylon" as the last-day conglomerate of all forces in opposition to God and His kingdom. The fact that it is a coalition of separate segments we find indicated by the reference in the previous chapter that the "city" is "divided into three parts" (Rev. 16:19). Apocalyptic Babylon represents the cooperative efforts of the "beast" (the historical Papacy), the "false prophet" (fallen Protestantism), and the "dragon" (spiritualism) that all work in confederacy with the "kings of the earth." Like Revelation 13's beast from the sea which shares similarities with many former enemies of God in that it was like a leopard, bear, and lion (code terms for the kingdoms of Greece, Medo-Persia, and Babylon in the past), the woman/beast symbol of Revelation 17 is the final-day combination of entities that fight against God.

The first part of Revelation 17's description (verses 1-6) emphasizes the "woman" of Babylon, while the latter part (verses 7-18) stresses the "beast" on which she rides. The symbol of the "woman" focuses on those entities that promote themselves as being spiritual. Scripture symbolizes God's people as wedded to its Lord. "I was a husband to them" (Jer. 31:32). "I have betrothed you to one husband, that I may present you as a chaste virgin to Christ" (2 Cor. 11:2).

When God's people strayed from their allegiance to their "husband," the Lord, Scripture described the situation as being that of a harlot. The heart-wrenching story of Hosea breathes this imagery. God indicted Judah of old "because you have gone as a harlot after the Gentiles, because you have become defiled by their idols" (Eze. 23:30). The Lord told Jerusalem that they had become guilty because "you trusted in your own beauty, played the harlot because of your fame, and poured out your harlotry on everyone passing by who would have it" (Eze. 16:15).

The apostle James clearly defines spiritual fornication or adultery. "Adulterers and adulteresses! Do you not know that friendship with the world is enmity with God? Whoever therefore wants to be a friend of the world makes himself an enemy of God" (James 4:4). When those who have pledged their love to God abandon that covenant relationship and seek alliances with the world, they commit spiritual harlotry.

When the Bible uses the word "harlot," expect that it will refer to an entity that at one time vowed to follow God, and no doubt did for some period of time, but later slipped from the relationship with its Husband and conducted an illicit affair with others. While it is a slightly different way of looking at the word "harlot," a study of the Scriptures containing the word confirms it. The Bible at one time describes Old Testament Israel as "the people of God," but the nation later fell from that position and became a "harlot." The New Testament church began with lofty principles, but capitulated by compromise into apostasy. "Harlot," as used in Scripture, indicates that at one time there was "marriage." Strictly speaking, the Bible does not apply the term to "the world"; that is, those who have never professed allegiance to God. Rather, Scripture reserves it to those who have professed that relationship, but have left their Master. Expect that the "harlot" of Revelation will be an entity professing to follow God, but not living up to the truths of Scripture.

Notice that Revelation 17 calls the woman not only a "harlot" but also the "MOTHER OF HARLOTS" (Rev. 17:5). Being a mother, she must have daughters. Long has the Church of Rome styled itself as the "mother church." Her daughters are those churches that have not relinquished the errors and deceptions Satan introduced into the church during its early centuries, and therefore they fall under the same indictment.

Yes, there was a Reformation, and it made many strides in regaining truths lost, obscured, or corrupted in the past. Martin Luther, John Calvin, and many more were God's mariners attempting to steer the ship of faith back on course, to plow the waters of Bible truth. The Protestant Reformation began in glory, yet in the succeeding centuries those churches that began with such brilliance have seen their light dimmed by worldliness and a failure to separate completely from the errors perpetuated by Rome, chief of which are the honoring of the first day of the week as the Sabbath and the belief in the immortality of the soul. Thus we must include apostate Protestantism in the mural of Babylon as portrayed in Revelation 17.

As previously mentioned, the first part of the chapter highlights the "woman" of Babylon, while the latter part emphasizes the "beast" that carries her. The sequence is appropriate, because it will be the religious forces that take the lead and instigate the last-day trial for God's people, but they will have to involve political forces in order to accomplish their goal of exterminating God's faithful.

Isn't this exactly what happened 2,000 years ago? It was the church—indeed, a fallen and apostate religious leadership—that led in the trial and execution of our Savior, Jesus Christ. Priests, scribes, and elders fomented and agitated for His death (Matt. 26:57-66). And yet the church had to solicit the assistance of the state, represented by Rome's governor, Pontius Pilate, in order to accomplish its intent. Under the rules of occupation, the Jews did not have the ability to carry out the death penalty—it could happen only through the complicity of Rome.

Listen to the voice of the mob, composed of religious leaders, demanding the crucifixion of the Messiah before the judgment seat of Pilate. Here's why that's so relevant to the message of Revelation: it was a union of church (by vote of the Sanhedrin) and state (the permission given by Pilate) that put Jesus on the cross. In a similar way, it will be a union of church (the "woman") and state (the political powers represented by the "beast," its "horns" and "kings") that will bring about Satan's last-day agenda of destroying Christ's followers.

In summary, the word "Babylon" has many facets, some rooted in history, some in symbol. The literal Tower of Babel was a "Babylon" constructed on the foundation of unbelief, defiance, and later confusion. The Babylon of Abraham's day had a law written on stone that was similar to, but not exactly the same, as God's law. The Babylon of Nebuchadnezzar's day began as the tool of God but ended up as a persecuting and apostate power, one condemned as blasphemous and reprobate. The "Babylon" of pagan Rome spilled the blood of Christ and His followers. And the "Babylon" of the church of the Middle Ages began in purity but declined into moral poverty and practiced intolerance to an unspeakable degree.

But there remains yet one more manifestation of Babylon. It will bring together all aspects into one last-day union of apostasy and blasphemy. Led by spiritual forces (the "woman") that will feature the Papacy and fallen Protestantism, it will shake hands with cooperative political forces, and thus Satan will seek to accomplish his design of ridding the earth of those faithful to God and His commandments.

---

[1] Robert Young, *Analytical Concordance to the Bible*, p. 66.

[2] See http://www.britannica.com/EBchecked/topic/401320/Nabopolassar.

[3] See http://www.cleveleys.co.uk/wonders/gardensofbabylon.htm.

[4] See Geoffrey W. Bromiley, *The International Standard Bible Encyclopedia*, vol. 1, p. 389.

[5] See http://www.cleveleys.co.uk/wonders/gardensofbabylon.htm.

[6] See http://en.wikipedia.org/wiki/Neo-Babylonian_Empire.

[7] www.cs.unc.edu~plaistered/estimate.doc.

[8] Uriah Smith, *Daniel and the Revelation*, p. 325.

[9] See http://en.wikipedia.org/wiki/Siege_of_Rome_(537%E2%80%93538).

[10] See http://www.newadvent.org/cathen/07006a.htm.

CHAPTER 13

"BABYLON IS FALLEN, IS FALLEN"

The message of the second angel is "Babylon is fallen, is fallen, that great city, because she has made all nations drink of the wine of the wrath of her fornication" (Rev. 14:8). We've discussed the varying manifestations of "Babylon." Now, what does the angel mean by its "fall"? And why does he mention it twice?

The concept of "fall" in Scripture is both sobering and mystifying. To understand the term "fall of Babylon," we need to begin with the one whom Scripture identifies as Babylon's king, none other than Lucifer himself. As we have already seen, Isaiah 14 begins as an address to the literal king of Babylon. God tells the prophet, "Take up this proverb against the king of Babylon" (Isa. 14:4), but then the message focuses on what clearly must be Satan, for we read, "How you are fallen from heaven, O Lucifer, son of the morning!" (verse 12). The form of the sentence in the NKJV expresses the thought of astonishment and incredulity. In the KJV it says, "How art thou fallen from heaven, O Lucifer, son of the morning!" Here the sentence structure also implies mysterious question, "How could you have fallen?"

The inception of sin has a mystery about it that baffles explanation. The Bible calls it the "mystery of iniquity" (2 Thess. 2:7, KJV). We find here in Isaiah 14 a wonderful beginning and unlimited potential, but a tragic and lamentable conclusion. It includes the concept that a creature could think it possible to achieve the status of the infinite Creator.

In analyzing Satan's fall, the Bible says, "For you have said in your heart: I will ascend into heaven . . . I will be like the Most High" (Isa. 14:13, 14). While His creatures were "made in His image" in character and feature, it is a gross mistake to think that the creature would ever

141

attain to the level of deity in all of its omnipotence. "Before Me there was no God formed, nor shall there be after Me" (Isa. 43:10). But that's what Lucifer wanted. It's what he thought he could become. He coveted the position and worship that belonged to the great Creator-God alone!

How one so beautiful, talented, and wise—so perfect in his ways—could become the devil and Satan defies reason. And yet it happened. Because the only allegiance acceptable to God is that given without coercion, free will was an integral component built into the character of all of His creatures. God made His creatures with the freedom of choice, knowing that it might happen that someday, someone might make the wrong decision. That being was Lucifer. Solomon put his finger on Lucifer's problem when he penned, "Pride goes before destruction, and a haughty spirit before a fall" (Prov. 16:18).

Although he began as the "covering cherub," he made himself into God's archenemy. He started as the "bearer of light" but transformed himself into the prince of darkness. Of him the Bible says, "You were the anointed cherub who covers; I established you" (Eze. 28:14). Reflecting on the construction of the ark of the covenant, with its cherubim above the mercy seat, it's not difficult to conclude that the expression "covering cherub" describes one whose position was next to God's throne. A highly honored and elevated position, it should have evoked gratitude and humility.

Not only that, but Scripture describes him as the "anointed cherub." The Hebrew word translated "anointed" is the root of "messiah." As they began their work, prophets, priests, and kings were anointed to inaugurate them into service. Each of them became a "messiah" in a very narrow sense, a dim reflection of the true Messiah. Cyrus, who liberated God's people from Babylon, was "anointed" (Isa. 45:1). He was in a limited scope a "messiah." In the fullest sense, Jesus is God's Anointed One. To a lesser degree Lucifer was also an "anointed one," a "messiah."

The Bible describes his beauty. "Every precious stone was your covering: the sardius, topaz, and diamond, beryl, onyx, and jasper, sapphire, turquoise, and emerald with gold" (Eze. 28:13). Could it be that the biblical writer mentions the stones because of their brilliance? Sometimes prophets struggled to find words to convey the incomparable things they saw. Human language can't adequately portray the glories of heaven. We know that God "wraps himself in light as with a garment" (Ps. 104:2, NIV). It's not too far a stretch to think that Lucifer, His "anointed" would also have a "garment of light." Could it be that what the prophet was trying to describe was Lucifer's garment of light whose flashing beauty and iridescence would make the throat of a hummingbird seem dull? Was this a "coat of many colors" given to the angel that stood closest to His throne?

His mysterious fall from glory became the template for later similar ones. We speak of the failure of Adam and Eve in the garden as the "Fall" (see 1 Tim. 2:14). They began in perfection but ended in ruin. We see the tragedy of "fall" in the life experience of Israel's first king. Saul enjoyed an outstanding beginning. "God gave him another heart" (1 Sam. 10:9) and "turned [him] into another man" (verse 6). The prophet Samuel anointed him for service. Yet he became a despotic paranoid tyrant who sought to spear his son Jonathan and his successor, David. Eventually, in a manner that typified his decline, he took his own life by falling on his sword. David lamented his tragic ending with the poignant words "The beauty of Israel is slain on your high places! How the mighty have fallen!" (2 Sam. 1:19).

That last phrase also captures Lucifer's story. He was a "mighty one," an "anointed one," and one day this same chorus will be sung of him: "How the mighty have fallen!" Adam was a "mighty one" who fell. The mighty nation of Israel "fell" from being the people of God, His chosen ones, only to have its leaders put God on a cross. A glorious beginning followed by a shameful decline is a narrative that all too often appears in Scripture and history. Lest we become haughty and high-minded, let us recognize that it is only through the grace and mercy of Christ that it is not also our story. "So, if you think you are standing firm, be careful that you don't fall" (1 Cor. 10:12, NIV).

We can see the "fall of Babylon" in the story of the Tower of Babel. Babel experienced its fall in a very literal sense. Because they denied the authority and promises of God, their building project came to a sudden end. The mighty Babylon of Belshazzar experienced a fall. Prophesied Isaiah (in words that obviously formed the backdrop for Revelation's warning), "Babylon is fallen, is fallen! And all the carved images of her gods He has broken to the ground" (Isa. 21:9). Said Jeremiah: "Shout against her all around; . . . her foundations have fallen, her walls are thrown down" (Jer. 50:15). "Babylon has suddenly fallen and been destroyed. Wail for her!" (Jer. 51:8). "I will punish Bel in Babylon, and I will bring out of his mouth what he has swallowed; . . . Yes, the wall of Babylon shall fall" (verse 44).

Through gluttony, debauchery, and idleness, the glory of Rome likewise departed and became the subject of books, as reflected in Gibbon's famous *The Rise and Fall of the Roman Empire.*

Paul predicted that the Christian church, whose establishment he gave his life for, would experience a fall. "Let no one deceive you by any means; for that Day will not come unless the falling away comes first" (2 Thess. 2:3). The church that began as the cradle of Christ's truth ended up punishing those who would own, read, or follow its precepts. How could such a thing happen?

The church became "Babylon," replicating all the unfavorable character traits of those entities that had opposed God in the past. Its fall from grace is both remarkable and mysterious. Well might the prophet have said regarding the ecclesiastical structure of the Middle Ages, "How you have fallen from heaven, you who were the bearer of light!" The first "fall" of the second angel refers to the incredible spiritual decline of the church of the first century, one clothed in purity and holiness, to the depths into which it descended through the centuries, its garments stained with the blood of martyrs.

A Second "Fall" of Babylon

At last, godly individuals led by His Spirit and through great travail inaugurated a Reformation in an attempt to change the church and correct its errors. For their efforts they endured every imaginable persecution: mockery, intimidation, the scaffold, the stocks, and the stake. They jeopardized life and limb in their endeavors to cleanse the church they loved and see a return to the truths and teachings of Scripture. Eventually, though not their original design, they broke from the Church of Rome, and those who saw light in their teachings formed other groups, other denominations.

Searching the sure Word of Scripture, they became convinced that the Bible taught salvation by grace, not by works. The believed that Scripture is above the church, not the other way around. Among their convictions was that the Church of Rome fulfilled all the prophetic specifications of Revelation's "Babylon," Paul's "man of sin," John's "antichrist," and Daniel's "horn power." (We will explore these aspects later.)

Keeping one's eyes focused on the earthly director, instead of Christ, can lead to trouble. In the Old Testament we read about Israel's departure from faithfulness after the demise of certain leaders. "So the people served the Lord all the days of Joshua, and all the days of the elders who outlived Joshua, who had seen all the great works of the Lord which He had done for Israel. . . . When all that generation had been gathered to their fathers, another generation arose after them who did not know the Lord nor the work which He had done for Israel. Then the children of Israel did evil in the sight of the Lord, and served the Baals" (Judges 2:7-11).

So it was also in the days of the Protestant Reformation. Those spiritual "Joshuas," who pioneered reform, at last were also "gathered to their fathers" and rested in the grave. Sadly, those who followed them refused to progress any further in the quest for truth than had their founders. Because the ship of truth had strayed so far from the Scriptures, Martin Luther was not capable, in his limited lifetime, to turn the vessel completely around, to accomplish all the reforms necessary.

God knows that total reformation requires time, and He is not impatient. But does that give license to remain stagnant in faith and refuse to advance? When Israel left Egypt, God overlooked some things that He hoped they would soon grow away from. The New Testament takes a tolerant stance on the issue of slavery (see the counsel in Philemon), yet today we recognize that it certainly has no place in God's ideal for society. God expected that the principle of *agape* love, finding root in converted hearts, would in time eliminate slavery, polygamy, and other things at one time tolerated.

Making spiritual progress is the goal of life. We do not expect a 2-year-old to use the language of a university professor. Parents are thrilled when their children speak their first words, though they be stumbling and imperfect. They are cherished and treasured and no doubt in many cases recorded. But if no development occurs beyond those first stammering attempts at speech, and throughout life and into adulthood he or she continues to speak as a 2-year-old, that would be most unfortunate. What Paul said about himself applies equally to the body of the church: "When I was a child, I spoke as a child, I understood as a child, I thought as a child; but when I became a man, I put away childish things" (1 Cor. 13:11).

Likewise, the Protestant Reformation in its infancy made great gains toward the ideals of scriptural truth, as God patiently sought to bring advancement to His people. But when the leaders of the various movements passed to their rest, their followers refused to go any further to search out and apply more of God's truths. They stagnated in the footsteps of their spiritual forefathers. In many cases not only was no forward progress achieved in the understanding of truth, but the vital spirituality that had sparked the movement in the first place began to fade or even vanish. Many truths that the earliest leaders had held, particularly in the area of prophetic interpretation, were later abandoned. Thus the Protestant Reformation "fell" from the high and holy ideal to which God had called it.

John Robinson was the pastor of America's Pilgrims. Hindered from making the voyage himself, he penned this remarkable counsel, to which all should take heed, recognizing the principle of the progressive revelation of truth. "Brethren, we are now erelong to part asunder, and the Lord knoweth whether I shall live ever to see your faces more. But whether the Lord hath appointed it or not, I charge you before God and His blessed angels to follow me no farther than I have followed Christ. If God should reveal anything to you by any other instrument of His, be as ready to receive it as ever you were to receive any truth of my ministry; for I am very confident that the Lord hath more truth and light yet to break forth out of His holy word."*

Had the children of the Reformation cherished that godly counsel, how different the story might have been. The Protestant Reformation might have led directly to the final promulgation of the gospel and the end of all things. But consistently its adherents allowed their feet to become glued to the tracks of their predecessors, refusing to take any additional steps beyond what the pioneers had taken. Thus today we have a multiplicity of Protestant churches, each claiming to follow the same book as their guide.

Sad to say, many of them no longer hold the convictions of their founders. The understanding of prophecy, so crystal clear in the minds of the Reformers, has dimmed into mist and fog in the minds of Protestants today. If you were to ask Martin Luther who the antichrist of Scripture is, he would have neither hesitated nor stammered. He would boldly affirm that the seat of Rome constituted the prophetic symbol. Today, however, those who identify themselves as Lutherans are not being taught what Martin Luther believed on the subject of prophecy.

Through the process of change brought about by the passing of time, a name given originally might later lose its significance. Not too far from where I now live in California is a place called Orange County. Some time ago it was a haven for citrus growing. Now it is planted with skyscrapers and freeways that long ago crowded out the orange groves. I often wonder if newcomers ask the question, Why is this metropolis called Orange County? In the same way, centuries ago there was a reason the followers of the Reformers were called Protestants. Does anyone today wonder about the derivation of the term? What exactly are current Protestants "protesting"?

The first "fall of Babylon" refers to the drifting away of the church founded by Christ and the apostles, representing the Papacy of the Middle Ages. The second "fall of Babylon" points to the decline of the Protestant Reformation, which began in such glory but eroded into traditionalism and formalism. Still, we recognize that God has countless children within the walls of Babylon. Many there are who have not yet heard the truths of the Scripture proclaimed with certainty and conviction. The Lord is calling "His people" out of Babylon.

And we must keep still another thing in mind. Though what we have seen in history is shown to be true regarding these two phenomena (that "Babylon has fallen, has fallen"), it doesn't completely fulfill the language of the second angel. A still greater fall of Babylon is yet to come. "Babylon is fallen, is fallen, that great city, because she has made all nations drink of the wine of the wrath of her fornication."

Not yet can it be said that Babylon has made all nations drink of her wine. The word "made" has the connotation of duress and compulsion. This speaks to the as yet future when the uniting of church and state will restrict religious liberty through legislation. Force and coercion, so long the implements of the past, will emerge from hidden and dusty tool chests and be laid in the hands of the state in order to bring about the desires of the church.

---

* William Carlos Martyn, *The Pilgrim Fathers of New England: A History*, vol. 5, p. 70. In Ellen G. White, *The Great Controversy*, pp. 291, 292.

CHAPTER 14

THE "WINE" OF "BABYLON"

The "wine" is Babylon's false teachings that it uses to intoxicate and confuse its subjects. False teaching is addictive. When thus "intoxicated," people "stumble." In a similar way, when Christ was here He referred to the doctrines of the Pharisees and Sadducees as being "leaven." "Then Jesus said to them, 'Take heed and beware of the leaven of the Pharisees and the Sadducees'" (Matt. 16:6). It took a while before the disciples caught on to what He was saying. "Then they understood that He did not tell them to beware of the leaven of bread, but of the doctrine of the Pharisees and Sadducees" (verse 12). Leaven, or yeast, is the agent that causes fermentation in bread, as it does in a similar way in the process of wine's fermentation. Jesus wanted to warn His disciples against the insidious principles of falsehood that the teachers of His day passed around like someone would alcoholic drinks.

At the root of Babylon's doctrine is the teaching that the church and its traditions wield the highest authority, above even the Word of God. The ecclesiastical leadership of the church of Rome has made it plain that it has the power to interpret or change Scripture. It argues that "the church has been responsible for the formulation and protection of Scripture, therefore it is above it and has the authority—the sole authority—to declare what it means or to change it at will." Which is it? Who has higher authority? The Bible or the church? Scripture or tradition? It is a watershed question, one that must be settled!

While it is true that the church was to occupy the role of being the custodian of Scripture, it is absolutely not true that this honored role has made the church superior to the Holy Bible. How do we know that? Actually, there's an easy way to find that out. Examine carefully the life and teachings of Jesus. His example would be a safe one to follow, wouldn't it? What we see recorded in the Gospels is a continuous conflict between Jesus and the religious teachers of His day, the latter a "church" that, one could argue, was the custodian of the Old Testament Scriptures. The substance of much of the conflict involved the concept of authority. To what did Jesus point as the final authority? Was it the tradition of the fathers—the "church"—or was it Scripture?

The evidence is clear and overwhelming. Jesus consistently upheld the authority of Scripture over the teachings and traditions of the religious leadership. It is true, as Paul says, that to them (the Jewish people, the "church") "were committed the oracles of God," and it was a great "advantage." It was to "profit" them (Rom. 3:1, 2). The church of His time was the custodian of Scripture, but it in no way placed its leaders above the authority of the Bible itself.

Notice carefully the dynamics of this issue as recorded by Matthew. Jesus said to the ecclesiastical leadership of His day, "Why do you also transgress the commandment of God because of your tradition? For God commanded, saying, 'Honor your father and your mother'; and, 'He who curses father or mother, let him be put to death.' But you say, 'Whoever says to his father or mother, "Whatever profit you might have received from me is a gift to God"—then he need not honor his father or mother.' Thus you have made the commandment of God of no effect by your tradition" (Matt. 15:3-6).

In other words, if a person was in a position to help his aged parents, in keeping with the principle of the fifth commandment, but instead chose to make a charitable contribution to the church, he was excused from obeying that commandment. The Pharisees had elevated tradition above Scripture—even the Ten Commandments. Jesus then quoted from Isaiah, saying, "In vain they worship Me, teaching as doctrines the commandments of men" (Matt. 15:9).

There can be no question as to which in Jesus' view had the higher authority. It was Scripture above tradition, the Bible above the teachings of the "church." To the chief priests and elders who challenged His authority, Christ appealed to the Bible. "Jesus said to them, 'Have you never read in the Scriptures: "The stone which builders rejected has become the chief cornerstone"?'" (Matt. 21:42). To the Sadducees, who manufactured a clever question to pose to Him concerning the teaching of the resurrection, something they rejected, He said, "You are mistaken, not knowing the Scriptures nor the power of God" (Matt. 22:29). When Jesus asked the lawyer who quizzed him about eternal life, "How readest thou?" (Luke 10:26, KJV), to what did He point him? Talmudic tradition or the Holy Scriptures? Obviously, the latter.

In His teachings Christ constantly referred to the Bible as the source of truth. He began His ministry by quoting the prophecy of Isaiah 61, saying "Today this Scripture is fulfilled in your hearing" (Luke 4:21). He closed His ministry by sharing truth from the Scriptures with the Emmaus travelers after His resurrection. "And beginning at Moses and all the Prophets, He expounded to them in all the Scriptures the things concerning Himself" (Luke 24:27). He did the same with His disciples. "'These are the words which I spoke to you while I was still with you, that all things must be fulfilled which were written in the Law of Moses and the Prophets and the Psalms concerning Me.' And He opened their understanding, that they might comprehend the Scriptures" (verse 44). No, there can be no question but that Jesus upheld Scripture over any teaching of the church based on tradition. His approach should be the example followed by all believers.

The Lord said, "Therefore I have hewn them [His people] by the prophets" (Hosea 6:5). It is the teachings of God, given through the prophets, that have carved and chiseled the church. What is it that Paul says is "profitable for doctrine, for reproof, for correction, for instruction in righteousness" (2 Tim. 3:16)? Was he speaking of tradition? Of church authority? No! He was referring to "the Holy Scriptures," which he said were "given by inspiration of God," or "God-breathed" (NIV). "God-breathed" is one word in Greek *(theopneustos)*. Nor did Paul pick and choose which "Scriptures" he favored above another. "All Scripture," he said was "God-breathed."

The phrase directs our minds back to humanity's creation in Eden, when God took the dust of the ground and breathed His breath into Adam's nostrils, and the man became a living being (Gen. 2:7).

So likewise, the Scriptures, though composed of paper and ink (the "dust of the ground"), are unlike any other volume on earth. They have been "God-breathed." "For prophecy never came by the will of man, but holy men of God spoke as they were moved by the Holy Spirit" (2 Peter 1:21). Thus invested with God's "breath" or Spirit, like Adam, the Word became "alive." The Bible is a living book. "For the word of God is living and powerful, and sharper than any two-edged sword, piercing even to the division of soul and spirit, and of joints and marrow, and is a discerner of the thoughts and intents of the heart" (Heb. 4:12).

Scripture is God's revealed will and must be the foundation of all Christian teaching, the standard by which we test all our beliefs. A friend of mine wished to build a house. Soon the contractor had the site graded, the trenches dug, the forms placed, and the sub-slab plumbing embedded. All was ready for the concrete trucks to roll in. Just before they did, my friend chanced to stop by and take a closer look at the footprint of his new house as defined by the forms. Imagine his shock and dismay when he realized that they came nowhere near the configuration of the drafted plans. When he mentioned the fact, the architect rather flippantly replied, "Oh, we'll fix all that later." Needless to say, my friend released both the contractor and the architect from the project.

Surprisingly, many are relying on an edifice of doctrine, a structure of belief, that doesn't conform with the Bible, the divine plan given by God. The widespread comment "It doesn't really matter what you believe" echoes the reply the architect gave my friend, except it has to do with something vastly more important than building a house. Jesus told a story about a man who "built his house" on the shifting sands of human theory, only to see it wash away when the storms of conflict arose (Matt. 7:24-27). God has graciously drafted a blueprint of salvation for us to learn about Him and His just requirements— Scripture. If we depart from His guidebook, we do so at our own peril. "To the law and to the testimony! If they do not speak according to this word, it is because there is no light in them" (Isa. 8:20).

It is the sacred Scripture that shapes and molds the teachings of the church. "I have hewn them by the prophets." In an amazing illustration, the wise man presents the beauty of the church thus constructed. "Wisdom has built her house, she has hewn out her seven pillars" (Prov. 9:1). By New Testament times "Wisdom" had become a metaphor for Christ. Jesus is Wisdom personified. "But of Him you are in Christ Jesus, who became for us wisdom from God" (1 Cor. 1:30).

The "house" that Wisdom built is the church. "Consequently, you are no longer foreigners and strangers, but fellow citizens with God's people and also members of his household, built on the foundation of the apostles and prophets, with Christ Jesus himself as the chief cornerstone. In him the whole building is joined together and rises to become a holy temple in the Lord" (Eph. 2:19-21, NIV).

The "pillars" are those teachings—those doctrines of truth—that uphold the structure and bind together the believers. Again, Paul spoke about "God's household, which is the church of the living God, the pillar and foundation of the truth" (1 Tim. 3:15, NIV). These "pillars" were "hewn" by the hand of God through the ministry of the prophets who revealed His truths.

God gave strict warnings against bringing into His sanctuary pagan "pillars"—fertility symbols borrowed from the false religions of the Canaanites. "You shall not plant for yourself any tree, as a wooden image, near the altar which you build for yourself to the Lord your God. You shall not set up a sacred pillar, which the Lord your God hates" (Deut. 16:21, 22). Pagan pillars in God's house? Say it couldn't be. Yet that is exactly what happened later in Israel's history. The wicked Manasseh "even set a carved image, the idol which he had made, in the house of God" (2 Chron. 33:7). Because human beings had made such idols and they represented human systems of religion, they were totally out of place in the house dedicated to the worship of the Creator-God. Is it any less disgusting to God to see "pillars" of false doctrine, borrowed from paganism, in His "house" today?

The wine of Babylon represents its false teachings, which issue from its belief that church tradition and practice are a more authoritative source of truth than the Holy Scriptures. Yes, it will tell you that the Bible plays a role, but there is no question that when push comes to shove, tradition is at the helm. All one has to do is look at the Ten Commandments in Exodus 20 of the Bible and compare it with the

Ten Commandments as taught in any Catholic catechism, and you will see what guides the papal ship of doctrinal belief—tradition.

We give credit to Catholicism for being consistent, for if one accepts the premise that the church is above Scripture, then everything its leaders say follows logically. If that be true, then it indeed is capable of interpreting or changing the Word of God. Thus by edict of the Papacy Sunday is the right day on which to worship. Should Catholicism be correct in its self-understanding, then let the world become converted to it.

If, on the other hand, the principle of *sola scriptura* holds, then those doctrines taught by the Papacy neither found in Scripture or that are contrary to them, must be discarded. They are equivalent to the "pillars" or "images" found in the "house of God" that must be removed. On this battleground the Reformers fought valiantly. And on this platform we encourage all to stand today. Certainly, as we have seen, the Savior cherished this concept. For Him, without question Scripture trumped tradition.

We cannot overestimate the importance of this issue. It is the watershed question facing the Christian community today. What is the ultimate source of authority? Geography has a feature known as the Great Divide, or the Great Continental Divide. It is an imaginary line stretching across the ridge of the Rockies upon which, if a theoretical drop of rain were to fall and split, one half of it would end up in the Atlantic Ocean, the other in the Pacific. In theology, the question of authority is the great divide. If you accept the premise of Catholicism that the church is above Scripture, then you will travel in one direction. But if you regard Scripture as the only source of authority, you will journey in the opposite direction. There can be no middle ground.

And yet while most Protestants claim to be following in the footsteps of the Reformers who stood for *sola scriptura,* at the same time they continue to follow many church traditions rather than the tenets of Scripture. To cite one example that we have already touched upon, where do we find in Scripture any authority for Sunday worship? It doesn't exist. Or where do we find in the Bible that human beings go to their reward immediately upon death? That doesn't exist either. Such things are teachings that Catholicism presents and claims as its own. Protestant churches that claim to accept the principle of *sola scriptura* nevertheless to a large degree still incorporate unscriptural teachings that long ago crept into the mother church.

When on the cross, undergoing excruciating (literally "out of the cross") pain, Jesus was offered "sour wine mingled with gall to drink. But when He tasted it, He would not drink" (Matt. 27:34). The wine would have acted as an anesthetic—it would have been a way out of His suffering. But wanting His mind to remain clear, He refused. So Christ's followers at the end, though put to the test, will not drink of the "wine" offered to them in the hour of their trial.

The "Babylon" of the second angel is a modern-day Jehoiakim, one-time king of Judah. The Lord commissioned Jeremiah to deliver a message from Him. "Now the king [Jehoiakim] was sitting in the winter house in the ninth month, with a fire burning on the hearth before him. And it happened, when Jehudi had read three or four columns, that the king cut it with the scribe's knife and cast it into the fire that was on the hearth, until all the scroll was consumed in the fire that was on the hearth. Yet they were not afraid, nor did they tear their garments" (Jer. 36:22-24). Like Jehudi, the church has dared to tamper with God's holy Ten Commandments, written by God's own finger. It has done so without shame.

In place of the teachings of Scripture, so vital for our understanding of God's character of love, the church has substituted its traditions, mixed with a generous dosage of ancient religious belief and philosophy that had infiltrated early Christianity. Stirred together, this doctrinal cocktail is intoxicating and addictive. It results in confusion, one of the biblical meanings of the term "Babylon." "Babylon was a golden cup in the Lord's hand, that made all the earth drunk. The nations drank her wine; therefore the nations are deranged" (Jer. 51:7).

Behind all this is the master deceiver, Satan, who has coveted the place of God from the beginning. Through the teachings that he has whispered into the ears of unsuspecting theologians, he seeks to occupy the place that belongs only to the Lord. By erroneous doctrines such as that of the immortal soul, he misleads humanity onto the path of deception and destruction. Through incorrect theology, such as the teaching of never-ending torment of the lost, he hopes to warp and distort the picture of God's character of love. Through the supplanting of God's holy Sabbath day, erecting in its place a false sabbath, Sunday, he attempts to sway the allegiance of humanity to himself and away from simple obedience to God, who alone deserves our loyalty.

"She has made all nations drink of the wine of the wrath of her fornication." Babylon's "wrath" is arm-twisting force applied to compel all to worship the way it dictates. Without the true power of *agape* love dispensed by God's Spirit, it finds that it needs to use the arm of the state. This is its "wrath." The Middle Ages saw it demonstrated in full force. But sometimes in Scripture "wrath" can also mean something else. God's "wrath" represents His allowing the sinner to reap the consequences of his or her stubborn choice. Unlike human anger, which is self-motivated and exhibited by raised voices, God's wrath is His stepping back when continuously repulsed, and letting the fruitage of sin become ripe.

Satan knows this and uses it as an opportunity to trick God's people into believing lies and engaging in illicit activity so that God will remove His blessing and exercise His "wrath." Like the influence of Balaam, a renegade prophet who induced Israel into idolatry, immorality, and apostasy, Satan seeks to introduce falsehood and disobedience into the camp, knowing that thereby he can cause the Lord to remove His blessing. We'll study God's "wrath" in greater detail when we review the words of the third angel.

This "wine" of false doctrine is not merely offered, but forced upon "all nations," the entire world. "She has made all nations drink of the wine." Notice the global impact of the measure. When it becomes completely fulfilled, the whole earth will feel the coercive imprint of Babylon's agenda. It falls under divine indictment for imposing the wine of its false teachings on others. "Woe to him who gives drink to his neighbor, pressing him to your bottle, even to make him drunk, that you may look on his nakedness! You are filled with shame instead of glory. You also—drink! And be exposed as uncircumcised! The cup of the Lord's right hand will be turned against you and utter shame will be on your glory" (Hab. 2:15, 16).

The cup of false doctrine from which Babylon will compel all to drink will focus on the substitute sabbath of Sunday, in the place of

God's true Sabbath, the seventh day. Loyalty to God, expressed by loving obedience to Him in obeying all His commandments, will be contrasted with loyalty to Satan, represented by observing his replacement day of rest. The message of the third angel will speak to this more directly.

An illicit relationship of church and state will demand that "all nations" drink the cup of disobedience. It is the "fornication" of political power enforcing religious dogma. In Old Testament times we saw this reflected in the false religion of Jezebel united with and enforced by the royal scepter of Ahab. Jezebel, the "woman," injected her pagan ideas by means of the authority of the crown. It formed a union of church and state destined for disaster and hardship for God's true followers. In Christ's day Jewish religious leaders twisted the arm of Pilate to crucify Christ. And it became the prescription for religious persecution during the Middle Ages as the power of the state implemented the edicts of the religious establishment.

Revelation predicts that this deadly marriage between church and state will repeat itself in the future. We have not yet seen this development, but rest assured that it will come. God's Word cannot be broken. Prophecy cannot lie.

When Babylon (the conglomerate of apostate religions, headed by the Papacy and fallen Protestantism) join together in "fornication" with the political powers of the state (the "kings of the earth") to enforce legislation in direct denial of God's holy law and compel the human conscience to disobey the Creator, then will its fall be full and complete. As it operates with a power not yet manifested, it will truly be stated, "Babylon is fallen, is fallen, that great city, because she made all nations drink of the wine of the wrath of her fornication." May God prepare us for the time that will soon be upon us!

CHAPTER 15

THE "BEAST" OF THE THIRD ANGEL'S MESSAGE

Then a third angel followed them, saying with a loud voice, 'If anyone worships the beast and his image, and receives his mark on his forehead or on his hand, he himself shall also drink of the wine of the wrath of God, which is poured out full strength into the cup of His indignation. And he shall be tormented with fire and brimstone in the presence of the holy angels and in the presence of the Lamb. And the smoke of their torment ascends forever and ever; and they have no rest day or night, who worship the beast and his image, and whoever receives the mark of his name. Here is the patience of the saints; here are those who keep the commandments of God and the faith of Jesus'" (Rev. 14:9-12).

Of all the messages of the Bible, none is more serious and somber than this one. Have you noticed that the Bible sometimes presents important messages in a package of three? God called out to little Samuel three times. Cyrus, Darius, and Artaxerxes issued a total of three decrees giving permission for Judah to return to her homeland. The Lord showed Peter the vision of the sheet filled with unclean animals three times. Here the threefold format of the messages of Revelation 14 suggests their supreme importance.

They contain warnings that every person on our planet should carefully and prayerfully consider. The third message raises several vital topics. We must ascertain what the "beast" is and identify its "mark." Along with that, a companion study of God's "mark" or "seal" is a natural and necessary addition. Then we must determine the significance of receiving the beast's mark in the "forehead" or in the "hand." Furthermore, what does it mean to drink of the "wine of

God's wrath," and what does the phrase "full strength" indicate? What about the "torment" that the angel speaks about as well as the "smoke that ascends forever and ever"? Why does the angel's message end with the spotlight focusing on those who "keep the commandments of God and the faith of Jesus"? All these questions deserve Bible answers.

What, or Who, Is the "Beast"?

We are familiar with the use of animals as mascots or symbols for various organizations, sporting teams, or nations. A bear calls to mind Russia or the state of California; a lion the United Kingdom. The practice goes back millennia, with archeological discoveries unearthing the same phenomena in ancient artwork and architecture.

The Lord made use of a similar scheme in His delivery of messages through His prophets. The vision of the wild beasts of Daniel 7 offers an excellent example. In this portrayal, the lion represented Babylon, the bear stood for Medo-Persia, the leopard for Greece, and the nondescript beast symbolized Rome. The angel told Daniel, "The fourth beast shall be a fourth kingdom on earth" (Dan. 7:23). Bible students clearly understood these concepts by the dawning of the Christian Era.*

Using Scripture as being the best source of interpretation for its symbols, we would look first, as we read the message of the third angel speaking of a "beast," to a kingdom or power as being its antitype. Does the Bible itself give us any clues as to what kingdom or power the beast might be? Since the messages of the three angels themselves do not provide any, we must go back a bit to find its antecedent and its identifying clues.

The previous chapter, Revelation 13, introduces us to a "beast" that has a "mark." Actually, we find two beasts, which immediately raises the question as to which of the two in chapter 13 Revelation 14 is speaking about. Revelation 13:1-10 focuses on the "beast from the sea," while verse 11 directs our attention to another "beast coming up out of the earth." Verses 12-18 portray the cooperative effort of the two beasts, culminating in the erection of an "image" of the first beast and the placement of a "mark of the beast," enforced upon all. It must be this "beast" and "mark" that the angel of Revelation 14 has in mind.

Which of the two beasts is the one that wields the mark? A careful reading of the last verses of the chapter reveals that they employ the word "beast" in reference to the second beast only once (verse 11). Thereafter, Scripture uses the pronoun "he" when speaking of the second beast (see verses 12, 13, 14, 15, 16). When the remaining verses of chapter 13 mention "beast," it is clear that it is speaking of the first beast. We don't have to guess about this. Verse 12 refers to it as the "first beast" and as "the first beast, whose deadly wound was healed." This is clear and unambiguous.

In verse 14 we find the word "beast" described as "the beast who was wounded by the sword and lived," again clearly indicating the first "beast" of the chapter. In the words just previous to that phrase, we find that it is this first beast of which an "image" will be made. Once more, there is nothing uncertain as to which of the two beasts it is speaking about. Then in verse 15 we find that "he" (consistently referring to the second beast) gives breath to the image of the "beast" (which must logically be the first beast), compelling the worship of the image of the "beast." Again, it is obvious that it is the first "beast" referred to.

Verse 16 reports that "he" (the second beast) causes all to receive a "mark," either on their right hand or forehead, mandating that no one may buy or sell except those who have the mark or the name of the "beast." Since John's use has consistently shown that, other than the first time when the prophet introduces the second animal as the "beast coming out of the earth," the pronoun "he" refers to the second beast and the remaining times the word "beast" appears in chapter 13 it is speaking of the "first" beast, the one "who was wounded by the sword and lived." The word "beast" in verse 16 (the one which has the "mark") therefore must also indicate the first beast revealed in the chapter.

What power or kingdom does the term "beast" symbolize in the first 10 verses of Revelation? This is absolutely vital to know, because it is this kingdom or power that will have the "mark" that, according to the third angel's message, we must avoid at all cost. If you don't know what the "beast" is, you will have no idea what the "mark of the beast" is. It's that simple.

As we study the clues given in the first 10 verses of chapter 13, we will also compare them with other prophetic pictures given in Scripture. Remember, as I mentioned earlier, there appear at least seven biblical references, employing various prophetic symbols, to this entity. Through the use of repetition the Lord gives emphasis to the subject. From heaven's viewpoint, it's very important to know about this!

The Danger of Excessive Literalism

One popular concept currently circulating is that the "beast" is a giant computer in Belgium, capable of storing and processing the names of everyone alive today. Is that what the Bible is speaking about? When seeking the identity of the beast of Revelation 14, whose deadly mark we must avoid, we must do serious and competent investigation to arrive at a reliable conclusion. Just because a theory sounds good isn't enough. And just because many people believe and promote an idea and many published books present it doesn't make it correct. We must allow the Scriptures to clarify and identify this prophetic term. Because it is such a pivotal point, we must spend some time studying how Scripture presents its truths. Remember, it was misinterpretation of prophecy that prepared the Jewish leaders to reject Jesus.

Here's a pitfall to watch out for. The Jewish expositors of Jesus' day tended to be too literalistic in their interpretations. For example, the Old Testament said, "You shall bind them [God's words] as a sign on your hand, and they shall be as frontlets between your eyes" (Deut. 6:8). Clearly what God really wanted was for them to have His words in their hearts and minds. Just before this He had pled, "Oh, that they had such a heart in them that they would fear Me and always keep all My commandments, that it might be well with them and with their children forever!" (Deut. 5:29). Then it was right after He had said this that He told them they should "bind them as a sign on your hand, and they shall be as frontlets between your eyes." We'll give more scrutiny to this passage when we study the mark of the beast and the seal of God a little later.

But what did they do? Taking the counsel literally, they made small boxes to contain Bible verses and mounted them on their foreheads. They inscribed scriptural passages and covered their forearms with them. The devices were called "phylacteries" or "tefillin," from a Greek word meaning "to guard" or "protect." Jesus addressed this when He spoke of their hypocrisy, saying, "They make their phylacteries broad and enlarge the borders of their garments" (Matt. 23:5). Excessive literalism caused them to miss the point.

Was God as interested in their making physical Scripture boxes to wear on their foreheads as He was in their allowing the Spirit to inscribe His law on their minds? Or was He as concerned with the physical wearing of verses on their arms as He was in their hands engaged in working righteousness?

Another example: when Jesus said "Beware of the leaven of the Pharisees" (Matt. 16:6), the disciples thought He was referring to the fact that they had run out of bread. Only later did they catch on that He was not speaking of literal leaven or bread. "Then they understood that He did not tell them to beware of the leaven of bread, but of the doctrine of the Pharisees and Sadducees" (verse 12). Excessive literalism had stood in the way of their understanding Jesus' meaning.

Jesus identified the ministry of John the Baptist as a fulfillment of Malachi's prophecy of the return of Elijah. "His disciples asked Him, saying, 'Why then do the scribes say that Elijah must come first?' Jesus answered and said to them, 'Indeed, Elijah is coming first and will restore all things. But I say to you that Elijah has come already, and they did not know him but did to him whatever they wished. Likewise the Son of Man is also about to suffer at their hands.' Then the disciples understood that He spoke to them of John the Baptist" (Matt. 17:10-13). Earlier He had said, "And if you are willing to receive it, he [John the Baptist] is Elijah who is to come" (Matt. 11:14).

This poses a puzzle, for when questioned as to his identity, John the Baptist denied being Elijah. "Now this is the testimony of John, when the Jews sent priests and Levites from Jerusalem to ask him, 'Who are you?' He confessed, and did not deny, but confessed, 'I am not the Christ.' And they asked him, 'What then? Are you Elijah?' He said, 'I am not'" (John 1:19-21). How can it be that Jesus said John was "Elijah" but John answered that he wasn't? Do we have a contradiction in Scripture?

It's not really that difficult of a question. Before John was born, the angel Gabriel appeared to his father, Zachariah, and said, "He [John] will also go before Him in the spirit and power of Elijah" (Luke 1:17). No, John the Baptist was not literally the reincarnation of Elijah, and he properly denied being him when asked by the delegation of priests. It is also true, though, that in another sense he was indeed "Elijah," for he came in the same Spirit and power of the Old Testament prophet and his role was similar. Just as Elijah did through his ministry, as the angel said, "He will turn many of the children of Israel to the Lord their God" (verse 16). But you would never understand the truth that Jesus spoke about John being "Elijah" if you saw it only through a literalistic lens. How much truth was lost because the people didn't understand Jesus' way of speaking! And how important for us in these last days to make sure we're "rightly dividing the word of truth" when it comes to interpreting the important prophetic symbols of Revelation.

We have a number of illustrations of this same principle at work in the Gospel of John. When the Jewish leadership asked Jesus for a sign, He replied, "'Destroy this temple, and in three days I will raise it up.' Then the Jews said, 'It has taken forty-six years to build this temple, and will You raise it up in three days?' But He was speaking of the temple of His body" (John 2:19-21). Notice how they missed Christ's point, because they were mired in a literalistic rut of interpretation.

In the next chapter Jesus told Nicodemus, "'Most assuredly, I say to you, unless one is born again, he cannot see the kingdom of God.' Nicodemus said to Him, 'How can a man be born when he is old? Can he enter a second time into his mother's womb and be born?'" (John 3:3, 4). The religious leader didn't yet understand the illustration Jesus was using, because he was stuck in literalism.

In the following chapter someone again misunderstood Jesus. As He rested beside Jacob's well, He spoke with a Samaritan woman who had come to draw water. He said to her, "'If you knew the gift of God, and who it is who says to you, "Give Me a drink," you would have asked Him, and He would have given you living water.' The woman said to Him, 'Sir, You have nothing to draw with, and the well is deep. Where then do You get that living water?'" (John 4:10, 11). The true meaning of Jesus' words did not penetrate her thinking at that time because she viewed them in a strictly literal sense.

Even those who walked with Him sometimes struggled with the mind-set. Later in that same chapter when the disciples returned from the village, they invited their Master to partake of some food. "In the meantime His disciples urged Him, saying, 'Rabbi, eat.' But He said to them, 'I have food to eat of which you do not know.' Therefore the disciples said to one another, 'Has anyone brought Him anything to eat?'" (verses 31, 32). Jesus was completely comfortable in using everyday things as illustrations of spiritual truth. Spiritual things are spiritually discerned (1 Cor. 2:14).

The fact that Jesus often employed parables confused the disciples, but He explained to them, "'To you it has been given to know the mysteries of the kingdom of God, but to the rest it is given in parables, that "seeing they may not see, and hearing they may not understand"'" (Luke 8:10). "And when they were alone, He explained all things to His disciples" (Mark 4:34). Sometimes the Bible presents its truths coded in symbolic format, but God will never leave the sincere, diligent, and obedient seeker of truth in ignorance. He will reveal truth to His "servants."

Such New Testament examples illustrate that the Jewish religious leaders had trapped themselves in a maze of excessive literalism that prevented them from understanding spiritual truth. This affected their understanding of Bible prophecy as well. Looking for a political redeemer, the Jews were unprepared to receive Christ, the suffering Lamb. Here's the point: their misunderstanding of Bible prophecy was fatal! It led to the rejection of God's plan and the crucifixion of His Son. Truly the angel spoke of them, "None of the wicked shall understand, but the wise shall understand" (Dan. 12:10).

Here's the all-important question: could it be possible that history will repeat itself? Could the overly literalistic mistakes prevalent at the First Advent be duplicated at the time of the Second Advent? Could it be that many of the professed followers of God in the last days will be as unprepared for His coming as were the Jews of old, being locked into a system of excessive literalism and false interpretations of prophecy? Is the devil trying to deceive people today, suggesting overly literalistic and incorrect interpretations of the "beast" and its "mark," and thus leading people to perdition?

Jesus' first words were, as He began His discourse on the signs preceding His return, "Take heed that no one deceives you" (Matt. 24:4). Such language assures us that the devil will indeed seek to twist the prophecies and signs that pertain to Jesus' second coming. What is the beast, and what is its mark? Is it some computer in Europe? Is the mark a visible tattoo, bar code, or as some now suggest, a microchip implanted under the skin? Let's not indulge in fanciful human theories on such matters, but allow Scripture to give us the answers to these most important questions. The Bible is its best interpreter.

---

* See, for example, the exposition of Hippolytus (d. A.D. 236). In L. E. Froom, *The Prophetic Faith of Our Fathers,* vol. 1, p. 272.

CHAPTER 16

CLUES IDENTIFYING THE "BEAST" OF REVELATION 13

We'll begin by looking at the clues given in the first 10 verses of Revelation 13. As we have seen, this passage contains the evidence to identify the beast that has the deadly mark. It was seen to be "rising up out of the sea." What does this signify? In the symbolic language of Bible prophecy, water stands for people. "The waters which you saw, where the harlot sits, are peoples, multitudes, nations, and tongues" (Rev. 17:15). So since this beast arises "out of the sea," we would expect it to emerge within a populated area. This will be in contrast, as we will see, to the second beast, which John observes "coming up out of the earth," or an unpopulated area.

John the revelator tells us that the beast has seven heads and 10 horns with crowns on the horns. Crowns represent kingship. The word in Greek here is *diademata*, or "kingly crown," as opposed to *stephanos*, the "victor's crown." Such crowns represent the monarchies, the political kingdoms that support the agenda of the beast power. What about the seven heads? They symbolize the various manifestations of Satan's tools of attack through the ages. In the next verse the beast has traits of a leopard, bear, and lion, echoing the beasts of Daniel 7.

Revelation 13:2

The second verse provides two clues. The beast was "like a leopard, his feet were like the feet of a bear, and his mouth like the mouth of a lion." Not only are these specific animals significant, but the order given is important. We know that the animals of Daniel 7 represented earthly kingdoms. They were a lion, a bear, a leopard, and another fourth beyond description. The lion stood for Babylon, the bear for

Medo-Persia, the leopard for Greece, and the fourth represented pagan Rome.

So the beast of Revelation 13 resembles the beasts that preceded it. It partakes of similar characteristics. Fragments of the philosophies and methods as well as the flaws of these kingdoms now appear in this beast. Also, notice that John sees them from the perspective of looking backward in history. In Daniel 7 the order is lion, bear, and leopard. Now, since those kingdoms have faded into the past, the sequence is in reverse order. It is leopard, bear, and lion. John's perspective in this verse is from the beast's "rising," which occurs subsequent to the downfall of the leopard, bear, and lion. (We'll discuss the name of blasphemy on its head later.)

"The dragon gave him his power, his throne, and great authority." Revelation 12 told us explicitly that the "dragon" is "the Devil and Satan" (Rev. 12:9). The devil was behind the establishment of this beast's power and authority. But we also recognize that the devil almost always gets people to do his work for him. That's how the story began in Eden, when the devil succeeded in getting Eve to tempt Adam. In chapter 12 the "dragon stood before the woman who was ready to give birth, to devour her Child as soon as it was born" (Rev. 12:4). When Jesus was born, what kingdom was in power when Herod issued the order to kill the babies of Bethlehem? Civil Rome. So while it is true that in the primary sense the dragon represents the devil, it is also the case that in a secondary sense the dragon who gave to the beast its power represents civil Rome.

Therefore, we must ask, When pagan Rome declined into obscurity and the empire moved eastward to Constantinople (the capital founded by Emperor Constantine), what took its place? To whom did civil Rome give its "power, throne and authority"? What entity stepped into the political vacuum left by pagan Rome? It was the ecclesiastical structure of papal Rome. Following the removal of the seat of the empire and the decline of civil Rome, the bishop of Rome gained more and more authority. He assumed the political powers vacated by the absent emperors and rose higher and higher in influence. As we noted before, when in A.D. 533 Emperor Justinian assembled his famous code, he identified the bishop of Rome as the head of the church and the corrector of heretics. Then Justinian dispatched his general Belisarius to implement the new reality.

So the dragon, in a secondary sense representing pagan Rome, gave to the church structure its authority and power, a historical fact that any history book or encyclopedia will confirm. It was as if civil Rome passed the baton of leadership to papal Rome. The popes of the Middle Ages occupied the place of the Caesars before them. They governed from the very seat formerly held by the rulers of pagan Rome.

The historian Abbott states, "The transfer of the emperor's residence to Constantinople was a sad blow to the prestige of Rome, and at the time one might have predicted her speedy decline. But the development of the Church and the growing authority of the bishop of Rome, or the pope, gave her a new lease on life, and made her again the capitol—this time the religious capital—of the civilized world."[1] The seventeenth-century philosopher Thomas Hobbes is credited with the quotation "The Papacy, is no other than the ghost of the deceased Romane Empire, sitting crowned upon its grave. For so did the Papacy start up on a Sudden out of the Ruines of that Heathen Power."[2]

What we will discover is that only one entity fulfills all the prophetic specifications of Revelation 13's beast from the sea, and that is the ecclesiastical structure that governs the Roman Catholic Church. It alone meets all the criteria. Not only that, it has all the specifications of the other six portraits of the beast in Scripture, which we'll note a little later.

"Hate Speech" or "Warning Message Given in Love"?

We need to pause here to consider a vital point. People talk a lot today about "hate speech." It has become a criminal act, punishable by fine or imprisonment. When someone identifies the ruling organization of the Roman Catholic Church as the beast of Revelation 13, others might wonder, "Isn't that harsh language? Isn't that 'hate speech'? What do you have against Catholics?" Let us be very clear on this matter. *This is not about Catholics* but about the authoritative structure that rules their church. It is not a message against individual believers but about a thought and administrative system. As noted before, that community of faith contains countless people who constitute God's people, as is the case with all communities of faith. They are those who will yet hear His call given in the messages of the three angels, and who will respond.

Realizing that we live in a world hijacked by a great and powerful deceiver, we pose the question: is a message given in love and designed to warn against and save from the devil's schemes "hate speech"? Absolutely not! Would the forceful and explicit warning of a New York firefighter giving directions to those trapped in the burning twin towers on September 11, 2001, be considered inappropriate? No! Messages such as those were borne of love, and yes, of sacrifice, but they had to be direct and unequivocal under the circumstances. Would the screaming sirens warning of a coming Kansas tornado be considered harsh and inappropriate? No! As unpleasant as those sounds might be to the ear, they seek to save lives.

Was it "hate speech" when Noah warned his world of the Flood and gave a message contrary to all the scientists and pundits of his day? Was it "hate speech" when the prophet Nathan looked King David in the eye and said, "Thou art the man"? Was it "hate speech" when John the Baptist rebuked the hypocrisy and excesses of his day? Was it "hate speech" when Jesus censured the unbelief and ungodliness of His times? No! Such messages, though stern and uncompromising, originated in love. The voice of the Savior had tears in it as He uttered those scathing rebukes. They represented a message of hope and salvation to a dying world. So also are the messages of the three angels.

Because the devil has infiltrated the church, as he did in Jesus' day, and twisted God's message so that it is hardly recognizable as being the gospel that Christ preached, the language that God used must be clear in order to save those who will listen and heed. When Peter preached to the Jews who put Christ on the cross, his message didn't cut corners—it "cut to the heart" (Acts 2:37). Strong language was necessary, but it led to the salvation of those who would listen.

"But," someone might protest, "you're talking about a Christian church, the largest Christian denomination in the world." Yes, the size of the Catholic Church is impressive, having more than a billion adherents. But is it a shocking thing to consider that evil has infiltrated it or any other church? It shouldn't be surprising. Jesus and His apostles gave clear warning about this. Christ said, "Watch out for false prophets. They come to you in sheep's clothing, but inwardly they are ferocious wolves" (Matt. 7:15, NIV). Think about the metaphor Jesus used: "sheep's clothing." Who in the Bible is the Lamb? It is Jesus. To wear "sheep's clothing" is to wear the garb of Christianity; to profess belief in the Savior. Yet Christ warned about such individuals as being "ravenous wolves." Hate speech? No, a warning presented in love.

Paul gave a similar caution to the elders of the church of Ephesus, saying, "For I know this, that after my departure savage wolves will come in among you, not sparing the flock. Also from among yourselves men will rise up, speaking perverse things, to draw away the disciples after themselves" (Acts 20:29, 30). Christianity would face danger both from without and from within. Paul wrote that such a power, representing a "falling away" from truth, "sits as God in the temple of God, showing himself that he is God" (2 Thess. 2:3, 4). Don't be shocked at the thought that the "beast" with the deadly "mark" would be an organizational structure claiming to be Christian. The Bible foretold it.

When we think of the startling language of prophecy, consider this example of how God used extreme measures to save one of His children. The same Peter who gave the "cutting" sermon on the day of Pentecost later found himself imprisoned and slated for execution. Look at the words of the following passage very carefully—let them speak to your heart. As he slept, "behold, an angel of the Lord stood by him, and a light shone in the prison; and he struck Peter on the side and raised him up, saying, 'Arise quickly!' And his chains fell off" (Acts 12:7). The text doesn't say that the angel "lightly touched Peter on the side." Nor does it tell us that he "gently tapped Peter on the arm." Rather, it declares that he "struck" him.

The KJV reports that the angel "smote" him. This word is emphatic. It's the very same word that Luke used to describe the action of Peter on the Thursday night before Christ's crucifixion. "And one of them [Peter] struck the servant of the high priest and cut off his right ear" (Luke 22:50). Thankfully, the angel of the Lord who "struck" Peter didn't have a sword in his hand. Sometimes, metaphorically speaking, what we need (as in Peter's case) isn't a gentle nudge—it's a "slap." We're sleeping so soundly that it takes a strong impact to awaken us.

That's what Peter needed to wake up from his sleep. It was the act of smiting him that brought him salvation. Do you think Peter complained that the angel "smote" him? Certainly not! Consider this story of Peter as an illustration. If the Lord graciously extends His "light" to those who are in the "prison" of falsehood and "strikes" them with a message of truth designed to "wake them up" from spiritual error, so that the "chains" of inaccurate doctrine fall off, should we consider it as hate speech, or should we regard it as a warning message given in love?

On November 5, 2009, one of the worst massacres in United States history occurred at Fort Hood, Texas, as Nidal Malik Hasan, an American military psychiatrist of Palestinian descent allegedly shot and killed 13 people and wounded another 29.[3] Were there no warning signs that this man "from within" could erupt into volcanic violence? Were there no red flags in the past that could have saved innocent individuals? Apparently there were many indicators. But not wanting to take direct action, perhaps to avoid charges of being prejudiced and engaging in hate speech, those who had seen the clues and should have known that he was dangerous withheld their warning voices.

What is the lesson of Fort Hood? When the clues are present, the warning message must be given, though it may seem stern to some. It would actually be a message of love to those whose lives would be saved. Talk to the families of those who died in the incident about how they feel that the authorities ignored clues that seem obvious to us now. The Bible says, "Have nothing to do with the fruitless deeds of darkness, but rather expose them" (Eph. 5:11, NIV).

We have proof that the warnings of Revelation originated in a spirit of love. Revelation 13 speaks of a "dragon" (the devil) and features two beasts who collaborate to bring about the construction of the image of the beast and the establishment of its mark. Scripture presents strong and stern warnings against the two beasts, one from the sea and the one from the land. But take notice that beside these two "beasts" and the "dragon," we encounter a fourth "beast." Verse 8 reads: "And all who dwell on the earth will worship him, whose names have not been written in the Book of Life of the Lamb slain from the foundation of the world."

Who is the "Lamb"? It is most certainly Jesus. He is the one to whom John the Baptist pointed from Jordan's shore and said, "Behold! The Lamb of God who takes away the sin of the world" (John 1:29). Within the context of the fierce warnings against the designs of the beasts from the sea and from the land under the influence of the dragon—in the very heart of this chapter—we find a reference to the Lamb. The language of the warning includes the message of salvation by His blood through faith in His atoning sacrifice! Scripture's warning messages begin in love and the hope that humanity will wake from its slumber and leave behind the deceptions conceived by the enemy of souls. God speaks in pity and love to His creatures who have been seduced by the master deceiver.

The Infiltration of Satan

We should not be shocked to learn that Satan has found a way to infiltrate Christianity. Remember how the story of sin on earth began? It was when the serpent of Eden succeeded in misleading the woman. He persuaded her to set aside the Word of God and replace it with something else. The devil led her to believe that what God said didn't matter. Then, after she had eaten the forbidden fruit, he used her as his tool to mislead her husband, Adam. Whether Adam would have fallen for the deceptions of the serpent without this happening, we can't say. The Scripture says, "Adam was not deceived, but the woman being deceived, fell into transgression" (1 Tim. 2:14).

Note the method well. Nowhere does Scripture tell us that the serpent spoke to or tempted Adam. He didn't have to—he could do something much better! Satan used the "woman" to do his work. (As we've seen, many times in the Bible a "woman" represents a church or God's people.) But don't forget this: how did God look upon Eve, deceived as she was? In pity and in love. Does it excuse what she had done? No, she should have relied on the Word of God instead of listening to the talking snake. Was there hope for Eve? Yes, through the mercy and grace of God.

In the same way Satan has employed God's professed people as his tool through the ages. He used Balaam, a renegade prophet, to induce Israel into idolatry and immorality at Baal Peor, on the very outskirts of the Promised Land, shutting out many from Canaan's blessing (Num. 25; 31:8, 16). Satan worked through the Jewish hierarchy, to put God on a cross. And he used unsuspecting church leaders of the Middle Ages to accomplish his goals of removing, replacing, or modifying the teachings of the Holy Scriptures and to persecute those who would abide by its precepts. This is not "hate speech"—it is historical fact.

Besides this, God's call is to His people in "Babylon" to come out and be saved (Rev. 18:1-4). The Lord still has countless people in "Babylon" who have not yet seen the truth for the last days. We find honest and sincere God-fearing saints even in those communities of faith most steeped in error. They are living up to all the light they presently have. It is God's desire that they hear and heed the messages of the three angels. Though clear and unvarnished, they are messages of love and salvation.

Revelation 13:3

Let's continue with the clues given in these 10 verses. In verse 3 we encounter two more. "I saw one of his heads as if it had been mortally wounded, and his deadly wound was healed. And all the world marveled and followed the beast." Bible prophecy has a pattern of giving a brief overview, then retracing with greater detail. (The prophecies of the companion book Daniel illustrate the principle.) Verses 1-3 of this chapter lay out the general outline, with the other verses filling in more details. Note how verse 10 has echoes of things in verse 3: "He who leads into captivity shall go into captivity; he who kills with the sword must be killed with the sword."

What about the "deadly wound" that was "healed"? We recognize that this entity would enjoy uninterrupted power for a prophetic period of 1260 "days," a period mentioned no less than seven times in the Bible (twice in Daniel and five times in Revelation: Dan. 7:25; 12:7; Rev. 11:2, 3; 12:6, 14; 13:5). It is the most frequently mentioned time prophecy in Scripture. To recapitulate, the period of time appears variously as three and a half years, 42 months, or 1260 days, but they all refer to the same period of 1260 literal years.

As we have also discussed previously, this period of time extended from A.D. 538 with the removal of the last remaining obstacles to full papal power, through 1798, when under the direction of Napoleon and the military leadership of Berthier, the French forces captured Pope Pius VI. What brought about such a shocking event? It was the culmination of many forces and reasons. For example, the people of France had long seen their treasuries depleted to embellish the coffers and cathedrals of Rome. They had become dissatisfied with the oppression and opulence of the priests and prelates. Thus their frustration became part of the circumstances leading to the French Revolution.

A major part of that revolution was a repudiation of religion. When Napoleon became emperor after the revolution, one of his priorities was the overthrow of the Papal States (territory long ruled by the Vatican) in Italy, because of the Vatican's opposition to the French state. On the tenth of February his general entered the Vatican without opposition. The pope's ring was forcibly removed as were all the papal arms and insignia. He demanded that the pope renounce all temporal powers, and when Pope Pius declined, took him prisoner and marched northward to the citadel of Valence, France, where Pius died in 1799. The "Vatican palace was entirely stripped of everything that could be taken away. The palaces at Monte Cavallo, Terracina, and Castel Gandolfo, I was told, underwent the same reverse of fortune; but of the Vatican I can speak with more confidence, as I was myself in that palace the whole time of its being plundered. The sacerdotal vestments of the Sistine Paolini, and other pontifical chapels were all burnt for the gold and silver of their embroidery."[4] Thus the Papacy suffered a deadly setback, a "mortal wound," just as prophecy had predicted.

It is of more than passing interest that some whose eyes were on the prophetic calendar predicted the event shortly before it happened. The Edinburgh *Missionary Magazine* for 1796 published the statement: "By the general consent of prophecy, the reign of Antichrist, is now hastening to an end."[5]

An article in a similar vein by George Bell appeared in the *Evangelical Magazine* of 1796. Analyzing the prophetic clues, he concluded, "If this be a right application of events to the prophecy, then Antichrist arose about the year 537, at the farthest about the year 553. He continues for 42 months, or 1260 prophetical days, that is, 1260 years [Revelation 13:5]; consequently we may expect his fall about the year 1797, or 1813."[6]

An even earlier voice pointed to the fulfillment of prophecy. Toward the end of the seventeenth century Drue Cressener identified the beast with these words written in 1689. "Where-ever was there an Empire since the writing of the Prophecy, but that of the Roman Church, that was so Universal for 1260 years together, as to have all that dwell upon the Earth, Peoples, and Multitudes, and Nations and Tongues, to worship it? What Ruling Power, but that, so Ancient, as to have the Blood of Prophets, and Saints, and of all that were slain upon Earth, of that kind for that space of time, to be found in it? What Rule but that, had ever so long a duration in the World, as to continue set upon an Hill, much less upon seven Hills, for so great a space of time . . . ?"[7]

Cressener anticipated the demise of the beast power, or at least the deadly setback, at the end of the eighteenth century. "The first appearance of the Beast was at Justinian's recovery of the Western Empire, from which time to about the year 1800 will be about 1260 years." He went on to say, "For if the first time of the Beast was at Justinian's recovery of the City of Rome, then must not it end till a little before the year 1800."[8]

Notice that these prophetic expositions by Protestant Bible students gave full faith and credence to the day for a year in symbolic prophecy rule founded on Ezekiel 4:6 and Numbers 14:34. Also observe a recognition that the "beast" and the "antichrist" refer to the same entity. Keep that in mind as we compare its seven prophetic portrayals in Scripture a little later. Protestants held such views in common from the time of the Reformation until about 100 years ago, when a gigantic shift in prophetic interpretation took place, as we discussed previously.

But the beast would experience a resurgence. Revelation 13:3: "His deadly wound was healed. And all the world marveled and followed the beast." History confirms its truth. The root still remained and sprouted again. Paul had prophesied that nothing would completely remove the entity and its power until the coming of Jesus destroyed it "with the brightness of His coming" (2 Thess. 2:8). So what happened in 1798 represented only a temporary diminishing of power.

Like the mythological phoenix, the Papacy began to rise again from the ashes. Gradually its authority grew. Finally, under the terms of the Lateran Concordat of 1929, it regained the 108 acres of the Vatican as an independent state, making it the smallest but one of the most powerful empires on earth. When this took place, the San Francisco *Chronicle* of February 11, 1929, reported, "The Roman question tonight was a thing of the past and the Vatican was at peace with Italy. In affixing the autographs to the memorable document *healing the wound . . .* extreme cordiality was displayed on both sides" (italics supplied).

The New York *Times* on the same day reported, "The Pope is again an independent sovereign ruler, as he was throughout the Middle Ages, though his temporal realm, established today, is the most microscopic independent State in the world, and probably the smallest in all history." The document was signed in behalf of King Victor Emmanuel III by Premier Benito Mussolini and in behalf of Pope Pius XI by Cardinal Gasparri.

The April 18, 1929, edition of the *Catholic Advocate* comments about the people anticipating the signing, saying, "A crowd, tense with excitement, is here to witness the passage of these two men, whose pens will *heal a wound* of 59 years" (italics supplied). The article celebrated the fact that "his [the pope's] Kingship has at last been acknowledged by Italy."[9]

Today the Vatican is a recognized world leader in both ecclesiastical and political affairs. Like a state, she issues her own postage and receives ambassadors. The United States under President Ronald Reagan sent William A. Wilson as an official ambassador representing the U.S. American presidents had used "personal representatives" beginning in 1848, but Wilson's appointment as ambassador opened a new era.

George W. Bush received many heads of state during his presidency. While he was cordial to all of them, only once did he actually go to the airport to meet his guest. That was when Pope Benedict XVI visited the U.S. for a six-day whirlwind tour beginning on April 15, 2008. If you question the phrase in Revelation 13:3, "all the world marveled and followed the beast," go to the link cited and view the pictures of the pope's short visit.[10]

See him welcomed by President Bush into the White House. Scroll down to view him as he celebrated Mass in Nationals Park in Washington, D.C., adored by thousands. Notice the warm welcome by Sayyid M. Syeed, secretary general of the Islamic Society of North America. View him as he signs the guest book of the United Nations, and then addresses the assembly. Two Jewish students present the pope with a matzo (unleavened bread used for Passover) under the beaming eyes of Rabbi Arthur Schneier as the pope prepares to speak at the Park East Synagogue in New York.

At an ecumenical prayer service at the Church of Saint Joseph in New York, the photos capture him with the daughter of the late Martin Luther King, Bernice King, and as he shakes hands with Archbishop Demetrios, primate of the Greek Orthodox Church of America. At Ground Zero, the former site of the twin towers of the World Trade Center, he meets the families of victims and prays. A crowd of approximately 60,000 gather to worship with him in Yankee Stadium. If you don't think the phrase "all the world marveled and followed the beast" has meaning today, just scan through those photos and notice the adoration written on the faces of those people.

Going back for a moment to Revelation 13:1, which speaks of the beast as having "seven heads," one way of understanding the seven heads is to recognize them as representing Babylon, Medo-Persia, Greece, Rome, the Papacy of the Middle Ages, the Papacy of the deadly wound, and finally the resurgent Papacy. This line of thought corresponds well with the language of Revelation 17 when it speaks of seven kings and says, "Five have fallen, one is, and the other has not yet come. And when he comes, he must continue a short time" (Rev. 17:10).

Revelation 13:4

"So they worshiped the dragon who gave authority to the beast; and they worshiped the beast, saying, 'Who is like the beast? Who is able to make war with him?'" (Rev. 13:4). Scripture exposes the shocking link between the worship of the beast and the worship of the dragon, the devil. Remember, verse 2 had said that "the dragon gave him his power." Although in a secondary sense the "dragon" represented civil Rome, in its primary sense the Bible affirms that the dragon is indeed Satan.

From the beginning of his fall, Satan has coveted God's position and craved the honor and prerogatives belonging only to the Deity. He has desired to be worshipped. Of Lucifer the Scriptures said, "For you have said in your heart: 'I will ascend into heaven, I will exalt my throne above the stars of God; I will also sit on the mount of the congregation on the farthest sides of the north; I will ascend above the heights of the clouds, I will be like the Most High'" (Isa. 14:13, 14).

When Jesus came to earth Satan tempted Him to bow at his feet and worship Him (Matt. 4:9). It is Satan who stands behind the beast and seeks to be worshipped. By worshipping the beast, human beings unwittingly worship the dragon, the devil. Scripture reveals that "they worshiped the dragon" (Rev. 13:4). It is his rebellion, his agenda, his evil principles that instigated the departure from God's ways. The devil uses human beings as his pawns to work out his craving to be worshipped. It has always been this way. Paul stated that "the sacrifices of pagans are offered to demons, not to God" (1 Cor. 10:20, NIV). Those who engaged in idolatry in Old Testament times, as well as those who worship the beast, would be shocked if they saw themselves bowing at the feet of the arch rebel himself, Satan. Yet that is precisely what took place back in history when people worshipped their idols, and what will occur as history concludes with human beings giving their homage to the beast and his image. Ponder well the words, "They worshiped the dragon."

The word "worship" is the key term in Revelation 13 and 14, appearing no less than eight times in the two chapters. In the end, each person on this planet will give his or her worship to either the sovereign God, the one rightfully due our adoration by virtue of creation and redemption, or to the master deceiver Satan.

What is "worship," anyway? Let's review for a brief moment what we discussed earlier about the meaning of this most important word. Sometimes words in our language become shortened for ease of pronunciation, and we lose their original significance. The word "bedlam," for example, is a corruption of the word "Bethlehem," which referred to the "Hospital of St. Mary of Bethlehem" in London, an insane asylum. Because of the chaos associated with that institution, the word "bedlam," an abbreviated form of "Bethlehem," came into use in the English language.

We noted before that the word "worship" appears to derive from "worthship," which emphasizes the truth that whatever it is that we consider of highest worth, that we worship. The suffix "ship" means "state of," as in friendship, fellowship, championship, and a host of other words. Because the combination of letters "thsh" in that original word "worthship" is not easy to pronounce, it became shortened to "worship," thereby diminishing its former sense. The question is, Upon what do we put our highest value, as evidenced by our life choices? Do we place it on the fleeting things of this age, or do we value as highest God Himself: His presence, His ways, His Word and His law? It's a matter of assessment.

David addressed this matter of evaluation when he wrote, "The fear of the Lord is clean, enduring forever; the judgments of the Lord are true and righteous altogether. More to be desired are they than gold, yea, than much fine gold; sweeter also than honey and the honeycomb" (Ps. 19:9, 10). "The law of Your mouth is better to me than thousands of coins of gold and silver" (Ps. 119:72). "I love Your commandments more than gold, yes, than fine gold!" (verse 127). His son King Solomon added, "How much better to get wisdom than gold! And to get understanding is to be chosen rather than silver" (Prov. 16:16). The comparisons filling such texts reveal the authors' higher evaluation of godly things (thus God Himself) than earthly things.

To worship God is to accord Him the most vital place in our lives and hearts. It is to give Him first priority in all that we think and do—to esteem His ways and His words as having the greatest value. Job said, "I have treasured the words of His mouth more than my necessary food" (Job 23:12).

This evaluation will result in loving and willing obedience to God's commandments. How could it be otherwise? Those who treasure His Word above all things will cherish in their heart His ways and will. As a loyal citizen of His kingdom, willing compliance is inevitable!

Thus obedience is the highest form of worship. All verbal claims, professions, and representations to worship God clatter in empty and meaningless confusion if the heart is not surrendered to be obedient to His will. To "say" but "do not" is the highest form of hypocrisy. "He who says, 'I know Him,' and does not keep His commandments, is a liar, and the truth is not in him" (1 John 2:4).

Thus Samuel said to Saul, "Has the Lord as great delight in burnt offerings and sacrifices, as in obeying the voice of the Lord? Behold, to obey is better than sacrifice, and to heed than the fat of rams. For rebellion is as the sin of witchcraft, and stubbornness is as iniquity and idolatry" (1 Sam. 15:22, 23). Consider what those words mean. To think that I'm worshipping God while openly disobeying Him means that I might as well be practicing witchcraft. The deception that a form of worship birthed by disobedience is nevertheless acceptable to God is the worst sorcery or enchantment of all!

Jesus tried to open the eyes of the religious leaders of His day to this truth, saying, "In vain they worship Me, teaching as doctrines the commandments of men" (Matt. 15:9). He made this principle crystal clear when giving His Sermon on the Mount. "Not everyone who says to Me, 'Lord, Lord,' shall enter the kingdom of heaven, but he who does the will of My Father in heaven. Many will say to Me in that day, 'Lord, Lord, have we not prophesied in Your name, cast out demons in Your name, and done many wonders in Your name?' And then I will declare to them, 'I never knew you; depart from Me, you who practice lawlessness'" (Matt. 7:21-23). It is incredible blindness that one would think he or she is rendering worship to God while in fact they are practicing lawlessness and rendering homage to the devil! Yet such is the deception that Satan has enmeshed so much of humanity. Make no mistake about it: true worship of God involves giving Him first place—worship is obeying His law.

Does the beast power invite people to worship it? Can it be that a human organization would think it proper to accept the homage that belongs to God alone? Has the papal system fulfilled this prophecy? Sad to say, the answer to those questions is yes. We'll study this a little more when reviewing Revelation 13:5.

Revelation 13:4 concludes with the question "Who is able to make war with him?" It suggests that the resurgent beast has achieved such a status of power that others consider it invincible. As far as earthly powers go, there are none to withstand it. Modern Babylon will bask in such authority and impregnability that it regards itself as unconquerable, just as ancient Babylon did with its sturdy walls and water and food supplies sufficient to withstand any siege. Nevertheless, Cyrus walked into her citadel and Babylon fell, just as prophecy had predicted.

Who can make war with the beast? While the question might seem to be without an answer in Revelation 13, Revelation 19 does provide one. Although no earthly entity appears able to muster forces to make war against it successfully, there is One fully capable of doing so. John reports, "Then I saw heaven opened, and behold, a white horse. And He who sat on him was called Faithful and True, and in righteousness He judges and makes war. . . . He was clothed with a robe dipped in blood, and His name is called The Word of God. . . . And I saw the beast, the kings of the earth, and their armies, gathered together to make war against Him who sat on the horse and against His army. Then the beast was captured, and with him the false prophet who worked signs in his presence, by which he deceived those who received the mark of the beast and those who worshiped his image. These two were cast alive into the lake of fire burning with brimstone" (Rev. 19:11-20). Who can make war against the beast? The Bible gives us the answer: only Jesus. But He will defeat the beast completely. When He comes in the sky as the rider upon the white horse, the beast will be defeated and destroyed.

Revelation 13:5

Here we find two more clues to identify the beast, one involving behavior and the other involving length of duration (at least in an uninterrupted reign). "And he was given a mouth speaking great things and blasphemies, and he was given authority to continue for forty-two months." Has the papal structure fulfilled this aspect of the prophecy? And what is "blasphemy" in the biblical sense?

Most people may think of blasphemy as involving profane language or uncouth words, but the Bible gives a more specific definition. When

Jesus Christ came to earth, He was God incarnate. "The Word became flesh" (John 1:14). Although from outward appearance it may not have seemed so, He was in fact the Creator-God in sandals. It was part of God's miraculous and bold plan to make salvation a reality. He would step from His throne, remove His diadem, and live here as a human being to die for our sins and serve as an example of how to live. The Scriptures make this abundantly clear.

But the "God in the flesh" truth was so unthinkable that the pagans would never have dreamed of it. When faced with the assignment of bringing back to life Nebuchadnezzar's forgotten dream, his counselors said, "It is a difficult thing that the king requests, and there is no other who can tell it to the king except the gods, whose dwelling is not with flesh" (Dan. 2:11). Yes, it's true that only God could reveal such secrets, but the Bible tells us that this very God did indeed make His dwelling with flesh. Almost as a direct rebuttal to the statement of Babylon's wise men, John tells us that "the Word became flesh and dwelt among us" (John 1:14). That is the beautiful fulfillment of the term Immanuel, "God with us" (Matt. 1:23).

Still, it was so difficult to comprehend that the Jewish religious leaders, themselves versed in Scripture, found it nearly impossible to accept, let alone grasp. They should have been prepared to welcome the birth of the Messiah and pave the way for His ministry, but Satan had blinded their hearts through pride and unbelief. Thus when Jesus affirmed His true status—His true identity—they reached for stones to silence the voice of what they determined to be "blasphemy."

Jesus said, "'My Father, who has given them to Me, is greater than all; and no one is able to snatch them out of My Father's hand. I and My Father are one.' Then the Jews took up stones again to stone Him. Jesus answered them, 'Many good works I have shown you from My Father. For which of those works do you stone Me?' The Jews answered Him, saying, 'For a good work we do not stone You, but for blasphemy, and because You, being a Man, make Yourself God'" (John 10:29-33).

Like the counselors of ancient Babylon, the Jewish leaders were both right and wrong. They were absolutely correct to define "blasphemy" as occurring when a "man makes himself God." But they were dead wrong in not realizing that the One who stood before them was God in the flesh! For another person to make such a claim would indeed be blasphemy. But it would have been inaccurate for Jesus to deny His divine nature.

The Jewish religious hierarchy became even more specific in their accusation of blasphemy on another occasion. Four friends of a paralyzed man lowered him through the roof and into the presence of the great Healer. As Jesus saw their faith, He said, "'Son, your sins are forgiven you.' And some of the scribes were sitting there and reasoning in their hearts, 'Why does this Man speak blasphemies like this? Who can forgive sins but God alone?'" (Mark 2:5-7). Again, they were right and yet so wrong!

It is true that only God can forgive sins, because ultimately all are done against Him. David prayed, "Against You, You only, have I sinned" (Ps. 51:4). Yes, Jesus said, "If your brother or sister sins, go and point out their fault, just between the two of you" (Matt. 18:15, NIV). But to do that to another human being is not the same thing as confessing them to God. James counsels us to confess our faults one to another (James 5:16), but nowhere does Scripture tell us to approach a human mediator and confess our sins to another mortal and expect that they are forgiven in the eyes of God. Scripture recognizes only one Mediator, and His name is Jesus. "For there is one God and one Mediator between God and men, the Man Christ Jesus" (1 Tim. 2:5). For a human being to pronounce divine forgiveness is to usurp the place of God Himself.

We see then, that the Bible identifies it as blasphemy when human beings set themselves up as God, and more specifically when anyone claims to be able to forgive sins in the way that God does. Remember that Satan has always wanted to be equal with God. It was that aspiration that caused his fall in the beginning. "I will be like the Most High" was his lofty and ambitious desire (Isa. 14:14). For that reason heaven had to expel him. But he has ever since attempted to achieve that goal. When Jesus was about to begin His ministry, Satan came to tempt Him, and the last temptation included an offer to give Him all if He would just bow and worship Satan. To this offer, Christ said, "No, thank you."

With sadness we read the boastful and arrogant claims that have fallen from the lips of pontiffs through the ages. They echo the great claim made by Lucifer himself ages ago: "I will be like the Most High."

Keep in mind that this matter of boastful, blasphemous claims is one of the hallmarks of the Bible's picture of apostasy. Daniel mentions it in his description of the horn power that it was "speaking pompous words" (Dan. 7:8). Daniel 11's king of the north "shall speak blasphemies against the God of gods" (Dan. 11:36). Paul includes it in his description of the "man of sin" who "sits as God in the temple of God, showing himself that he is God" (2 Thess. 2:4).

John underscores this point in identifying this power as "antichrist," the prefix "anti" having the meaning of "in the place of," or "instead of."[11] It is the Greek equivalent of the Latin vicar, which means "in the place of," or "instead of." (We'll study this in greater detail later in chapter 18.) In Revelation 17's picture of the harlot the beast upon which she rides is full of the "names of blasphemy" (Rev. 17:3).

As we noted previously, the very title "pontiff" hails back to the priests of ancient Babylon who styled themselves the ones who made the connection between heaven and earth. The root of the word is "*pont*," or "bridge." The pope's title *Pontifex Maximus* might be translated "the greatest bridge maker." Thus anyone who wears this label is claiming to be the "bridge" between the "here" and the "hereafter," the connecting link between God and humanity. But the Bible makes it plain that Jesus is the link between heaven and earth. He is the mystical "Ladder" of Jacob's dream (Gen. 28:12-19; John 1:51). When we read, "Therefore He is also able to save to the uttermost those who come to God through Him, since He always lives to make intercession for them" (Heb. 7:25), of whom is it speaking? Does it have in mind a human being—a pope or priest? Certainly not! Jesus, the divine Son of God, is the only mediator!

Nonetheless, notice a few of the claims made by popes and prelates. Pope Leo XIII in his Encyclical Letters said, "We hold upon this earth the place of God Almighty."[12] Elsewhere we read, "The Pope has power to change times, to abrogate laws and to dispense with all things, even the precepts of Christ."[13]

Cardinal Bellarmine stated, "All names which in the Scriptures are applied to Christ, by virtue of which it is established that he is over the church, all the same names are applied to the Pope."[14] In an 1895 article appearing in the *Catholic National* we find this startling statement: "The Pope is not only the representative of Jesus Christ, but he is Jesus Christ, Himself, hidden under the veil of flesh." In 1512 Christopher Marcellus told Pope Julius II: "Take care that we lose not that salvation, that life and breath which thou has given us, for thou art our shepherd, thou art our physician, thou art our governor, thou art our husbandman, thou art finally another God on earth."[15]

"The Pope is of so great dignity and so exalted that he is not a mere man, but as it were God, and the vicar of God. . . . The Pope alone is called most holy. . . . Hence the Pope is crowned with a triple crown, as king of heaven and of earth and of hell. Moreover the superiority and the power of the Roman Pontiff by no means pertains only to heavenly things, but also earthly things, and to things under the earth, and even over the angels, whom he is greater than. So that if it were possible that the angels might err in the faith, or might think contrary to the faith, they could be judged and excommunicated by the Pope. The Pope is as it were God on earth, sole sovereign of the faithful of Christ, chief of kings, having plenitude of power."[16]

The Papacy's claim to divine attributes reaches its zenith in the Mass, in which the priest is said to have the power to bring to life the actual body of Christ in the wafer he holds. At the climax of the service, He raises the host high in the air and pronounces the words *"Hoc est corpus,"* "This is [My] body," and lo, that which was mere bread moments before has now become the Sovereign God of the universe. Think of the absurdity of the creature creating the Creator! (Ironically, strong evidence suggests that the phrase *"Hoc est corpus"* evolved into the magical phrase "hocus pocus.")

Earlier we pointed out that when Jesus spoke the words "Your sins are forgiven" to a lame man, the Pharisees charged Him with "speaking blasphemies. Who can forgive sins but God alone" (Luke 5:20, 21). As we said, they were correct in their understanding of the definition of blasphemy, but woefully ignorant of the divine nature of the One who had proclaimed those words. Yet the theology of the Catholic Church states that its priests have the power to forgive the sins of those who come to them in the confessional—a forgiveness binding in heaven.

The ecclesiology of Catholicism maintains that the church and its traditions supersede Scripture. "As the Catholic yields his judgment in spiritual matters implicitly, and with unreserved confidence, to the voice of his church, so, too, the Protestant recognizes no teacher but the Bible."[17]

My wife and I love our pets and have had several to enjoy through the years. And I can assure you that they get their share of treats! But I notice that our dog, Sully, though he loves and trusts us dearly, will almost always sniff what I hold out to him before he gobbles it up, just to check to see that it's edible. Are humans as careful with what they let enter their minds? Something to think about!

A while back I pulled into the parking lot of a local food store and parked behind a vehicle whose bumper had an interesting sticker on it. It was obviously a Christian symbol including a cross, and I thought, as I walked up to the entrance of the store, that I might leave a card or piece of literature on the windshield of the car when I left. As I departed the store with my groceries in hand and walked toward my car, I noticed that the owner of the vehicle parked in front of mine was just then placing her bags into the trunk.

I slowed as I passed her car and waited for the right moment, then said, "I couldn't help noticing your bumper sticker," pointing to it. "You must be a Christian."

"Oh, yes, I am a Christian."

"What faith do you practice?" I inquired.

"Oh," she said, "I go to the church right over there," gesturing to the Catholic church across the street.

"Wonderful!" I said. "So you believe in the Bible, right?"

"Oh yes, the Bible!"

"And the Ten Commandments, you believe in them too, don't you?"

"Oh yes, the Ten Commandments!" she responded.

I ventured to go one step further and proceeded cautiously. "Have you ever compared the Ten Commandments in the Bible with what you find in the catechism? Do you know that the Bible tells us the seventh day is the Sabbath, but that the church changed the day of worship from Saturday to Sunday?"

"Oh," she replied with a wave of her hand. "I don't get into all that. I just do what they tell me to do."

How sad! I pray that she will come to know Scripture.

Consider the following quote: "**Q.** What if the Holy Scriptures command one thing, and the Pope another, contrary to it? **A.** The Holy Scriptures must be thrown aside. **Q.** What is the Pope? **A.** He is the Vicar of Christ, King of kings, and Lord of lords and there is but one judgment seat belonging to God and the Pope."[18]

A bumper sticker I saw recently reminds me of those who allow themselves to be led without adequate research or careful searching of the Scriptures on their part. The slogan was on a trailer, and it said, "I go where I am towed."

Revelation 13:6

Here we find blasphemy directed against God in three ways: to "blaspheme His name, His tabernacle, and those who dwell in heaven" (Rev. 13:6). We've examined a few papal statements that ascribe to themselves names and titles that belong to God alone. And we've seen how the Papacy claims to have the power to forgive sins. The "tabernacle" in ancient Israel was where sins were forgiven and human beings put right with God and thus relates to the issue of forgiveness of sins.

But what about the third category: involving "those who dwell in heaven"? One way is by presuming that it has the power to elevate to sainthood those whom it wishes. The Papacy blasphemes those "who dwell in heaven" in the sense that it proclaims that certain individuals are now in heaven (whereas the Bible teaches that the dead rest unconsciously in the grave) and that they have been accorded the mantle of sainthood as well as the capacity to render assistance to humans on earth. Catholic teaching has placed one individual in particular—Mary, the mother of Jesus—on a pedestal that rivals the position of the Lord Jesus Christ. Yet the Bible teaches that Jesus is the door through which we gain access to the Father (John 10:9).

Through Scripture we understand that Mary, a mortal being, is dead and asleep in the grave awaiting the resurrection at Jesus' coming and thus cannot be presently in heaven. "For the living know that they will die, but the dead know nothing; they have no further reward, and even their name is forgotten" (Eccl. 9:5, NIV). "For there is no work or device or knowledge or wisdom in the grave where you are going" (verse 10). That would include the "work" of rendering mediation and providing spiritual or material assistance, wouldn't it?

What purpose would be served to pray to one who is dead in the grave, in which there is no "work . . . knowledge, or wisdom." Mary cannot conduct the work of intercession, nor does she any longer have any wisdom in her to give answers to prayers. You might as well be praying to an inanimate rock. Jesus is the only one able to offer salvation and by whose name we are saved. "Salvation is found in no one else, for there is no other name under heaven given to mankind by which we must be saved" (Acts 4:12, NIV).

Note that Peter, adjudged to have been the first "pope," is the one who spoke these words. This same Peter affirmed that Jesus (not Peter) is the rock. "Coming to Him [Jesus] as to a living stone, rejected indeed by men, but chosen by God and precious. . . . Therefore it is also contained in the Scripture, 'Behold, I lay in Zion a chief cornerstone, elect, precious, and he who believes on Him will by no means be put to shame.' Therefore, to you who believe, He is precious; but to those who are disobedient, 'The stone which the builders rejected has become the chief Cornerstone,' and 'A stone of stumbling and a rock of offense' " (1 Peter 2:4-9). A quick review of a few Bible passages will reveal that many other individuals in Scripture understood and taught that Jesus is the rock of our salvation.

The patriarch Jacob knew it. "By the hands of the Mighty God of Jacob (From there is the Shepherd, the Stone of Israel)" (Gen. 49:24). Moses proclaimed it. "Give ear, O heavens, and I will speak; and hear, O earth, the words of my mouth. Let my teaching drop as the rain, my speech distill as the dew, as raindrops on the tender herb, and as showers on the grass. For I proclaim the name of the Lord: ascribe greatness to our God. He is the Rock, His work is perfect" (Deut. 32:1-3). David declared it. "The Lord is my rock and my fortress and my deliverer; my God, my strength, in whom I will trust; my shield and the horn of my salvation, my stronghold. I will call upon the Lord, who is worthy to be praised; so shall I be saved from my enemies" (Ps.

18:2, 3). "He only is my rock and my salvation; He is my defense" (Ps. 62:2).

Isaiah prophesied it. "The Lord of hosts, Him you shall hallow; let Him be your fear, and let Him be your dread. He will be as a sanctuary, but a stone of stumbling and a rock of offense to both the houses of Israel" (Isa. 8:13, 14). Daniel foresaw it. "You watched while a stone was cut out without hands, which struck the image on its feet of iron and clay, and broke them in pieces. . . . And the stone that struck the image became a great mountain and filled the whole earth" (Dan. 2:34, 35). Paul preached it. They "all drank the same spiritual drink. For they drank of that spiritual Rock that followed them, and that Rock was Christ" (1 Cor. 10:4). How shocked these prophetic spokespeople would be to learn that human lips and pens have ascribed this lofty title to mere mortals!

But didn't Christ give Simon the name "Peter"? According to Christ's words he was "*Petros*," or a "small, rolling stone."[19] But the rock against which the gates of Hades could not prevail could not be the apostle Peter, for just moments later Peter tried to dissuade Christ from His mission. At that point Christ "turned and said to Peter, 'Get behind Me, Satan! You are an offense to Me, for you are not mindful of the things of God, but the things of men'" (Matt. 16:23). No, Peter was not the "rock." He never claimed to be. When he later used that term in his epistles, he reverently applied it to his Lord, Jesus Christ. And he would be mortified to learn that those in later ages thought of him as pope. The rock upon which Jesus built the church was the confession of Peter and all Christians that Jesus is the foundation of the church.

Revelation 13:7

"It was granted to him to make war with the saints and to overcome them. And authority was given him over every tribe, tongue, and nation" (Rev. 13:7). Has this been fulfilled? Has the papal ecclesiastical system made "war with the saints" and overcome them? Unfortunately, the blood of martyrs stains the pages of history. How many? We don't really know, since the records are incomplete. As mentioned before, conservative estimates place the number at somewhere between 50 and 100 million who gave their lives for their faith.

John Foxe published in 1563 a book entitled *Actes and Monuments of These Latter and Perilous Days, Touching Matters of the Church.* Better known by the shorter title *Foxe's Book of Martyrs,* it was the most prodigious publishing project undertaken in Great Britain up to that point, with numerous woodcut illustrations. The book recounts the afflictions and persecutions of Christians from the first century to his day, with emphasis on the fourteenth to sixteenth centuries. Outside of the Holy Bible, it is said that no book had as profound an influence on Protestant Christianity as the volume penned by John Foxe. (And it is available online free.)[20] Peruse some of the chapters and become acquainted with the characters whose faith survived the persecutions heaped upon them in the name of religion. What John saw in Revelation 12 literally became true. "And they [the saints] overcame him by the blood of the Lamb and by the word of their testimony, and they did not love their lives to the death" (Rev. 12:11).

The Vatican does not deny the facts as historians have recorded them. The inquiring student can find voluminous evidence to substantiate the prophecy of Revelation. The dungeon, the rack, the Inquisition, and the stake are all a part of the sad heritage of the power that thought itself to be in the role of "corrector of heretics."

Jesus predicted that when He said, "The time is coming that whoever kills you will think that he offers God service" (John 16:2). The word "service" in that passage is sobering: it is the Greek *latreia,* which means "reverential worship."[21] In other words, Jesus said that people would think that executing someone for his or her religious convictions would be equivalent to an act of worship. Can you imagine a mind so corrupted by the devil that it would assume that torturing others to death because of their belief in the Scriptures would constitute an act of homage or obeisance to God? But it did happen countless times in the medieval church.

The text says that "it was granted" to him to make war with the saints. The word "grant" signifies that it was "given." Who gave permission, and for what reason? The obvious answer is that God, who is ultimately in control of all things, allowed it to happen. But why would He permit such atrocities to take place? Why didn't He stop it? To answer that, we must remember that God is looking toward a long-range solution to the problem of sin. He didn't stop Adam and Eve from eating the forbidden fruit. Nor did He prevent Cain from killing Abel or the religious leaders from demanding the crucifixion of Christ. And He didn't halt the martyrdoms of the Middle Ages.

Although the omniscient Lord knows full well the lethal nature of sin and the insanity of iniquity, He must allow the actions of those who have given their minds over to satanic influences to work out the results of what they have done so that the universe can see that there is nothing good in sin or the proposal set forth by the archrebel Lucifer. Evidence, as painful as its production must be, has to accrue. It must demonstrate how deadly disobedience is.

When Satan brought his charge against God, it was twofold in nature. Essentially he said, "You'll be better off if you disobey God and disregard His laws. My way will give you freedom and happiness." The second part of the charge was that "God's way is impossible. No one can keep His law. If they were to try, they would discover only restriction and confinement." Satan accused the loyal angels of God of being slaves.

Consequently, God has allowed him room in which to operate so as to expose his charges for what they are: lies. Though it pains His great heart deeply, He has allowed sin to grow and flourish, with the ugly fruits of destruction and sorrow being the result. He also seeks to reveal that Satan's second charge is equally unfounded. Through the lives of committed saints, God desires to demonstrate that righteousness brings peace and joy and that through the indwelling Spirit and from the motive of love obedience is indeed possible.

The two harvests of Revelation 14 will resolve the conflict that has torn the universe apart. Understanding the truth of the two harvests gives significant meaning to the condition and perplexities of life that we struggle with now. The book of Revelation speaks of the harvest of the grain and the harvest of the grapes. The harvest of the grain in Revelation 14:14 depicts Christ coming with His sickle in hand. Verse 5 portrays the righteous as being the "firstfruits," a reminder of the wavesheaf offering presented after the Passover. The harvest of the grain represents the saved.

In symbolic terms, it is speaking of those who have yielded their lives to His Spirit and allowed the "fruits of the Spirit" to develop in their lives. "Transformed by the renewing" of their minds, they reflect the gracious character attributes of Jesus. As a result, they prove that Satan's charge is false, in that by God's strength they have become overcomers. Their lives demonstrate that, through His power, obedience is possible. They are both "happy" and "holy," two words that the devil claimed didn't belong together. The harvest of the grain represents the maturation of the growth of grace in their hearts. "When the grain ripens, immediately he puts in the sickle, because the harvest has come" (Mark 4:29).

On the other hand, Revelation also describes a second harvest—that of the grapes (Rev. 14:17-20). It represents the ripening of the character of sin, the full development of the heart absent of God's Spirit and in rebellion against His government. Those who belong to it have taken on the character of the devil. Devoid of God's Spirit, they manifest all the attributes of their leader, Satan. The prophecy of Ezekiel will come to pass: "See, the day! See, it comes! Doom has burst forth, the rod has budded, arrogance has blossomed! Violence has risen, a rod to punish the wicked" (Eze. 7:10, 11, NIV). "Another angel" brings the sickle for their harvest. "So the angel thrust his sickle into the earth and gathered the vine of the earth, and threw it into the great winepress of the wrath of God" (Rev. 14:19).

Before God can wrap up the saga of Planet Earth, the two harvests have to be ready for reaping. There can be little doubt but that the effects of sin have manifested themselves. Who could argue that sin is good or that anything positive can ever result from disobeying God? Yet before Jesus comes, as the angels release the figurative winds of strife and God withdraws His Spirit from the wicked, there will be an even greater demonstration of what sin brings. The harvest of iniquity will be fully ripe. Worldwide chaos on a scale not yet seen will burst forth.

God is waiting patiently for His people to surrender their wills to Him so that the harvest of righteousness—the harvest of the grain—will be ready. He is desirous of His people providing the exhibits for His courtroom rebuttal of Satan's charge. Is it possible to live a righteous and holy life? God is waiting to point to His true children and say, "Here is the patience of the saints; here are those who keep the commandments of God and the faith of Jesus" (verse 12). From our perspective it seems that the conflict has already raged long enough. "How long?" is the question that has been on the minds and lips of His people for a sizable period of time. It seems, from our point of view, as if it's already been an eternity. But when the harvest ripens, immediately He will put in the sickle.

The good news is that God's solution will be a permanent one. "Affliction will not rise up a second time" (Nahum 1:9). What He has accomplished will effectively cleanse the entire universe of the sin problem for time and eternity. Though it may seem long and painful now, ultimately the safety of the universe will be assured through His response to the sin problem.

Remember, these things were not a part of God's plan in the beginning. He created a perfect world in which sin, pain, and death did not exist. It was because the human race chose to sell out to Satan that the effects of sin came to overshadow the peaceful world that the Creator had made. But the Lord, praise His name, stepped in and provided a solution to the problem. He would Himself take the penalty of our sin and give us another chance to be faithful to Him.

And when you think of all the pain the martyrs endured, don't forget that what they went through didn't reach the level that Christ, God's dear Son, experienced. He suffered beyond what any human being has been asked to endure. It was "granted" to him, the beast, to make war against the saints so that all could see the heinous nature of sin.

When you meet God's warriors in heaven, those whose lives were extinguished in the name of religion, you might be surprised to learn that they considered it an honor to walk the footsteps of their Lord. Bearing the cross of Christ was to them similar to the privilege given to Simon of Cyrene who carried the cross of Jesus. Is sin ugly, painful, and horrific? Yes. Were the martyrdoms conducted by the church wrong? Yes. We would minimize neither the agony nor the culpability of these things. But God has a way of bringing good out of bad, triumph from tragedy. "Surely your wrath against mankind brings you praise" (Ps. 76:10, NIV). These who gave the last ounce of their blood as a sacrifice on the altar of misled zeal will one day live to praise and honor the God for whom they died.

Revelation 13:18

One final clue appears in the last verse of Revelation 13. "Here is wisdom. Let him who has understanding calculate the number of the beast, for it is the number of a man: His number is 666" (Rev. 13:18). Few verses of Revelation, let alone the whole Bible, have attracted as much attention and speculation as this one. What does the mysterious number "666" signify?

Many languages of the world have a set of characters that serve a dual purpose: that of alphabetic sounds used to assemble words for speech, and at the same time representing numbers. English is an anomaly in that regard in that the character "a" has no numerical significance, nor does the integer "8" have any phonic significance.

In many other languages (Hebrew and Greek, for example) certain characters double as letters and numbers. However, we do have something in English that corresponds to this, but we seldom use it today. We speak of "Roman numerals." In this system some English letters do have numerical value. "I" is equal to one; "V" or "U" stands for five; "X" for 10, "L" for 50, "C" for 100, and so on. In the past, it was not uncommon for people to refer to the numerical value of their name as a type of nickname. There is actually a word that describes this phenomenon: *gematria*. A young boy in school might scribble "98 loves 256" for a cryptic substitute of "Johnny loves Mary." The phrase "number of his name" refers to this practice of adding up the numeric value of the letters of a specific name.

One of the titles that has been used in reference to the pope is "*Vicarius Filii Dei,*" which means "Vicar of the Son of God."[22] It appeared long ago in the "Donation of Constantine," a document that someone fabricated to establish the authority of the papal see. For many centuries some touted the document and the title it contained as representing official sanction for the rule of the Roman pontiff. Later, scholars determined that the document was a forgery, but that in no way removes the fact that it, and its contents, served as a source of authority for the Papacy, being quoted by many popes and included in numerous documents and encyclopedias. Since the Vatican never retracted the language, it has implied its approval to the usage of the phrase. And why not? The pope indeed claims to be the Vicar of Christ.

More recently, a lively discussion has surfaced surrounding the question as to whether it is an "official title" of the pope or not, and whether it meets the prophetic specifications of Revelation 13:18. Those who see in this title a fulfillment of "the number of his name," point out that although the "Donation of Constantine" was indeed a fake, the Papacy endorsed and did not refute its contents for many centuries. The only reason church leadership discarded it was because of its questionable origin. They note that this very question was asked in the April 18, 1915, edition of *Our Sunday Visitor*. "What are the letters supposed to be in the Pope's crown, and what do they signify, if anything?" The answer was: "The letters inscribed in the Pope's mitre are these: *Vicarius Filii Dei*, which is the Latin for Vicar of the Son of God."[23]

Those who wish to deny the title as being the subject of Revelation's prophecy point to the fact that it is not currently approved as being an official title of the pope, that the "Donation of Constantine" was a forgery, thus diminishing the effect of the title's inclusion, and that the copy of *Our Sunday Visitor* containing the above referenced question and answer has been lost from the official archives.

Briefly, the first word of the title, *Vicarius*, comes from the same root as "vicar," which means "instead of," or "in place of." "*Filii*" means "Son" and refers to Jesus Christ. The last term *Dei* means "God." The title therefore means "Vicar of the Son of God," or "The one who stands in the place of the Son of God." As to the title's authenticity, its applicability to the Papacy, and its fulfilling the prophecy of Revelation 13:18, the reader must decide for himself or herself.

There is no question that this title has been used at one time or another in reference to the pope. Even if it was never sanctioned as an official title or actually inscribed on the crown of the pope, the concept that it conveys accurately and clearly represents the claims of the Papacy today. It correctly reflects the spirit of the papal claims, which are numerous and well documented. Most certainly the pope does indeed regard himself as the "vicar" of the Son of God, the one who is "in the place of" Jesus. Concerning that there is no dispute. Finally, this item appears last in the list of clues to identify the "beast" of Revelation 13. The conclusion that the beast represents the historical Papacy rests on solid footing, whether or not the title *Vicarius Filii Dei* currently appears on the pope's crown.

A quick examination of the letters of this title reveals that the value of its letters does indeed add up to 666, the "number of his name."

V	5
I	1
C	100
A	
R	
I	1
U	5
S	
F	
I	1
L	50
I	1
I	1
D	500
E	
I	1

Total 666

Some might question why "u" and "v" both receive the value of 5. It is because they were essentially the same letter. In many towns still today you may find the inscription on an old city "pvblic library."

Even if we discard this particular title, when we put all the clues together the identity of the beast is unmistakable. One entity on earth fits all the specifications of Revelation 13:1-10, and that is the ecclesiastical structure known as the Papacy. It arose according to the prophetic timetable. Its conduct and behavior fit the Bible picture.

Its intolerance of dissenters meets the specifications of prophecy. The length of its duration, lasting 1260 years, then suffering a deadly setback followed by a dramatic resurgence to a position of worldwide power and worship sufficient to evoke the claim "Who is like the beast? Who is able to make war with him?"—all correspond to the prophetic portrayal.

[1] Frank Frost Abbott, *A Short History of Rome,* pp. 235, 236.

[2] Thomas Hobbes, *Leviathan*, part 4, chapter 47, p. 516.

[3] http://en.wikipedia.org/wiki/Fort_Hood_shooting.

[4] Richard Duppa, *A Brief Account of the Subversion of the Papal Government* (1798), pp. 59, 60.

[5] *Missionary Magazine,* vol. 1, p. 185.

[6] George Bell, *The Evangelical Magazine* (1796), vol. 4, p. 56.

[7] Drue Cressener, *A Demonstration of the First Principles of the Protestant Applications of the Apocalypse* (1690), pp. viii, ix.

[8] Drue Cressener, *The Judgments of God Upon the Roman Catholick Church* (1689), pp. 309, 312. See L. E. Froom, *The Prophetic Faith of Our Fathers*, vol. 2, pp. 591-596.

[9] See, for example, http://biblelight.net/wound.htm.

[10] http://www.catholicvoiceoakland.org/2008/08-04-21/popevisitphotos.htm.

[11] W. F. Arndt and F. W. Gingrich, *A Greek-English Lexicon of the New Testament*, pp. 72f.

[12] http://www.papalencyclicals.net/Leo13/l13praec.htm.

[13] Decretal De Translat. (For references for these and the following quotes, see http://amazingdiscoveries.org/AD-Articles-TotalOnslaught-ThePopeIsGodOnThisEarth.html.)

[14] Robert Bellarmine, *On the Authority of the Councils*, vol. 2, p. 266.

[15] Christopher Marcellus addressing Pope Julius II, in *Fifth Lateran Council*, Session IV (1512), Council Edition. Colm. Agrip. 1618 (J. D. Mansi, ed., Sacrorum Conciliorum, vol. 32, col. 761). Also quoted in Philippe Labbe and Gabriel Cossart, *History of the Councils,* Vol. XIV, column 109.

[16] Lucius Ferraris, "Concerning the Extent of Papal Dignity, Authority, or Dominion and Infallibility," *Prompta Bibliotheca Canonica, Juridica, Moralis, Theologica, Ascetica, Polemica, Rubristica, Historica,* Vol. V.

[17] *Catholic Mirror,* Sept. 9, 1893.

[18] Roy Livesey, *Understanding the New Age,* p. 101.

[19] See, for example, *Vine's Expository Dictionary of Old and New Testament Words,* vol. 4, p. 76, or M. Vincent, *Word Studies in the New Testament,* vol. 1, p. 91.

[20] http://www.ccel.org/f/foxe/martyrs/home.html.

[21] W. F. Arndt and F. W. Gingrich, *A Greek-English Lexicon of the New Testament*, p. 468.

[22] For a discussion of the history of this title, see http://biblelight.net/envoy.htm.

[23] *Ibid.*

CHAPTER 17

THREE OLD TESTAMENT PROPHETIC PICTURES OF THE "BEAST"

The six other biblical portrayals share many of the same clues that we find in Revelation 13:1-10. Three of them appear in the book of Daniel and the other three in the New Testament. Since He devoted so much prophetic material to it, God must have felt that it was of great importance for people to be aware of this matter. Scripture admonishes: "By the mouth of two or three witnesses, every word shall be established" (2 Cor. 13:1). What shall we say when God provides no less than seven "witnesses" to a truth?

Daniel 7's "Horn Power"

Of necessity, our look at the six other pictures will be a very brief one. Daniel 7 contains the first snapshot. It introduces four wild beasts coming from the windwhipped sea, a symbol of the strife and war occurring in areas of large population from which emerged kingdoms and empires. First, a winged lion represented Babylon. Then a bear raised up on its side pictured the kingdom of Medo-Persia, followed by a winged leopard with four heads standing for the empire of Greece and the four parts into which it divided following the death of Alexander the Great. Finally, a ferocious beast that defied description sprang forth with iron teeth, devouring and trampling. The iron teeth aptly portrayed the Roman Empire with its longevity and crushing power.

The fourth beast sports 10 horns. Daniel reports: "I was considering the horns, and there was another horn, a little one, coming up among them, before whom three of the first horns were plucked out by the roots. And there, in this horn, were eyes like the eyes of a man, and a mouth speaking pompous words" (Dan. 7:8). This horn power, which began small but became great, features some of the very same characteristics that we've encountered in Revelation 13's beast from the sea. The "pompous words" reported by the angel in Daniel's book correspond to the "blasphemy" of Revelation. Like the first beast of Revelation 13, the horn power is a persecuting entity. Said the prophet, "I was watching; and the same horn was making war against the saints, and prevailing against them" (Dan. 7:21). It continues in its uninterrupted reign for the same period as does the beast of Revelation 13. "The saints shall be given into his hand for a time and times and half a time" (Dan. 7:25). This period is equivalent to three and a half "years," which, according to the prophetic yardstick of a "day for a year in symbolic prophecy," translates to the same 1260 literal years that we saw in Revelation 13's "42 months," extending from A.D. 538 through A.D. 1798.

What about the phrase "And there, in this horn, were eyes like the eyes of a man"? It refers to a system that depends on human wisdom rather than divine revelation. Throughout history God has always directed His people by His appointed messengers, the prophets. "Surely the Lord God does nothing, unless He reveals His secret to His servants the prophets" (Amos 3:7). The prophet then became God's "mouth" or spokesperson to share the information divinely revealed to them (see Ex. 4:16; 7:1, 2; Deut. 5:5). The very word "prophet" comes from a Greek background with the prefix *pro,* meaning "in behalf of" or "for" combined with the verb *phemi,* meaning "to speak."[1] Thus a prophet is one who speaks for, or in behalf of, the Lord.

Those who occupied the role of prophet were also called "seers." "Formerly in Israel, if someone went to inquire of God, they would say, 'Come, let us go to the seer'; because the prophet of today used to be called a seer" (1 Sam. 9:9, NIV). While the word "prophet" focuses on the messengers *sharing* the communication to others, as they "speak for" God, the term "seer" emphasizes the aspect of his ministry *receiving* the messages from God. The word "seer" simply means "one who sees."

Often prophets would literally "see" a vision or a dream, by which God communicated with them. The Lord graciously provided such insight to guide and safeguard His people from the deceptions of

Satan. The prophet, or seer, would present to the people of God the divinely revealed messages as the "word of the Lord." Through time, some of them were preserved and compiled in the collection known as the Sacred Writings, or the Holy Scriptures. We are on safe ground when we follow the teachings of the Bible, the revealed Word of God. The Bible presents divine insight. "Your word is a lamp to my feet and a light to my path" (Ps. 119:105). It is by His Word that we can "see" our way in this darkened world of sin. "And so we have the prophetic word confirmed, which you do well to heed as a light that shines in a dark place" (2 Peter 1:19).

The system brought to view by Daniel—the horn power—is distinguished by it having the "eyes of a man." It is a system that rejects the messages of the "seers," those given divine insight into God's ways and His will, and instead relies on human wisdom to guide its spiritual feet. But that is a most dangerous thing to do. "If they do not speak according to this word, it is because there is no light in them" (Isa. 8:20). Spiritual blindness is the inevitable result of ignoring the truths of His Word. Necessarily, a human-oriented system is prone to error and falsehood.

The Papacy—the highest leadership of Catholicism—has openly averred that its traditions and teachings have authority over the Sacred Scriptures. It has ignored many plain teachings of the Bible and supplanted them with a cocktail of paganism and human philosophy. The "eyes of a man" describe a system that walks in spiritual darkness, not in the light of God's truth.

Later in Daniel 7 prophecy specifically reveals the little horn's defiance against the law of God. "He . . . shall intend to change times and law" (Dan. 7:25). A matter of changing human law would certainly not be the subject of Bible prophecy, for that routinely occurs when one kingdom takes over for another. No, we have here a prediction that this power would intentionally attempt to change divine law.

The Papacy is neither embarrassed nor diffident about its position. It confidently and boastfully affirms that its authority must exceed that of Holy Scripture and divine law, pointing out that nearly all in Christianity, including Protestants who claim to follow the Bible and the Bible only, have followed many of its practices.

This issue surfaced a century or so ago, when certain questions arose and called forth a response from the *Catholic Mirror,* the official organ of James Cardinal Gibbons. The city of Chicago had outbid its rivals St. Louis, Washington, D.C., and New York to obtain the privilege of holding the 1892 World's Fair, to be a commemoration of the four hundreth anniversary of Christopher Columbus' arrival in America. (Because of delays, it didn't actually open until 1893.)

Because it would be Chicago's chance to compete with the larger and more famous cities of the eastern seaboard, its promoters desired something spectacular that people would associate with their city. Alexandre-Gustave Eiffel proposed building a large tower for them. The fair's managers declined his offer, because they wanted someone American. They selected George Washington Gale Ferris, Jr., to translate into steel and cable an idea he had come up with. It would be a giant wheel 26 stories tall to which were attached 36 cars, each capable of holding 60 people at a time. Thus was born the Ferris Wheel.

But the Chicago World's Fair ran into problems. The promoters wanted to open and close it on a Sunday, which evoked the hue and cry of clergymen and churches. Apparently the question was not settled, at least to the satisfaction of those who objected to a Sunday opening of the fair. Not too long beforehand the United States Supreme Court had handed down a decision dated February 29, 1892, *Church of the Holy Trinity v. the United States,* in which the court identified the United States as being a "Christian nation." The ruling stated: "These, and many other matters which might be noticed, add a volume of unofficial declarations to the mass of organic utterances that this is a Christian nation."[2] Emboldened by such rhetoric, church leaders in Chicago went to Congress and succeeded in persuading them to pass legislation halting a Sunday opening of the fair.

From a Web site that chronicles the history of Chicago, we read, "The most spectacular struggle over Sunday closing in Chicago occurred when city organizers sought federal support to host the World's Columbian Exhibition in 1893. Effective petitioning by

Protestant church leaders ensured a Sunday closing requirement in the fair's 1892 enabling legislation. The fair's directors filed suit and won a partial victory. Although the fair opened on Sundays, no machines were allowed to operate and most exhibits remained closed."[3]

Because the Supreme Court's declaration that the U.S. is a "Christian nation" involved the fact that the U.S. Supreme Court collaborated with Congress in forcing the World's Fair to close on Sunday at that time, thus, in effect, making Sunday "Sabbath," the official religious day of the nation, it put the Seventh-day Adventist Church into action. Seventh-day Adventists objected to that nomenclature of America as a "Christian nation." They felt that label to be a dangerous one. So on February 24, 1893, the General Conference of Seventh-day Adventists passed resolutions appealing the declaration of the United States as a Christian nation and the action of Congress in legislating upon the subject of religion.

In March of 1893 the International Religious Liberty Association published the resolutions in a small tract called "Appeal and Remonstrance." The subject of the day of worship was implicit in this pamphlet. When the editor of the *Catholic Mirror* of Baltimore, Maryland, caught wind of this, he published four articles on the subject during September of 1893. At that time the *Catholic Mirror* was the official organ of James Cardinal Gibbons and the Papacy in America.

Although Cardinal Gibbons did not author the articles himself, they received his approval. They represent papal dogma accurately. In its four issues of September 1893 they addressed this issue head-on. I invite you to read the articles carefully and completely. You can access them by going to the Web site www.romeschallenge.com.

With unvarnished clarity they note that the day specified by Scripture is the seventh day of the week, the Sabbath. The Bible brings no other day to view as being God's designated day of worship. The Sabbath was embedded in the Old Testament and affirmed by the New Testament. Neither the Lord nor His apostles whispered a word of a change in the command of the Decalogue. Carefully the articles examine some 50 or 60 New Testament texts to determine if there is a scintilla of evidence to support the transference of sacredness from the seventh day to the first. They find none.

Their conclusion: "Protestantism recognizes no rule of faith, no teacher, save the 'infallible Bible.' As the Catholic yields his judgment in spiritual matters implicitly, and with unreserved confidence, to the voice of his church, so, too, the Protestant recognizes no teacher but the Bible. All his spirituality is derived from its teachings. It is to him the voice of God addressing him through his sole inspired teacher. It embodies his religion, his faith, and his practice. . . .

"Hence the conclusion is inevitable; . . . that of those who follow the Bible as their guide, the Israelites and Seventh-day Adventists have exclusive weight of evidence on their side, whilst the Biblical Protestant has not a word in self-defense for his substitution of Sunday for Saturday."[4]

"The Catholic Church for over one thousand years before the existence of a Protestant, by virtue of her divine mission, changed the day from Saturday to Sunday. . . . The Protestant world at its birth found the Christian Sabbath too strongly entrenched to run counter to its existence; it was therefore placed under the necessity of acquiescing in the arrangement, thus implying the Church's right to change the day, for over three hundred years. The Christian Sabbath is therefore to this day, the acknowledged offspring of the Catholic Church as spouse of the Holy Ghost, without a word of remonstrance from the Protestant world. . . .

"The Bible alone as the teacher" "most emphatically forbids any change in the day for paramount reasons. The command calls for a 'perpetual covenant.' The day commanded to be kept by the teacher has never once been kept. . . . Their pretense for leaving the bosom of the Catholic Church was for apostasy from the truth as taught in the written word. They adopted the written word as their sole teacher, which they had no sooner done than they abandoned it promptly, as these articles have abundantly proved; and by a perversity as willful as erroneous, they accept the teaching of the Catholic Church in direct opposition to the plain, unvaried, and constant teaching of their sole teacher in the most essential doctrine of their religion, thereby emphasizing the situation in what may be aptly designated 'a mockery, a delusion, and a snare.'"[5]

The leadership of Catholicism upholds the concept that the church has authority over Scripture and heralds the practice of professed Protestantism of worshipping on Sunday as *prima facie* evidence of that fact.

Before leaving this brief discussion of Daniel 7's horn power, it is vital to note how Scripture identifies the time and place of its origin. Correctly understood, the information in this verse would prevent many misinterpretations from gaining traction. "I was considering the horns, and there was another horn, a little one, coming up among them, before whom three of the first horns were plucked out by the roots" (Dan. 7:8). The horns unquestionably represent those Germanic tribes of the fourth, fifth, and sixth centuries that chewed away at the Roman Empire. Later many of them would become the modern nations of Europe. But three would disappear under the attacks of Justinian's forces led by Belisarius, their destruction working in favor of the Papacy.

The point is that the prophecy pictures the horn power as emerging during the time of the downfall of civil Rome. This is crucial! The horn power was "coming up among them," that is, the tribes that caused Rome's fall. Any identification of the horn power that places its inception in any other time period is necessarily inaccurate. It must arise during the downfall of ancient Rome. Can the activities of Antiochus Epiphanes meet the criteria of this prophecy? Absolutely not! The Roman Empire had not yet been born when he conducted his abominable atrocities. Antiochus IV cannot be the horn power, and the theory of preterism fails completely to conform to the biblical picture. Can we look for the horn power to surface in some future distant day? Of course not! The specifications of Daniel 7:8 are too precise to ignore. The horn power arose when pagan Rome fell. It's as simple as that. The hermeneutical concept of futurism fails to answer to the specifications of the prophecy.

Needless to day, the Papacy's fulfillment of this prophetic detail is unmistakable. No other entity fits the descriptions of Daniel 7's horn power. It emerged where and when prophecy specified. It persecuted

God's faithful and made boastful claims that it can change God's law. And it had an uninterrupted reign for the precise time allotted. The image of horn power is one picture of many bringing to view the sad chronicle of apostasy written against the church that Jesus Himself established.

Daniel 8's "Horn Power"

Daniel 8 contains a similar prophecy as Daniel 7. That they cover the same basic time frame is undeniable. Because the kingdom of Babylon was slipping off the screen of divine importance, we find in chapter 8 no corresponding animal to represent the winged lion of chapter 7 or the head of gold in the statue dream of chapter 2. Scripture specifically tells us that the ram represented Medo-Persia and that the goat stood for Greece (Dan. 8:20, 21). The vision of chapter 8 depicts a horn power that bears a striking resemblance to that of the previous chapter. To be technically correct, the "horn power" of Daniel 8 is a combined symbol, representing both civil and papal Rome. This makes sense since they both ruled from the same geographical location. The vision introduces it as a "little horn" that came up from one of the "winds of heaven" (verse 8), but which "grew exceedingly great" (verse 9).

Some commentators have attempted to show that the horn power of this vision is an outgrowth of the goat kingdom, Greece, and that the horn was an extension of one of the four horns depicting the breakup of Greece's empire following the death of Alexander. Those who use this approach offer the view that Antiochus IV was the horn power. However, it requires that we understand the antecedent of the word "them" ("out of one of them came a little horn") as being "notable ones," thus referring to the four horns that emerged in place of the "large horn" symbolizing Alexander.

When pronouns are used, such as the word "them" in verse 9, it is a well-established grammatical rule that the pronoun should agree with the noun it represents in gender and number. Also there is the presumption that, for the purpose of clarity, the pronoun will be in close proximity to the noun it replaces. For both reasons the word "winds" is a better choice as being the antecedent of "them" than "notable ones." What the text is telling us is that from one of the "winds," or directions of the compass, there came forth this "little horn which grew exceedingly great." Notice how the rest of the verse repeats the emphasis on "direction" as it describes the success of this little horn "toward the south, toward the east, and toward the Glorious Land."

To regard the little horn as representing the kingdoms of Rome, pagan and papal, is an interpretation that finds perfect harmony within the text of the vision of Daniel 8, as well as being in harmony with the vision of chapter 7. But to interpret the horn power of Daniel 8 as depicting Antiochus IV Epiphanes ruptures the harmony of the two visions of chapters 7 and 8.

What does this horn power do, as revealed in the vision of chapter 8? It "grew up to the host of heaven; and it cast down some of the host and some of the stars to the ground, and trampled them. He even exalted himself as high as the Prince of the host" (Dan. 8:10, 11). Furthermore, it "cast truth down to the ground" (verse 12), and "the place of His sanctuary was cast down" (verse 11).

Both pagan and papal Rome persecuted God's people. And both exalted themselves against the Prince. It was under Roman rule that Jesus, the Prince (Hebrew *tsar*), was crucified. Papal domination led to claims that fulfill the prophetic specifications of this verse. In addition, both pagan and papal Rome trampled the sanctuary. The Roman general Titus desolated the city of Jerusalem and its Temple in A.D. 70. Papal theology has substituted an earthly priesthood for the high priestly ministry of Jesus in the heavenly sanctuary and replaced the way to salvation, taught by the Scriptures as being "by grace through faith," with a system that includes human merits and works.

The phrase "cast truth down to the ground" deserves special attention. During one period the Papacy banned the use of the Bible without its guidance and made it a crime to possess, study, and apply Scripture differently than what it taught.

Later in the vision the angel explains to Daniel how the horn would exercise its power. "He shall destroy fearfully, and shall prosper and thrive; he shall destroy the mighty, and also the holy people. Through his cunning he shall cause deceit to prosper under his rule;

and he shall exalt himself in his heart. He shall destroy many in their prosperity. He shall even rise against the Prince of princes; but he shall be broken without human means" (verses 24, 25).

The scope of the entity's tenure does not allow for a one-person fulfillment. It must represent a kingdom, a power, an organizational system that stretches across many centuries. This is made clear by the fact that the horn power (representing both pagan and papal Rome) would exercise its power directly against the "Prince," and yet Gabriel informed Daniel that the subject of the vision "refers to the time of the end" (Dan. 8:17). How could just one king fulfill the prophecy? The angel repeats the point: "Look, I am making known to you what shall happen in the latter time of the indignation; for at the appointed time the end shall be" (verse 19). Only a self-perpetuating organizational system, and not a single individual, can meet the criteria given in Gabriel's explanation.

Its final destruction occurs at the end of the age, for Scripture describes its fate as being "broken without human means," a phrase that leads our minds back to the statue dream when a "stone was cut out without hands" and struck the statue and its earthly kingdoms, grinding them to powder (Dan. 2:34). That happens when Jesus returns the second time in glory. We will see that Paul builds his analysis in 2 Thessalonians on the concepts of Daniel in this regard. Like the horn of Daniel 8, the "man of sin" perishes at the second coming of Christ.

It is similar to what Daniel saw in the previous vision. In chapter 7 the end of the horn power was different than the three beasts preceding it. "I watched then because of the sound of the pompous words which the horn was speaking; I watched till the beast was slain, and its body destroyed and given to the burning flame. As for the rest of the beasts, they had their dominion taken away, yet their lives were prolonged for a season and a time" (Dan. 7:11, 12). The kingdoms of Babylon, Medo-Persia, Greece, and pagan Rome all had their "dominion taken away," that is, they lost their first-place position in world leadership, yet they remained on the stage for a period of time. A Babylon survived till the time of Alexander. Persia (Iran), Greece, and a Rome still exist, though they certainly do not enjoy the power they once wielded. But when the horn power reaches its final end, there will be no prolonging of its life. Its "dominion" and its very existence will come to a climactic conclusion at the return of Jesus.

So we see that Daniel 8 brings to view a "horn power" that features many of the same characteristics as the horn power of Daniel 7. It persecutes, it rises against the Prince, and it utters bombastic and blasphemous claims. Without question the two visions present the same entity through the symbol of a little horn. And it is also without question that those two pictures comprise part of a larger scriptural collage that highlights the origin and activities of the historical Papacy.

Daniel 11's "King of the North"

There remains one more picture in Daniel's book that we must study. It is the vision that begins in chapter 10 and continues through chapter 12. Daniel 11 reveals details concerning two of the rival factions of Greek rule, that of the Seleucids in Syria and the Ptolemies of Egypt, both of which vied for control of the territory between them, that of Palestine. The early verses of the chapter vividly depict some of those violent struggles. The closing verses take us down to the very last days and the triumphant return of Christ.

This vision parallels some other portrayals in Scripture, in that the one who is first in the spotlight might not remain there through the entire drama. Both Isaiah 14 and Ezekiel 28 employ this scheme. Isaiah 14 starts by addressing the "king of Babylon," but then progresses seamlessly into a discussion of "Lucifer." Why, we might ask, does the biblical author do it this way? It is simply because the king of Babylon had so identified himself with the same attitudes as Lucifer that it was not difficult to move beyond the literal king of Babylon to the one who had inspired him with those thoughts. We see the same thing in Ezekiel 28, which first places the king of Tyre on the stage, but then slides into a description of the one who stood behind him, the "anointed cherub" in the Garden of Eden—Lucifer.

Likewise, Daniel 11 commences by describing the conflict between Egypt and Syria for the coveted Promised Land. Judah found itself caught in the crosshairs. Both forces opposed God's plans and His people. They both were enemies of the faithful, and Israel suffered at their hands. The heroic story of John Hyrcanus and the Maccabees took place within these struggles. Somewhere in the discussion of the vision of chapter 11 new players take on the stage. They are still the enemies of God's people, but their identities have changed. It is not surprising for Bible prophecy to exhibit this format. The Scriptures look at the bigger picture and lump together those who share common ideas and philosophies—especially when they oppose the divine plans.

The king of the north—who occupies the most prominent role in the visions of Daniel 7 and 8—became first pagan Rome and then papal Rome. By the time the vision reaches its end, the identity of the king of the north has shifted completely to that of papal Rome. Many prophecies of the Old Testament use "north" as a code word for the location of the enemy (see Jer. 1:13; 4:6; 6:1, etc.). Because of geographical and topographical considerations, Judah's enemies, including Israel, Syria, Assyria, and Babylon, literally invaded from the north.

Familiar phrases and attributes surface in the portion of the vision relating to the activities and policies of the Papacy. The destruction of the sanctuary, highlighted in Daniel 8:11, again emerges to view in Daniel 11:31: "And forces shall be mustered by him, and they shall defile the sanctuary fortress; then they shall take away the daily sacrifices, and place there the abomination of desolation."

We see here the story of the countless martyrs and others who suffered while fearlessly declaring the truth of God during the Middle Ages. "And those of the people who understand shall instruct many; yet for many days they shall fall by sword and flame, by captivity and plundering" (verse 33). This power's uninterrupted tenure of 1260 years again forms a prominent part of the picture. "It shall be for a time, times and half a time; and when the power of the holy people has been completely shattered, all these things shall be finished" (Dan. 12:7).

Such persecution will reach fever pitch as time rushes to its close. "But news from the east and the north shall trouble him; therefore he shall go out with great fury to destroy and annihilate many" (Dan. 11:44). This verse seems to echo closely the closing sentiments expressed in another great prophetic chapter, Revelation 12:17. "And the dragon was enraged with the woman, and he went to make war with the rest of her offspring, who keep the commandments of God and have the testimony of Jesus Christ."

As God's people spread the true gospel that includes the call to obey all of His commandments (that's the "news" of which the prophecy speaks), the "king of the north" (the Papacy) is "troubled," just as Herod was "troubled, and all Jerusalem with him" at the news of Christ's first coming (Matt. 2:3). There was "news from the east and from the north" when Christ arrived the first time. Just before His second coming, the Papacy, working in cooperation with the nations of the world, will attempt to annihilate all those who obey God, just as Herod raised his sword against the Bethlehem infants at Christ's birth. That's the "fury to destroy and annihilate many."

We see arrogant blasphemies once more brushed on the canvas of prophecy. "Then the king shall do according to his own will; he shall exalt and magnify himself above every god, shall speak blasphemies against the God of gods, and shall prosper till the wrath has been accomplished; for what has been determined shall be done" (Dan. 11:36).

The final climactic surge against God's kingdom, followed by the finality of its divinely appointed end, is also part of the narrative. "And he shall plant the tents of his palace between the seas and the glorious holy mountain; yet he shall come to his end, and no one will help him" (verse 45). What does it mean when it says: "He will plant the tents of his palace between the seas and the glorious holy mountain"? It is a picture of an invasion. In the original context it referred to the king of the north placing his standard and erecting his palace in the territory that belonged to God and His people Judah. That's the place "between the seas and the glorious holy mountain," the holy mountain referring to Jerusalem. And it is the same thing that Daniel foresaw as being the "abomination of desolation" that Jesus alludes to in Matthew 24:15.

A partial fulfillment of the prophecy took place when ancient Rome attacked Jerusalem in A.D. 70. Titus invaded the sacred territory surrounding Jerusalem and planted his idolatrous banners in its holy precincts. They depicted the various pagan deities in which Rome placed its trust. Not only an "abomination," they represented

Rome's design to bring "desolation." Jesus clearly equated the phrase "the abomination of desolation" with the description of the armies of Rome surrounding Jerusalem, intent on its destruction (Matt. 24:15; Luke 21:20).

But there will be a more complete fulfillment of Daniel's prophecy of the assault by the king of the north at the end of time. A clear reference to the invasion of the Papacy into sacred territory that belongs only to God, it points to the attack against God's holy law and the use of the arm of the state to enforce a substitute sabbath. In what more effective way could Satan, through human institutions, wage war against the government of God than by attacking His holy law? It is the same picture given by Paul in 2 Thessalonians 2:3, 4 in which he tells us that the "man of sin" would sit in the temple of God, "showing himself that he is God." The time will soon come when the Papacy will plant the tents of its palace squarely within the precincts of God's holy territory.

Daniel 11:40, 41 introduce the invasion: "He shall enter the countries, overwhelm them, and pass through. He shall also enter the Glorious Land." As the last-day king of the north begins his assault, carrying forward his attempt to enforce by law teachings that conflict with Scripture, some will recognize the danger and escape. In the symbolic words of Daniel 11, "many countries shall be overthrown; but these shall escape from his hand: Edom, Moab and the prominent people of Ammon" (verse 41). We needn't attempt to arrive at a specific identification of these countries who "escape." They stand for those who were at one time under the domination and control of the king of the north but who will free themselves from the tyranny and deception of his reign. They represent those who will discover Bible truth and heed the invitation, "Come out of her ["Babylon"], my people, lest you share in her sins, and lest you receive of her plagues" (Rev. 18:4).

It is when this final affront commences against God's kingdom and His commandments, when this last offensive takes place against His sanctuary, that the final movements will begin. At that time the Scripture will be fulfilled: "It is time for You to act, O Lord, for they have regarded Your law as void" (Ps. 119:126).

We believe that this verse should be read in the light of Revelation 13, in which prophecy outlines the collaborative efforts of the two beasts working together to revive the policies of oppression prevalent during the Middle Ages. They will restrict conscience and elevate, under pain of law, the day of human appointment, to the position belonging only to the day God specified: the seventh day Sabbath. In this way the king of the north will "plant the tents of his palace between the seas and the glorious holy mountain." It will be the modern-day fulfillment of what Jesus predicted would take place when Titus would place the abomination that makes desolate in the holy place.

Thus Daniel 11's king of the north is one more piece of the prophetic puzzle, which, when put together, clearly reveals the face of the Papacy. Though now enjoying a prominence like few others, it will one day reach its full and complete end. But that won't happen till Christ arrives in the clouds. Until that time it will continue to "prosper" until the "wrath" (the final outpouring of the seven last plagues) has been accomplished. The last phrase of the verse corresponds to what we read in Daniel 8: "He shall be broken without human means" (verse 25).

---

[1] W. F. Arndt and F. W. Gingrich, *A Greek-English Lexicon of the New Testament,* pp. 708, 864.

[2] http://supreme.justia.com/us/143/457/case.html.

[3] http://www.encyclopedia.chicagohistory.org/pages/1221.html.

[4] *Catholic Mirror,* Sept. 9, 1893.

[5] *Catholic Mirror,* Sept. 23, 1893.

CHAPTER 18

THREE NEW TESTAMENT PROPHETIC PICTURES OF THE "BEAST"

We turn now to three additional pictures in the New Testament that portray the church of the Middle Ages, beginning with the "man of sin" brought to view in 2 Thessalonians 2. Paul was an excellent student of the Scriptures and thoroughly conversant in the prophecies of the Old Testament. As he matured in his understanding of God's plan, he realized that the coming of Jesus in glory could not take place until after certain prophetic prerequisites.

When writing to the believers at Thessalonica who had lost sight of the grand climax of all things—when God will give immortality to those laid to rest in the graves—the apostle encouraged them that one day Jesus will come back and we'll see our loved ones again (1 Thess. 4:13-18). It appears that some of his readers misinterpreted his message, or at least read more into it than he intended. They understood him to say that the return of Jesus was in the immediate future.

The apostle therefore composed a second letter to spell out in greater detail the prophecy and its sequence. He argued that the second advent of Christ could not happen before certain events happened. "Now, brethren, concerning the coming of our Lord Jesus Christ and our gathering together to Him, we ask you, not to be soon shaken in mind or troubled, either by spirit or by word or by letter, as if from us, as though the day of Christ had come. Let no one deceive you by any means; for that Day will not come unless the falling away comes first, and the man of sin is revealed, the son of perdition, who opposes and exalts himself above all that is called God or that is worshiped, so that he sits as God in the temple of God, showing himself that he is God" (2 Thess. 2:1-4).

Paul understood that before Jesus' return there would be a "falling away," an apostasy. As a matter of fact, our English word "apostasy" comes directly from the Greek word he used in predicting this "falling away." This would result in the emergence of one called the "man of sin," or the "son of perdition." The apostle specifically notes that the entity would bear the garb of Christianity. A wolf in sheep's clothing, it would sit "in the temple of God, showing himself that he is God." Keep in mind that only one other time does Scripture use the phrase "son of perdition," and that is to refer to Judas Iscariot (John 17:12). Judas walked with the Lord and purported to be His disciple, yet planted the betrayer's kiss on the Savior's cheek. Paul could not have employed clearer language to indicate that the "man of sin" would put on the mantle of religion. Don't look for a power that outwardly curses Christianity. This is an entity that claims to be Christian.

But it goes far beyond what Bible Christianity stands for in that it presumes to take the very place of God. He "sits in the temple of God, showing himself that he is God." It seeks for itself the titles, authority, and position of God. That it would be fulfilled in the historical Papacy, which has laid claim to being above the Written Word and the Ten Commandments, even to being equal with Christ and having authority to forgive sins, should not come as a great surprise to anyone who has studied biblical prophecy.

Paul lays out the timing sequence of the birth of this apostate power. "And now you know what is restraining, that he may be revealed in his own time. For the mystery of lawlessness is already at work; only He who now restrains will do so until He is taken out of the way. And then the lawless one will be revealed, whom the Lord will consume with the breath of His mouth and destroy with the brightness of His coming" (2 Thess. 2:6-8). Notice carefully that such a power will emerge after the apostle's time, though he detected the roots of it already growing. According to him, "the mystery of lawlessness is already at work," although its full revelation is still in the future.

This is similar to what we will find John speaking about the antichrist. Though when John wrote the complete manifestation of the antichrist was still in the future, its embryonic spirit was present in his day. "Dear children, this is the last hour; and as you have heard that the antichrist is coming, even now many antichrists have come" (1 John 2:18, NIV).

Paul continues: "He who now restrains will do so until he is taken out of the way. And then the lawless one will be revealed" (2 Thess. 2:8). The clearly enunciated fact that the power emerges subsequent to Paul's time period completely rules out the possibility that it could have been pre-Christian. There is no chance that Antiochus IV could have been the "man of sin" described by the apostle.

Notice a definite sequence in its emergence. There is an entity that is in power "now," that is, as Paul writes, and then when he is "taken out of the way" the "man of sin" would be "revealed." Mentally review the statue of Daniel 2. The chest of silver followed the head of gold. The legs of iron succeeded the waist of bronze. Here we find a definite order that history confirmed. The chest of silver kingdom, Medo-Persia, couldn't have its dominance until the empire represented by the head of gold, Babylon, had completed its time.

It is as if you're at the stoplight, waiting to proceed forward, and your young child is in the car with you. "When do we get to go, Daddy?" he or she asks. You explain that right now the cars that are crossing the road in front of you have the green light, and then when that light becomes red for them, then the cars wishing to make left-hand turns will get a green arrow. After that happens, you can expect that we will see the green light allowing us to continue. One thing must follow another. What Paul is saying is that there is definite structure to the prophetic timeline. One thing in prophecy must follow another in its proper sequence. The blasphemous and destructive horn power, which turned out to be papal Rome, couldn't step up to the stage until civil Rome had completed its performance.

Paul was thoroughly familiar with the progression of empires symbolized by the statue of metal and clay. He was totally conversant with the wild animals of Daniel 7's vision. Thus he well knew that the horn power of Daniel 7 came after the demise of the fourth beast. The fourth world empire, Rome, would have to decline before the horn power would emerge. Since in Paul's day Rome was at its height, he could foresee that it might be a while before its power would diminish. Right now the presence of Rome was "retarding" the birth of the "man of sin." But someday "he," that is, the Roman Empire, would be "taken out of the way," and at that time one could expect the revealing of the apostate power. Daniel 7:8 and 2 Thessalonians 2:7, 8 show a flawless harmony. They dovetail perfectly in their presentation of the anticipated timing of the coming of the power described as the "man of sin" as occurring during the downfall of pagan Rome.

Students of Scripture who lived during this time of transition understood this progression clearly and looked toward the fall of Rome, which would be followed by the emergence of the antichrist, the horn power of Daniel. An impressive array of commentators of the second through fifth centuries expressed the view that the continuing presence of the Roman Empire was blocking the full manifestation of the "man of sin." They included Irenaeus, Tertullian, Cyril, Chrysostom, Jerome, Theodoret, and the majority of the Church Fathers.[1]

For example, Jerome wrote, "He [Paul in 2 Thessalonians 2] shows that that which restrains is the Roman empire; for unless it shall have been destroyed, and taken out of the midst, according to the prophet Daniel, Antichrist will not come before that."[2]

Along with Daniel's portrayal, Paul also agrees that the apostate religious system will continue until the return of Jesus. Said Daniel, "I watched then because of the sound of the pompous words which the horn was speaking; I watched till the beast was slain, and its body destroyed and given to the burning flame" (Dan. 7:11). Likewise in Paul's account, the "lawless one" will be consumed and destroyed "with the brightness of His coming." Its reign would persist until the Second Advent.

Significantly, as we noted previously, the time span contemplated by this sequence overrules it being a "one person" entity. For it to emerge at the demise of civil Rome and then exist until the return of Jesus demands that it be understood as a system, a "kingdom," rather than one individual. Again, the empire of the Papacy is a perfect fit for Paul's prophecy.

His descriptive expression "lawless one" is worthy of note. "And then the lawless one will be revealed." It derives from the Greek *anomia,* a combination of the negative "alpha" ("alpha privative") and the word for "law," *nomos,* hence "one without law," or "lawless one." The kingdom of Satan is built upon the platform of rejection of God's law.

You need sever only one link of a chain to render it useless. Imagine a thief, bolt cutters in hand, approaching a gate secured by a chain. He places the bolt cutter on an exposed link of the chain and presses the handles together. With a "chink" the link falls away. The chain is now separated. But then the criminal proceeds to sever another link. Do you think that that would ever happen? No! Why? Because it takes only one broken link to destroy a chain's usefulness.

James said, speaking directly of the Ten Commandments, "For whoever shall keep the whole law, and yet stumble in one point, he is guilty of all. For He who said, 'Do not commit adultery,' also said, 'Do not murder.' Now if you do not commit adultery, but you do murder, you have become a transgressor of the law" (James 2:10, 11). Without question he has in mind the Ten Commandments. Might we extrapolate James to say, "He who said, 'Honor your father and your mother,' also said, 'Keep the Sabbath holy.' Now if you do honor your father and mother, but break the Sabbath, you have become a transgressor of the law"? Would that not be in the spirit of what the apostle is stating? Who has the right to say that one of the Ten Commandments is of less importance than another? Were not all 10 inscribed by the finger of God?

Notice that James here speaks of one "stumbling," a word that suggests a nonintentional and perhaps inadvertent act. What would he say regarding any entity that blatantly promotes an open attack against God's law, teaching and even compelling a disregard of it?

Paul states that the emergence of the "man of sin" is a "mystery" (the "mystery of iniquity" [KJV]). Scripture reveals two primary "mysteries." Along with this one, Paul wrote to Timothy, "Without controversy great is the mystery of godliness: God was manifested in the flesh" (1 Tim. 3:16). The "mystery of godliness" speaks to God becoming man, through the incarnation of Jesus. The Divine took on the form of the human, an act profoundly beyond human comprehension. The "mystery of lawlessness," or the "mystery of iniquity," is exactly the opposite. According to the very context in which this term appears, it is man becoming God, or at least claiming to be God. He "sits as God in the temple of God, showing himself that he is God."

The "mystery of godliness" is an act of self-sacrificing revelation of truth that results in salvation for humanity. The "mystery of lawlessness" is an act of self-exaltation clothed in deception that results in the destruction of humanity. "The coming of the lawless one is according to the working of Satan, with all power, signs, and lying wonders, and with all unrighteous deception among those who perish, because they did not receive the love of the truth, that they might be saved" (2 Thess. 2:9, 10).

Both have their respective time of "revealing." The lawless one, Paul predicted, would be "revealed in his own time." The word translated "time" is from the Greek *kairos,* a word that denotes "appropriate" or "correct" time. It is the same word we noted in Galatians 4:4: "But when the *fullness of time* had come, God sent forth His Son, born of a woman." Both the "mystery of godliness" represented by the birth of Christ, the true Messiah, and the "mystery of lawlessness" represented by the birth of antichrist, the false system, came according to the divine timetable.

The word *kairos* is more specific than the word *chronos* (also translated as "time"). Paul was aware of the sequence of prophecy. He knew that God had a timetable into which the various components fit. History confirms that civil Rome was "taken away" by the transfer of its capital to Constantinople and by the diminishing of its power through the attacks of the Germanic tribes. Into that vacuum, at the "specific time," stepped the bishop of Rome, and the Papacy was born. As we have seen, the uninterrupted reign of this power (the seven-time mentioned period of 1260 years) has been fulfilled with pinpoint accuracy.

A sad parallel exists between the "revealing" of the man of sin (the antichrist, the apostate power who brings deception) and the "revealing" of the true Christ, the Lord Jesus. The apostle John opened the last book of the Bible with the words: "The Revelation of Jesus Christ." Both the word "revealed" in Paul's description of the mystery of iniquity and the word "revelation" in John's opening remarks identifying the one who is the mystery of godliness come from the same Greek word, *apocalypses*. There is an *apocalypses* of the man of sin, and there is an apocalypses of the Man of righteousness. We mentioned this word at the very beginning of our study. Two "revelations"—but how different!

Paul's first words as he opened his discussion of the man of sin ("let no one deceive you" [2 Thess. 2:3]) echo Christ's as He revealed the signs of the end. "And Jesus answered and said to them: 'Take heed that no one deceive you'" (Matt. 24:4). Such warnings indicate that the devil will most certainly attempt to mislead human beings on this vital subject. How can we prevent that? By studying and applying the Word of God!

The "Antichrist" of 1 John

Few words in all the Bible have elicited more curiosity and notoriety than the term "antichrist" as used by John in his epistles. Writing toward the sunset of both his life and the first century, John wrote, "Dear children, this is the last hour; and as you have heard that the antichrist is coming, even now many antichrists have come. This is how we know that it is the last hour. . . . Who is the liar? It is whoever denies that Jesus is the Christ. Such a person is antichrist—denying the Father and the Son" (1 John 2:18-22, NIV). "By this you know the Spirit of God: Every spirit that confesses that Jesus Christ has come in the flesh is of God, and every spirit that does not confess that Jesus Christ has come in the flesh is not of God. And this is the spirit of the Antichrist, which you have heard was coming, and is now already in the world" (1 John 4:2, 3).

John had apparently instructed his audience on the falling away as had Paul. Like Paul, who had said that "the mystery of lawlessness is already at work," John had noticed the roots of apostasy even in his time. The rejection of scriptural truth—in his immediate day being the heresy of Gnosticism and its denial of the truth of the Incarnation— is the essence of apostasy. Though Scripture had clearly taught that Jesus was God in the flesh, some in John's day refused to accept this doctrine. They set aside Scripture in favor of the human theories they preferred.

As time went on, the principle of setting aside the Word of God and advancing human philosophies and concepts would take on slightly different garb than the Gnostic teachings. Nevertheless, the principle of the rejection of Bible truth prepared the way for the great falling away and the appearance of the medieval antichrist.

There is a most amazing thing about this term that we must understand, something that most are ignorant of today but one that we have already alluded to a number of times. We will now discuss it in greater depth. It allows us to see how perfectly the term that John chose fits harmoniously with the description that Paul gave to the Thessalonians. How did the apostle Paul portray this system? It would be that it would purport to be Christian. Instead of outwardly condemning or cursing Christianity, it would be a system that would seek to sit in the seat of Christ. The antichrist would attempt to take the place rightfully belonging to God alone. Keep that in mind as we explore the meaning of the word "antichrist."

We can trace a large proportion of English language words that we use today back either to Greek or Latin. It can sometimes be tricky because it may be that a word root or prefix appears in both languages, and we must exercise great care to make sure that we get the appropriate source and connotation for a particular word.

When most people think of the word "antichrist," they conceive of an entity (unfortunately, too often a single person) that is *against* Christ. They give the prefix *anti* the meaning of "in opposition to," like many other English words. For example, if someone is referred to as being "anti-government," we understand that they have attitudes that are against or in opposition to government. Coming from a Latin background, the prefix *anti* can certainly mean that.

But the New Testament was written in Greek rather than Latin, and the prefix *anti* has a different connotation when coming from that background. While it can sometimes have the implication of "against," it most certainly has another meaning. It is crucial for us to see this difference! Let us look at how the Bible uses this term *anti* in other passages, and we will see the distinctive flavor of the word.

Mary and Joseph were warned, after the visit of the Wise Men, to flee to Egypt because of Herod's wrath that found voice in the edict to kill the Bethlehem babies. This they did, and remained there until they received divine instruction that it was safe to return to Judea. Joseph, Mary, and the young Child went back to Israel. However, "when he heard that Archelaus was reigning over Judea *instead of* his father Herod, he was afraid to go there" (Matt. 2:22). Take careful note: the phrase "instead of" is translated directly from the Greek word *anti*. It wasn't that Archelaus was reigning "against" his father but rather *in the place of* him. There's a big difference!

The King James Version of the New Testament translates *anti* by the word "for" numerous times. (The New King James Version consistently parallels the KJV, and we will quote from it.) Jesus said, "The Son of Man did not come to be served, but to serve, and to give His life [for] a ransom for many" (Mark 10:45). The idea of "in place of" is the emphasis, not "against" or "in opposition to." In Hebrews we read of "Esau, who *for* one morsel of food sold his birthright" (Heb. 12:16). Again, the concept is one of "substitution," or "in place of."

The Septuagint, the ancient Greek translation of the Old Testament, uses *anti* to describe the succession of kings. "It happened after this that the king of the people of Ammon died, and Hanun his son reigned *in his place*" (2 Sam. 10:1). Making sure that his throne was going to be transferred to Solomon, King David said to Zadok the priest, Nathan the prophet, and Benaiah the son of Jehoiada, "Take with you the servants of your lord, and have Solomon my son ride on my own mule, and take him down to Gihon. There let Zadok the priest and Nathan the prophet anoint him king over Israel; and blow the horn, and say, 'Long live King Solomon!' Then you shall come up after him, and he shall come and sit on my throne, and he shall be king *in my place*" (1 Kings 1:33-35). There are more than 80 examples of this type of use in the Septuagint, describing a king ruling in another's place. In Genesis 36 *anti* appears in every verse between verses 33 and 39. First Chronicles 1:44-50 has it constantly.

We observe other interesting samples of *anti* in the Greek translation of the Old Testament, some of which foreshadow in a limited way the substitutionary role of our Savior. Notice this one as King David lamented the death of his rebellious son Absalom. "Then the king was deeply moved, and went up to the chamber over the gate and wept. And as he went, he said thus: 'O my son Absalom—my son, my son Absalom—if only I had died *in your place!* O Absalom my son, my son!'" (2 Sam. 18:33). When Abraham ascended Mount Moriah and was prepared to plunge the knife into his son Isaac, an angel seized his arm, and Abraham was pointed to a ram caught in a thicket. "So Abraham went and took the ram, and offered it up for a burnt offering *instead of* his son" (Gen. 22:13). As Judah offered his eloquent plea to pledge his life in behalf of his half-brother, after Joseph's servant revealed the silver cup in Benjamin's sack, Judah declared to Joseph, "Please let your servant remain *instead* of the lad as a slave to my lord, and let the lad go up with his brothers" (Gen. 44:33).

After Samson's anger at his fiancé for disclosing the secret to his riddle had abated, he went to receive her, only to have her father tell him that she had been given to Samson's best man. But the father suggested a compromise: "I really thought that you thoroughly hated her; therefore I gave her to your companion. Is not her younger sister better than she? Please, take her *instead*" (Judges 15:2). To serve at the Temple, the Lord told His people, "I have taken the Levites *instead* of all the firstborn of the children of Israel" (Num. 8:18). Shortly after the split of the kingdom, Egypt attacked Rehoboam and carried away the gold shields installed in the Temple by King Solomon. "King Rehoboam made bronze shields in their place and committed them to the hands of the captains of the guard" (2 Chron. 12:10). In all of these verses the Septuagint employs the word *anti* for the phrase appearing in italics.

Without question the Greek word *anti* conveys the meaning "in the place of" or "in the stead of." While the concept of "against" or "in opposition to" might also sometimes be present, the primary sense seems to be that of substitution. When John wrote about the coming antichrist, we must incorporate that central idea of *anti* into our understanding of the term. We must look for an entity which, though its overall policies would stand in opposition to God, one of its key characteristics would be to stand *in the place of* God, or at least attempt to do so.

The Papacy has claimed to be in the place of God by assuming titles and names that belong to Him alone. In addition, it has abrogated to itself authority over Scripture and God's holy law as well as the right to forgive sins, a prerogative that according to the Bible belongs only to God. In essence, such interpretations put the Papacy in the position of God in the prophecy of the seventieth week of Daniel 9. This is taking the place that belongs to Jesus, whose death on the cross is the legitimate subject of that prophecy!

Daniel, Paul, and John predicted all this. Satan, working through a human institution, has challenged the authority and role of God. He seeks the worship and adoration that belong to God and the place and power of Jesus. The term antichrist, correctly understood as meaning "the one in the place of Christ," brings such aspirations and goals into sharp focus.

In one of the stranger ironies of all time, the Papacy has applied the title "Vicar of Christ" to the pope. What is the etymological root of the word "vicar"? It comes from a Latin origin (since the Vatican is in Rome) and translates as "one in the place of." (Consider the adjective "vicarious" and the adverb "vicariously.") But give this thought careful consideration. What if the pope wanted to express that idea of being "the one in the place of Christ," but have the title reflect a Greek rather than a Latin background? What Greek word would convey the concept of "the one who is in the place of"? It would be "antichrist," since that is what the word literally means!

The "Impure Woman" of Revelation 17

The last of the seven pictures of the Papacy we find in Scripture appears in Revelation 17's portrayal of the impure woman. "Then one of the seven angels who had the seven bowls came and talked with me, saying to me, 'Come, I will show you the judgment of the great harlot who sits on many waters, with whom the kings of the earth committed fornication, and the inhabitants of the earth were made drunk with the wine of her fornication.' So he carried me away in the Spirit into the wilderness. And I saw a woman sitting on a scarlet beast, which was full of names of blasphemy, having seven heads and ten horns. The woman was arrayed in purple and scarlet, and adorned with gold and precious stones and pearls, having in her hand a golden cup full of abominations and the filthiness of her fornication. And on her forehead a name was written: MYSTERY, BABYLON THE GREAT, THE MOTHER OF HARLOTS AND OF THE ABOMINATIONS OF THE EARTH. I saw the woman, drunk with the blood of the saints and with the blood of the martyrs of Jesus. And when I saw her, I marveled with great amazement" (Rev. 17:1-6).

The picture of Babylon here combines the images of a woman, a beast, and a city. In Scripture, as we have seen, often a "woman" stands for a church or religious body. A pure woman, pictured in Revelation 12, represents the true church while an impure one, a false church. The woman rides on a beast, which in prophetic sign language symbolizes a kingdom. She bears the name "Babylon," an ancient capital that defiantly oppressed God's people.

The imagery represents a threefold union of last-day conspirators against God's throne, who along with the "kings of the earth" attempt to establish a one-world religious front in opposition to God's law. "Now the great city was divided into three parts, and the cities of the nations fell. And great Babylon was remembered before God, to give her the cup of the wine of the fierceness of His wrath" (Rev. 16:19).

The context in which this picture of Babylon emerges is intriguing. Indicted for her crimes, she has fallen under divine judgment. Said the angel to John: "I will show you the judgment of the great harlot" (Rev. 17:1). We'll take a brief look at four aspects of the "judgment" that Babylon experiences, all reflections of divine justice administered against the enemies of God in the past. They have to do with desolation, with self-destruction, with the "feast of the birds," and with a "song of lamentation." The four themes are very familiar to students of Old Testament eschatological literature since divine justice in the past included all of the elements.

First, let's look at the concept of "desolation." Significantly, Revelation tells us that John was taken in Spirit into the "wilderness" (verse 3), a most interesting and instructive term. The word "wilderness" is the Greek word *eremos,* which means a "desert or desolate place."[3] For a student of Scripture, "desolate" immediately sends our minds back to the prophecies of the Old Testament. When many of the nations, including Judah, fell under divine judgment, God declared that they would be made desolate.

What God is saying, by depicting Babylon in the "wilderness" or "desolate place," is that apocalyptic Babylon, though it has "prospered" for a very long time and has seemed to be invincible (remember the question posed in Revelation 13:4: "Who is able to make war with him?"), has now reaped the same judgment as pronounced on all the ancient kingdoms who rebelled against God's throne. It is made desolate and empty, because its support has collapsed. All of this occurs in the time frame of the sixth and seventh plagues, just before Christ returns.

Notice these uses of the same word *eremos* as it appears in the Greek Old Testament, the Septuagint, as well as Christ's pronouncement against the Jerusalem of His day. While we find many examples; we'll look at just a few. Again, we'll quote from the NKJV, since in each example it reflects the same understanding. In all cases the italicized word is *eremos* in the Septuagint. We will plainly see that the word "desolate" is a term integrally associated with divine judgment administered against those who rebelled against God. One of the key words of the Old Testament, Revelation will apply it to the grand climax of all things and the downfall of apocalyptic Babylon, the last-day conglomeration of apostate powers. The fact that John is being shown the judgment of the great whore in a *desolate place* is huge! Although used to riding high on the platform of power, now she finds herself in the wilderness.

Isaiah asked the penetrating question, "'Lord, how long?' And He answered, 'Until the cities are laid waste and without inhabitant, the houses are without a man, the land is utterly *desolate*'" (Isa. 6:11). Later the prophet said, in words that definitely have last-day significance, "Behold, the day of the Lord comes, cruel, with both wrath and fierce anger, to lay the land *desolate;* and He will destroy its sinners from it" (Isa. 13:9).

In Jeremiah's day the Lord used Babylon as His tool to discipline Judah. "The lion has come up from his thicket, and the destroyer of nations is on his way. He has gone forth from his place to make your land *desolate*" (Jer. 4:7). Divine judgment loomed over Judah. "'Thus I will make the land *desolate*, because they have persisted in unfaithfulness,' says the Lord God" (Eze. 15:8). "I will make the land most *desolate,* her arrogant strength shall cease, and the mountains of Israel shall be so *desolate* that no one will pass through. Then they shall know that I am the Lord, when I have made the land most *desolate* because of all their abominations which they have committed" (Eze. 33:28, 29; cf. Micah 6:13, 16).

This prophesied desolation of Judah became reality. "So the Lord could no longer bear it, because of the evil of your doings and because of the abominations which you committed. Therefore your land is a *desolation,* an astonishment, a curse, and without an inhabitant, as it is this day" (Jer. 44:22). "So My fury and My anger were poured out and kindled in the cities of Judah and in the streets of Jerusalem; and they are wasted and *desolate,* as it is this day" (verse 6). However, though Babylon assaulted Jerusalem no less than three times and indeed left her desolate, there was hope for later restoration. "The whole land shall be *desolate;* yet I will not make a full end" (Jer. 4:27).

A similar proclamation was issued against other nations, including Edom. "Therefore thus says the Lord God: 'I will also stretch out My hand against Edom, cut off man and beast from it, and make it *desolate* from Teman'" (Eze. 25:13). "Behold, O Mount Seir, I am against you; I will stretch out My hand against you, and make you most *desolate.* I shall lay your cities waste, and you shall be *desolate.* Then you shall know that I am the Lord" (Eze. 35:3). "The whole earth will rejoice when I make you *desolate*" (verse 14).

Because of their sins, Egypt would receive the same punishment. "And the land of Egypt shall become *desolate* and waste" (Eze. 29:9. "They shall be *desolate* in the midst of the desolate countries, and her cities shall be in the midst of the cities that are laid waste" (Eze. 30:7). One day ancient Babylon would itself be judged. "Because of the wrath of the Lord she [Babylon] shall not be inhabited, but she shall be wholly *desolate*" (Jer. 50:13).

Jesus used the very same word when indicting the Jerusalem of His day. Leaving the Temple precincts for the last time that Tuesday before Calvary, sadness filled His voice as He said, "O Jerusalem, Jerusalem, the one who kills the prophets and stones those who are sent to her! How often I wanted to gather your children together, as a hen gathers her chicks under her wings, but you were not willing! See! Your house is left to you *desolate*" (Matt. 23:37, 38). In this He quoted from Jeremiah 22, spoken against the Jerusalem of six centuries previous: "'If you will not hear these words, I swear by Myself,' says the Lord, 'that this house shall become a *desolation*'" (Jer. 22:5).

To anyone acquainted with the prophecies of the past, *eremos* would flash the message that divine judgment has at last been invoked. Isaiah's question, "How long?" has finally been answered! The divine gavel has fallen. All of the incidences of "desolate" in the past were but a foretaste, a foreshadowing, of the desolation that apocalyptic Babylon would experience. Though it mount up to the sky, yet God will bring it down.

The woman Babylon of Revelation, being the summation and epitome of all the rebellions of the past, partakes of all the classic components of God's divine retribution as illustrated in biblical history. We have seen that she is made desolate, as were the ancient kingdoms who raised their arm against the Almighty. She also suffers the other aspects of God's justice as seen in those stories that serve as types of last-day developments. "Now all these things happened to them as examples, and they were written for our admonition, on whom the ends of the ages have come" (1 Cor. 10:11). The book of Revelation is a "collage," stitching together the salvation/destruction accounts of the past and applying them to the final scenes of the drama.

In many of the accounts and prophecies of deliverance recorded in Scripture the enemy's panic, confusion, and self-destruction play a significant role in the story. When Jonathan defeated the Philistines, the Lord sent a panic among the enemy. "And there was trembling in the camp, in the field, and among all the people. The garrison and the raiders also trembled; and the earth quaked, so that it was a very great trembling. Now the watchmen of Saul in Gibeah of Benjamin looked, and there was the multitude, melting away; and they went here and there" (1 Sam. 14:15, 16). The panic that broke out precipitated a significant defeat of the Philistines, the enemies of God and His people.

The Lord sent panic and confusion among the ranks of the Syrians in the days of Elisha. "The Lord had caused the army of the Syrians to hear the noise of chariots and the noise of horses—the noise of a great army; so they said to one another, 'Look, the king of Israel has hired against us the kings of the Hittites and the kings of the Egyptians to attack us!' Therefore they arose and fled at twilight, and left the camp intact—their tents, their horses, and their donkeys—and they fled for their lives" (2 Kings 7:6, 7). Again, the panic originating from the Lord brought about the collapse of His enemies.

In the story of Gideon's warfare against Midian, as he and his 300 broke their pitchers and shouted, we read that the enemy, in a confused state of mind, destroyed themselves. "The Lord set every man's sword against his companion throughout the whole camp" (Judges 7:22). The enemies engaged in self-destruction. In the great victory that God gave to Jehoshaphat we read, "Now when they began to sing and to praise, the Lord set ambushes against the people of Ammon, Moab, and Mount Seir, who had come against Judah; and they were defeated. For the people of Ammon and Moab stood up against the inhabitants of Mount Seir to utterly kill and destroy them. And when they had made an end of the inhabitants of Seir, they helped to destroy one another" (2 Chron. 20:22, 23).

In a prophecy against Egypt God declared, "I will set Egyptians against Egyptians; everyone will fight against his brother, and everyone against his neighbor" (Isa. 19:2). The Lord told Haggai, "Speak to Zerubbabel, governor of Judah, saying: 'I will shake heaven and earth. I will overthrow the throne of kingdoms; I will destroy the strength of the Gentile kingdoms. I will overthrow the chariots and those who ride in them; the horses and their riders shall come down, every one by the sword of his brother'" (Haggai 2:21, 22). Zechariah's great prophecy declares: "It shall come to pass in that day that a great panic from the Lord will be among them. Everyone will seize the hand of his neighbor, and raise his hand against his neighbor's hand" (Zech. 14:13).

Such examples teach us how the end will come upon God's enemies in the last days. The Bible predicts that end-time Babylon will self-destruct. "And the ten horns which you saw on the beast [representing other political powers that join hands with Babylon], these will hate the harlot [when it becomes clear that they have been deceived by Babylon's policies], make her desolate and naked, eat her flesh and burn her with fire" (Rev. 17:16). As the world begins to realize that

Babylon has peddled falsehood and deception, there will be a gigantic reaction against the leaders who have been instrumental in misleading humanity. Swords raised against the saints will turn against the false shepherds who have been the tools of Satan.

Third, another familiar theme in Old Testament eschatology is the ravaging of wild animals on the abandoned corpses of the slain. In the mind of the ancient world, to die an untimely or premature death would be terrible, but not to have a proper burial, and have your corpse become the food of wild scavengers would be the ultimate humiliation. Moses warned the Israelites that if they were unfaithful in the Promised Land the Lord would remove His protection and their enemies would defeat them. "Your carcasses shall be food for all the birds of the air and the beasts of the earth, and no one shall frighten them away" (Deut. 28:26).

David said to Goliath, "This day the Lord will deliver you into my hand, and I will strike you and take your head from you. And this day I will give the carcasses of the camp of the Philistines to the birds of the air and wild beasts of the earth, that all the earth may know that there is a God in Israel" (1 Sam. 17:46).When the prophet Ahijah pronounced judgment against the house of Jeroboam, he declared, "The dogs shall eat whoever belongs to Jeroboam and dies in the city, and the birds of the air shall eat whoever dies in the field" (1 Kings 14:11). "And concerning Jezebel the Lord also spoke, saying, 'The dogs shall eat Jezebel by the wall of Jezreel. The dogs shall eat whoever belongs to Ahab and dies in the city, and the birds of the air shall eat whoever dies in the field'" (1 Kings 21:23, 24).

Jeremiah received strong messages to deliver against Judah. "Then the carcasses of this people will become food for the birds and the wild animals" (Jer. 7:33, NIV). "They shall die gruesome deaths; they shall not be lamented nor shall they be buried, but they shall be like refuse on the face of the earth. They shall be consumed by the sword and by famine, and their corpses shall be meat for the birds of heaven and for the beasts of the earth" (Jer. 16:4). "I will cause them to fall by the sword before their enemies and by the hands of those who seek their lives; their corpses I will give as meat for the birds of heaven and for the beasts of the earth" (Jer. 19:7).

The prophet Ezekiel bore a similar message against Egypt. "I have given you as food to the beasts of the field and to the birds of the heaven" (Eze. 29:5). Isaiah warned Ethiopia, "They will be left together for the mountain birds of prey and for the beasts of the earth" (Isa. 18:6). Ezekiel's prophecy against Gog and Magog included this theme. "And as for you, son of man, thus says the Lord God, 'Speak to every sort of bird and to every beast of the field: "Assemble yourselves and come; gather together from all sides to My sacrificial meal which I am sacrificing for you, a great sacrificial meal on the mountains of Israel, that you may eat flesh and drink blood. You shall eat the flesh of the mighty, drink the blood of the princes of the earth"'" (Eze. 39:17).

The divine invitation for the wild birds and beasts to feast on the unburied corpses of the slain enemies of God reaches its final fulfillment when Babylon falls at the coming of the Lord and there is no one to bury her. "Then I saw an angel standing in the sun; and he cried with a loud voice, saying to all the birds that fly in the midst of heaven, 'Come and gather together for the supper of the great God, that you may eat the flesh of kings, the flesh of captains, the flesh of mighty men, the flesh of horses and of those who sit on them, and the flesh of all people, free and slave, both small and great'" (Rev. 19:17, 18).

Finally, another oft-repeated theme in the Old Testament is the composing of a "song of lament" written at the destruction of an enemy. King David's "Song of the Bow," sung after the fall of Saul, is a classic example (2 Sam. 1:17-27). David penned a song of lament for Abner (2 Sam. 3:31-34) and sang a song of lament when Absalom died. "Then the king was deeply moved, and went up to the chamber over the gate, and wept. And as he went, he said thus: 'O my son Absalom—my son, my son Absalom—if only I had died in your place! O Absalom my son, my son'" (2 Sam. 18:33). Ezekiel 28:11-19 is a poem of lamentation concerning the fall of ancient Tyre. The fall of Jerusalem at the hand of Nebuchadnezzar elicited laments (see Jer. 4:8 and the entire book of Lamentations). The destruction of Egypt produced one (Eze. 32:18-32) as well as the overthrow of Nineveh (Nahum 3:7). All these were subjects of a "song of lament" at their unfortunate fall.

Likewise apocalyptic Babylon has its song of lamentation. "The kings of the earth who committed fornication and lived luxuriously with her will weep and lament for her, when they see the smoke of her burning, standing at a distance for fear of her torment, saying, 'Alas, alas, that great city Babylon, that mighty city! For in one hour your judgment has come'" (Rev. 18:9, 10). Thus we see four components of divine justice, as illustrated in the stories of the past, fall upon Revelation's Babylon: desolation, self-destruction, corpses left as food for birds and beasts of prey, and a song of lament.

Revelation's Babylon is a false trinity. We can identify its three parts as the "beast" (referring to the beast of Revelation 13, the Papacy), the "false prophet" (apostate Protestantism) and the "dragon," which can be seen as spiritualism or any other form of non-Christian religion. Satan will work mightily through this confederacy to try to accomplish his goals as his time runs out. The picture of Babylon in Revelation 17, this last-day triumvirate, seems to focus mainly on the papal power, in that it has spearheaded the movement against God through much of the post-cross era. The clues that we will examine in these verses pertain to all aspects of the various parts of Babylon, but to the Papacy especially.

Without question the woman shares many of the same characteristics of the papal power represented in the six other symbolic pictures in Bible prophecy. We see her exercising great authority and worldwide influence. She wears the garb of royalty, being arrayed in purple, is labeled as "Babylon the Great," and is pictured as sitting on "many waters." The angel explicitly explains the latter imagery: "The waters which you saw, where the harlot sits, are peoples, multitudes, nations, and tongues" (Rev. 17:15). Here is a power of global impact, echoing the thought of Revelation 13:3: "All the world marveled and followed the beast." The posture of her sitting on "many waters" can depict both the worldwide support she receives and the manner in which she oppresses the people of the world.

It is an ecclesiastical system that has relied on the power of the state to accomplish its policies. We see a woman (a church) riding or being supported by a beast (representing a political power). The union of church and state forms a relationship that God does not condone. It is an illicit relationship, hence the use of the word "fornication." History has shown that when church and state unite it diminishes the spiritual power of the church, forcing it to rely on political power. Restriction of conscience and the loss of freedoms are the inevitable consequences.

Revelation presents a picture of a combined religio-political entity: a "woman" on a "beast." The "woman" aspect highlights the religious persona of the Papacy, while the "beast" features its political facade. Thus it is both. The Papacy enjoys a unique position in the world, for it is indeed both a church and a state at the same time. As a church, it boasts the largest membership in the Christian community, having some 1.2 billion congregants. And as a state, though it occupies only about 108 acres, it receives ambassadors and issues its own postage and frequently participates in international issues.

You might say that the entity has a dual nature. Think of that concept for a moment. Our Redeemer, Jesus Christ, was both divine and human, for the purpose of bringing salvation. The antichrist likewise has a dual nature, but it is far different. It has an ecclesiastical aspect and a political one—a deadly combination.

Back in the Old Testament, the false systems of worship promoted by the pagan Queen Jezebel received support from the political authority of King Ahab. In type it was a union of church and state. During the Middle Ages what Jezebel had accomplished through Ahab on a smaller scale ballooned to be the horrors of medieval persecution and martyrdom. The reality of the illicit union of church and state manifested itself when the arm of the state enforced the dogma of the church, resulting in the persecution of those who refused to violate their consciences.

Many shed their blood as they gave their final testimony of faith. Hence we see the woman as "drunk with the blood of the saints and with the blood of the martyrs of Jesus." We've encountered the prophetic picture of persecution in many of the other pictures of papal domination contained in Scripture. This snapshot is no different.

Other clues pointing to the papal ecclesiastical structure include the woman sitting on seven mountains. For centuries Rome has been nicknamed the "city on seven hills." Whereas in Revelation 13 the beast was "given a mouth speaking great things and blasphemies," in chapter 17 the beast is "full of names of blasphemy." In other words, the disease of blasphemy has metastasized from being a condition of the mouth to spreading through the entire body.

As the indictment continues, we see her clothed in scarlet or crimson, the biblical color of sin. "Though your sins are like scarlet, they shall be as white as snow; though they are red as crimson, they shall be like wool" (Isa. 1:18, NIV). The distinctive red color is an allusion to Revelation 12 with its vision of the "fiery red dragon," Satan working through pagan Rome.

The woman holds a golden cup full of abominations and filthiness. It contains her wine, the intoxicating cocktail of false doctrine that she forces the world to drink, resulting in confusion and stumbling. On her forehead she bears: "MYSTERY, BABYLON THE GREAT, THE MOTHER OF HARLOTS AND OF THE ABOMINATIONS OF THE EARTH." Scripture describes God's last-day saints, the sealed ones, as having the "Father's name written on their foreheads" (Rev. 14:1). In contrast, the impure woman in chapter 17 has the signature of apostasy on her forehead. Paul in 2 Thessalonians, a passage we studied earlier, explains the term as referring to a human claiming the position and authority of the divine.

The book of Revelation calls her the "mother of harlots." Those other churches that initially broke away from the Papacy on the platform of *sola scriptura,* but which eventually drifted back to the "mother church" in doctrinal teachings, particularly on the identification of the day of worship, are the "daughters" of Babylon. The churches of the Protestant Reformation that began in such glory but later refused to walk in all the full light of Scripture and behaved as if God's holy law has indeed been modified by human hand, are the spiritual offspring of the great harlot of Revelation.

The beast has seven heads, which no doubt represent the different manifestations through the ages by which Satan has worked to attempt to achieve his goals. Scholars have offered varying interpretations as to exactly which kingdoms might qualify as the seven heads, and it might be that the number "seven" here simply stands for "completeness" and "totality." If it is necessary to identify the seven, we favor the view that they represent ancient Babylon, Medo-Persia, Greece, Pagan Rome, Papal Rome of the Middle Ages, Papal Rome of the "deadly wound," and finally Papal Rome in combination with fallen Protestantism and other world religions.

The phrase "the beast that you saw was, and is not, and will ascend out of the bottomless pit and go to perdition" (Rev. 17:8), resulting in those who dwell on earth marveling at it, is closely linked with the description of the beast of Revelation 13, which has a mortal wound but recovers to the "marvel" of the whole world (Rev. 13:3), making it logical to see the beast of chapter 13 and the woman/beast of chapter 17 as the same entity. It appears that at this particular point the picture reflects the chronological perspective of the beast during its deadly setback. It "was [the 1260 reign of the Papacy during the Middle Ages], is not [the Papacy during the period of the "mortal wound"], and yet [it will be resurrected and regain power]."

Likewise we may think of the seven "kings" as a parallel description of the seven heads of the beast. "Five have fallen [Babylon, Medo-Persia, Greece, pagan Rome, and papal Rome), one is [the Papacy during the deadly setback], and the other has not yet come [the resurgent Papacy]. And when he comes, he must continue a short time. The beast that was, and is not, is himself also the eighth, and is of the seven, and is going to perdition [the last-day manifestation of this apostate power, which will feature the resurgent Papacy, but technically be different in that it also includes fallen Protestantism and other religions]" (Rev. 17:10, 11).

We note a sad parallel regarding the beast that was, then was not, then will be again, in that it draws our minds to similar language used to describe Jesus. Perhaps we shouldn't be surprised since Satan's policy has always been to copy what God does. Jesus describes Himself as the one who "lives, and was dead, and behold, I am alive forevermore" (Rev. 1:18). Christ suffered a "mortal wound" on the cross, and for three days He "wasn't," being asleep in Joseph's tomb. But then He arose in triumph and glory. The history of the antichrist employs somewhat comparable language. But then the antichrist has always sought to counterfeit the true Christ.

The "kings of the earth" are those political powers that join hands with the religious agencies in bringing about the establishment of the image of the beast and the enforcement of the spurious sabbath, the mark of the beast. For a short time, laying aside their varying points of view, they, in a false revival, a false "Pentecost," join together to establish a one-world religious front, though it means the crushing of those who hold to God's true Sabbath.

"These are of one mind, and they will give their power and authority to the beast" (Rev. 17:13). It isn't necessary that all these factions reach total agreement on all issues. In the days of Christ's execution, there was a "coming together" of Pharisees, Sadducees, Herodians, and others. They retained their individual identities, but joined together and became of "one mind" regarding the crucifixion of Jesus. So it will be at the end. How sad that the unity achieved is within the confines of false religion. Paul spoke of Christians being of "one mind," but that was the mind of Christ (2 Cor. 13:11). How tragic that their being of one accord results in their carrying out the impulses of the archdeceiver, Satan!

Jesus said, "By the mouth of two or three witnesses every word may be established" (Matt. 18:16). Here we have heard seven witnesses! Three from the book of Daniel, one from Paul, and three from John. The Lord must have wanted this matter to be confirmed beyond any doubt. The historical papal organization is the "horn power" of Daniel 7 and Daniel 8, the "king of the north" of the latter part of Daniel 11, the "man of sin" of 2 Thessalonians 2, the "antichrist" of 1 John, the "beast from the sea" in Revelation 13, and the "harlot" of Revelation 17. Seven different pictures of apostasy!

---

[1] See L. E. Froom, *Prophetic Faith of Our Fathers*, vol. 1, p. 407.

[2] Jerome, *Commentaria in Jeremaim*, book 5, chap. 25, in J.-P. Migne, *Patrologia Latina*, vol. 24, col. 1020. In Froom, vol. 1, p. 444.

[3] W. F. Arndt and F. W. Gingrich, *A Greek-English Lexicon of the New Testament*, pp. 308, 309.

CHAPTER 19

PROTESTANT REFORMERS AND THE "BEAST"

In addition to all this, we have the testimony of the great Protestant Reformers who in virtual unanimity concluded that the Papacy of history fit the symbols of these prophecies. They likewise believed that the horn power of Daniel 7, the man of sin of 2 Thessalonians, the antichrist of 1 John, and the leopard beast of Revelation 13 all represented the same thing. The Reformers regarded them as different views of the same organizational and thought system.[1]

More specifically, they agreed that the little-horn power of Daniel 7, which grew out of the 10 horns of the fourth beast and removed three of the 10 horns, persecuted the saints, had the eyes of a man and spoke great things against the Most High, thought to change times and laws, and continued for a time, times, and half of a time, as representing the ecclesiastical Papacy.

The Reformers held that the man of sin spoken of in 2 Thessalonians 2, which brought about a great apostasy, who opposes and exalts himself above all, who sits in the temple of God, showing himself that he is God, symbolized the Papacy. The early Protestants believed that the antichrist spoken of in 1 John 2 who was to appear in the last time and stand "in the place of Christ" constituted the Roman church leadership. And they also concluded that the leopard-like beast of Revelation 13, which opened his mouth in blasphemy against God, made war against the saints, and continued for 42 prophetic months depicted the papal organization.

Second, the Reformers believed that these symbolic prophecies (the singular-sounding "little horn," "man of sin," "antichrist," and "leopard beast") represented a large-scale system, not an individual.

Much modern prophetic interpretation, in contrast, looks for a one-person antichrist. Such a view totally disagrees with the understandings of the Reformers. The Bible is clear that in prophecy a "beast" represents a kingdom and is not restricted to one person or monarch (cf. Dan. 7:23). Because the time span contemplated by these prophecies is 1260 years and more, it is obvious that only a self-perpetuating system can fulfill all the specifications of prophecy regarding this entity, unless one tosses aside the well-established day for a year in symbolic prophecy rule.

The confusion begins when one attempts to apply the latter concept in certain circumstances, but not in others. Many modern prophetic scholars wish to apply the "day for a year" principle when talking about the period following the rapture as being seven "years," based on a misunderstanding of Daniel 9:25-27 (the seventieth "week") which they unjustifiably wrest from the other 69 "weeks." But they then consider the day for a year concept as not applicable when discussing the great prophecies of Daniel 7 and Revelation 11-13. Why can one half of the seventieth week of Daniel 9 be understood as referring to three and a half literal years (based on a "day for a year"), but the 1260 days or 42 months of Revelation 12 not receive the same day for a year interpretation as 1260 literal years? Such inconsistency is a big problem.

The Reformers built the Reformation on a foundation of the views we have been exploring in this book. They did not create them from a vacuum, but from carefully studying the types and symbols of Scripture. Putting together the specifics of the prophecies, their conclusions were inescapable. They were the result of comparing Scripture with Scripture, meticulously assembling the jigsaw pieces of prophecy, with the knowledge that their conclusions would likely cost them position, property, and as unfortunately proved true in many cases, their lives. Though the Reformers recorded their research and conclusions in countless books, we will give only a few quotations as examples.

Eberhard II, archbishop of Salzburg (1200-1246), drawing largely from 2 Thessalonians 2, wrote about the Papacy: "They cannot tolerate an equal, they will not desist until they have trampled all things under their feet, and until they sit in the temple of God, and until they are exalted above all that is worshiped. . . . He who is servant of servants, desires to be lord of lords, just as if he were God. . . . He speaks great things as if he were truly God. He ponders new counsels under his breast, in order that he may establish his own rule for himself, he changes laws, he ordains his own laws, he corrupts, he plunders, he pillages, he defrauds, he kills—that incorrigible man (whom they are accustomed to call anti-Christ) on whose forehead an inscription of insult is written: 'I am God, I cannot err.' He sits in the temple of God, and has dominion far and wide."[2]

John Milicz of Bohemia became a priest in 1350, then secretary to the emperor Charles IV, king of Bohemia, and finally canon and archdeacon of the Cathedral of Prague before resigning his important position and becoming a humble but powerful preacher whose main thrust was the coming of the antichrist. He said he was "moved contrary to his own will by the Holy Spirit to search the Scriptures concerning the time when antichrist would appear. While doing so, he found that this antichrist had already appeared and is dominating the church of Christ."[3]

Milicz asked the Lord to free him from his convictions, but finding no rest he undertook a pilgrimage to Rome, addressed a number of cardinals, and fearlessly proclaimed that the antichrist had come. He waited for the pope to arrive but, since the pontiff was delayed, Milicz gave himself to prayer, study, and fasting for a full month. Still the pope did not arrive, whereupon Milicz could not restrain himself any longer, but posted a placard on the very doors of St. Peter's in Rome that on a certain day he would address the crowd. In this announcement Milicz stated, "The antichrist is come; he has his seat in the church."[4]

The influence of Milicz on later Bohemian Reformers such as Huss and Matthias of Janow is unmistakable. The latter wrote: "The antichrist has already come. He is neither Jew, pagan, Saracen, nor worldly tyrant, but the man who opposes Christian truth and the Christian life by way of deception—he is, and will be, the most wicked Christian, falsely styling himself by that name, assuming the highest station in the church, and possessing the highest consideration, arrogating dominion over all ecclesiastics and laymen; one who, by the working of Satan, assumes to himself power and wealth and honor, and makes the church, with its goods and sacraments, subservient to his own carnal ends."[5]

John Wycliffe (c. 1330-1384), the "morning star of the Reformation," professor at Oxford, and later leader of the religious group known as the Lollards, spoke openly of the papal antichrist. "Why is it necessary in unbelief to look for another antichrist? Hence in the seventh chapter of Daniel antichrist is forcefully described by a horn arising in the time of the fourth kingdom (which has) eyes and a mouth speaking great things against the Lofty One, and wearing out the saints of the Most High, and thinking that he is able to change times and laws."[6] After quoting Daniel 7:25 concerning the horn, Wycliffe expressly states: "For so our clergy forsee the lord Pope."[7]

One of Wycliffe's followers, Sir John Oldcastle (1360-1417), also called Lord Cobham, wrote: "But as touching the Pope and his Spirituality, I owe them neither suit nor service, forsomuch as I know him by the Scriptures to be the great Antichrist, the Son of Perdition, the open Adversary of God, and the Abomination standing in the holy place."[8]

John Purvey (1354-1428) was a student at Oxford when the influence of Wycliffe was at its height. He later became the leader of the Lollards after Wycliffe's death and wrote an impressive commentary on Revelation, a copy of which found its way 100 years later into the hands of Luther. Luther had it reprinted and wrote in the new edition: "This preface, noble reader, you may understand was written by us for this reason—that we might make known to the world that we are not the first who interpret the Papacy as the kingdom of Antichrist. For many years prior to us, so many and so great men (whose number is large, and their memory eternal) have attempted this so clearly and openly, and that with great spirit and force, that (those) who were driven by the fury of the papal tyranny into the farthest boundaries of the earth, and suffering the most atrocious tortures, nevertheless bravely and faithfully persisted in the confession of the truth."[9]

Elsewhere Luther stated: "We here are of the conviction that the Papacy is the seat of the true and real antichrist, against whose deceit and vileness all is permitted for the salvation of souls. Personally I declare that I owe the Pope no other obedience than that to Antichrist."[10]

Virtually all Protestant Reformers, including Andreas Osiander of Bavaria, Zwingli, Leo Judah, Theodor Bibliander and Heinrich Bullinger of Switzerland, William Tyndale, Robert Barnes, George Joye, Nicholas Ridley, John Philpot, John Hooper, John Jewell, and Thomas Cranmer of England, all shared Luther's opinion. Many of them gave their lives as martyrs for their faithful witness. John Knox and John Napier from Scotland joined the rising chorus identifying, on the basis of Scripture, the Papacy as the antichrist of prophecy. Because it recognized the historical Papacy as the antichrist, this teaching became known as historicism.

The Catholic Church understood clearly the role that prophetic interpretation had in the Reformation. With such clear and powerful preaching taking its effect, as witnessed by the success of the Reformation movement, we would not expect the Papacy to sit idly by while its adherents deserted it. And indeed they did not. The Jesuit order, founded by Ignatius of Loyola and authorized in 1540, became the leader of the Counter-Reformation movement. The Confession of Augsburg, the battle cry of the Reformers, was met by the Catholic Church's Council of Trent. The church responded to the charge of the pope as antichrist through the teachings of the Jesuits, Francisco Ribera of Spain, Robert Bellarmine of Italy, and Luis De Alcazar of Spain.

Alcazar said, in essence, "The Church cannot be the antichrist, because the antichrist already came long ago." In his view the antichrist was the twofold attack made on the early church by unbelieving Jews and pagans. Because this view sees the antichrist in the past, it has been called "preterism." Later, preterism adopted the teaching that the horn power of Daniel 7 and 8 represented the activities of Antiochus Epiphanes, a Greek ruler who persecuted Jews and violated the sanctity of the Temple in Jerusalem during second-century B.C.[11]

Ribera and Bellarmine took a different perspective: "The church cannot be the antichrist, because the antichrist has not come yet. The antichrist will come in the future, will be a single individual and not a system, will be an infidel, will have power for three and a half literal, not prophetic years, will rebuild the temple in Jerusalem, abolish the

Christian religion, be received by the Jews, pretend to be God, and conquer the world." Because this concept regards the antichrist as yet in the future, scholars refer to it as "futurism."[12]

Notice how the two schools of thought are basically self-contradicting, yet were initiated by the same church. One declares, "Look for the antichrist in the past," while the other announces, "Look for the antichrist in the future." Yet the Papacy taught both Counter-Reformation teachings simultaneously. By pushing the identity of the antichrist either backward into distant history (preterism), or forward into the future (futurism), the church was able to counterattack the Reformation.

By no means, though, is that the end of the story. Ironically, much of Protestantism itself has also embraced the two views of prophetic interpretation. If you go to virtually any current Protestant commentary or school and ask, "What or who is the antichrist of Scripture?" the answer you get will be based on either the concepts of preterism or futurism. The antichrist either came and went long ago, or he is not here yet but will manifest himself in the future. He is not here among us today. Protestantism itself is vigorously undermining the heritage of the Reformation.

The author Joseph Tanner has put it this way: "It is a matter of deep regret that those who hold and advocate the Futurist system at the present day, Protestants as they are for the most part, are thus really playing into the hands of Rome, and helping to screen the Papacy from detection as the Antichrist. It has been well said that 'Futurism tends to obliterate the brand put by the Holy Spirit upon Popery.' More especially is this to be deplored at a time when the Papal Antichrist seems to be making an expiring effort to regain his former hold on men's minds."[13]

It is important to keep in mind that if one is not clear as to who the "beast" of Revelation 13 is, it is likely that one will also be uncertain as to the "mark of the beast." This cannot be overemphasized. Many Protestants today hold that the beast is some giant computer in Belgium, and that the mark of the beast will be a visible thing such as a barcode, tattoo, or implanted microchip. Such concepts unfortunately miss the spiritual meaning of the prophetic symbols.

242 Three Angels, One Message

As we scan the horizon of time, it may be said that with regard to prophetic interpretation, particularly the identity of the scriptural antichrist, most Protestants today do not believe as did their spiritual forefathers, the original Protestants. The Counter-Reformation theologies of preterism and futurism, created to forestall the inroads of Protestantism, have become more successful than their originators ever would have dreamed, in that Protestantism itself has become their leading spokesman. The very name "Protestant" has a diminished meaning in the current context of ecumenism.

Historicists today, upon viewing the history of prophetic interpretation, have nothing to be embarrassed about. The scriptural foundation upon which these prophetic interpretations are based are well-placed, crafted by masons over many centuries, including many of the heroes of the Reformation. While others may look upon such teachings as being insensitive, uncaring, unkind, or even unchristian, a broad historical outlook puts them in an extremely favorable light. The picture emerges of a long succession of torchbearers. Wycliffe, Knox, Zwingli, Calvin, Huss, Jerome, Luther, Melanchthon, and a host of others witnessed to them.

Sometimes it's hard to see what is right in front of us. A lonely woman of Sychar came at noon to get water and met a man who opened her mind to spiritual truth as she had never seen it before. She went and told her neighbors, "This couldn't be the Christ, could it?" (see John 4:29). The form of her question in Greek grammar anticipates a negative answer. She was saying, "He couldn't really be the Messiah, could He?" It seemed impossible to grasp. Yet Jesus, the one who sat in front of her, met all the prophetic requirements. He really was the one!

And so today many wonder with respect to the historical Papacy, "This couldn't be the antichrist, could it? This couldn't be the one of which prophecy has spoken, could it?" It would be easier to look back into the yellowed pages of history to find his uncomfortable existence far in the past, removed from us by millennia, or shove his appearance into the far distant stretches of the future. That would be easier, wouldn't it? And yet, right before our eyes, we see that prophecy has spoken and history has confirmed. And yes, the institution's own statements corroborate the fulfillment.

Having said that, and recognizing that it is important to know about the "beast," it is far more important to know the "Lamb." You can have all the prophetic symbols correctly identified, but without knowing Jesus it will do you no good. It's not what you know, it's *whom* you know. The prophecies of Daniel and Revelation are soon to be completely fulfilled. If you listen carefully today, you can hear the echo of those sentiments that will soon result in the formation of the deadly "image to the beast" foretold in Revelation 13. Today we must make sure of our salvation. Today we must establish an unbreakable personal relationship with Christ. Today we must study, pray, work, and wait for the fulfillment of God's plan, which surely will soon come to pass.

---

[1] See L. E. Froom, *Prophetic Faith of Our Fathers*, vol. 2, pp. 528ff.

[2] Johannes Turmair, *Annalium Boiorum Libri Septem* (1554), p. 684 (note the allusions to 2 Thessalonians 2 and 1 John 2). In Froom, vol. 1, p. 800.

[3] George Cunrad Rieger, *Die Alte und Neue Bohmische Bruder*, vol. 1, pp. 68, 69. In Froom, vol. 2, p. 33.

[4] E. H. Gillett, *The Life and Times of John Huss,* vol. 1, p. 23. In Froom, vol. 2, p. 34.

[5] *Ibid.,* vol. 1, pp. 30, 31. In Froom, vol. 2, p. 40.

[6] John Wyclif, *De Veritate Sacrae Scripturae*, vol. 3, pp. 267, 268. In Froom, vol. 2, p. 55.

[7] *Ibid.*

[8] John Foxe, *The Acts and Monuments of John Foxe: A New and Complete Edition; With a Preliminary Dissertation*, by the Rev. George Townsend, vol. 1, p. 636. In Froom, vol. 2, p. 88.

[9] Martin Luther, preface in *Commentarius in Apocalypsin Ante Centum Annos Editus*. In Froom, vol. 2, p. 94.

[10] Martin Luther, *Sammtliche Schriften*, vol. 15, col. 1639. In Froom, vol. 2, p. 256.

[11] See Froom, vol. 2, p. 506ff.

[12] See Froom, vol. 2, pp. 484ff.

[13] Joseph Tanner, *Daniel and the Revelation*, p. 17. In Froom, vol. 2, p. 511.

CHAPTER 20

THE "MARK OF THE BEAST" AND THE "SEAL OF GOD"

W e have seen, then, that the beast that is the subject of the third angel's warning is the historical institution known as the Papacy. We have confirmed it by identifying the clues given in prophecy and comparing the six other pictures in Scripture that portray the same entity. The angel said with a loud voice, "If anyone worships the beast and his image, and receives his mark on his forehead or on his hand, he himself shall also drink of the wine of the wrath of God, which is poured out full strength into the cup of His indignation" (Rev. 14:9, 10).

The beast is the Papacy. The "image" is the copy of the style of compulsion of conscience that characterized the church during the Dark Ages that will revive in this last time period. But what is the "mark" of the beast? Having established what the beast power represents and having studied the identifying clues, understanding the "mark of the beast" is quite simple. You might have already figured it out.

What is the issue brought to light in Revelation 13 and 14? It is that of worship, a word that appears eight times in the two chapters. To what does the Papacy point, as being proof of its authority and superiority over Scripture? It is the changing of the Ten Commandments, written by God's own finger in stone. To give proof of its earthly authority in ecclesiastical matters the Papacy boldly cites its modification of the fourth commandment. It claims to have transferred the day of worship from the seventh day, the day that God ordained, to the first day of the week, a change for which, according to its own acknowledgment, there is no scriptural basis. Some may object that Sunday worship evolved long before the rise of the papal institution itself, but the Papacy upholds the change and claims it for its own.

We have noted the September 1893 articles in the *Catholic Mirror* in which Rome challenged the professed Protestant world as to why they worship on Sunday. The roots of this argument go back all the way to the Council of Trent, when Caspar del Fosso, archbishop of Reggio di Calabria, confronted the newly birthed Protestant movement on the issue of scriptural authority for the observance of Sunday as against the Sabbath of the Ten Commandments.[1] It is a practice the Papacy has always affirmed, one that while it has no biblical basis, was done by the church. Those who regard themselves as *sola scriptura* Protestants must then follow the Bible in this most important matter of when to worship. On the other hand, those who choose to continue to worship on Sunday should be honest and acknowledge to whose authority they bow to. It is ecclesiastical tradition, not Scripture.

The attempt to transfer the day of worship from Saturday to Sunday—an act predicted by Daniel and accepted by nearly all the Christian world—the Papacy presents as the sign of its power. "Sunday is our mark of authority. . . . The Church is above the Bible, and this transference of Sabbath observance is proof of that fact."[2]

The newsletter of the Rectory of St. Catherine's of May 21, 1995, announced: "Perhaps the boldest thing, the most revolutionary change the Church ever did happened in the first century. The holy day, the Sabbath, was changed from Saturday to Sunday . . . not from any directions noted in the Scriptures, but from the Church's sense of its own power."

No one has the mark of the beast yet, for it has not yet become law. Not yet has Babylon "made [coerced by legislation] all nations drink of the wine of the wrath of her fornication." That event is still future today. But it will come, rest assured. Don't be lulled to sleep with the thought that something like this could never happen in America. After all, we have constitutional guarantees of the freedom of religion. But I'm quite sure that if you had interviewed Eve the morning of the Fall and asked her, "Are you planning to disobey your Creator despite all that He's done for you?" she would have replied, "Absolutely not!" But Satan caught her off guard and deceived her.

The Lord told His disciple Peter that before the rooster crowed twice, he would deny Him three times. Peter protested against the prophetic word of Jesus. "No, my Lord! Why, I'm willing to die for You!" And yet, caught off guard in the pressure of the moment, the disciple did exactly that. And I'm quite certain that if you had interviewed certain citizens of Jerusalem 2,000 years ago and asked, "Are you planning to crucify your Messiah? Are you planning to put God on a cross?" they likewise would have recoiled in horror. "Of course not!" Yet, caught up with the demon-led mob, they did just that! Under Satan's leadership, the unthinkable happened.

Don't think that what prophecy predicts can't happen. Don't think that when Satan inspires men who are not founded on the Word of God that the unthinkable can't become reality. And don't think that this picture of the revival of persecution on the scale of the Middle Ages is an impossibility. When under the control of the master of evil, without the controlling and restraining power of the Holy Spirit, human beings will do unimaginable things.

Someday exactly what Revelation 13 predicts will become reality. It will result as fallen Protestantism of America joins hands with Catholicism to cause the United States to legislate laws restricting freedom by giving honor to the first day of the week as a national rest day. Perhaps it could sneak in the back door posing as a "National Family Day," or a "National Worker Rest Day." Or it could come about as an economic measure to restrict the purchasing of gasoline or other scarce commodities on the first day of the week.

But along with the mark of the beast, we need to study the seal of God, for they are contrasting signs. At the last day, every person on this earth will have either the seal of God or the mark of the beast. There will be no middle ground, no chance to sit on the fence.

We express allegiance and loyalty through obedience. As we've affirmed many times throughout this book, obedience is the highest form of worship. God is looking to populate His kingdom with subjects who obey Him. How could He possibly take to heaven those who persist in rebellion? That would only perpetuate the sin problem forever. Just as it was a simple test in Eden that gave our first parents opportunity to express their loyalty to God, so at the end of the age it will be a simple test by which we can demonstrate our allegiance to our Creator-God. It will be whether we choose to worship on His day.

Notice how the symbols of the mark of the beast and the seal of God compare and contrast each other perfectly. In a sense they fit together like a dovetailed joint. In contrast to those who receive the mark of the beast, the sign of disobedience, the third angel points to those who are loyal to God and declares, "Here is the patience of the saints; here are those who keep the commandments of God and the faith of Jesus" (Rev. 14:12). Obedience to God stands in contrast with those who receive the mark of the beast. The ones who listened to the message of the angel heard and responded to the invitation to "worship Him who made heaven and earth, the sea and springs of water" (verse 7).

As we saw before, it is God's creatorship that uniquely qualifies Him to be the one we worship. Proclaimed the 24 elders, "You are worthy, O Lord, to receive glory and honor and power; for You created all things, and by Your will they exist and were created" (Rev. 4:11). God's creatorship and worship are inseparable. "Thus you shall say to them: 'The gods that have not made the heavens and the earth shall perish from the earth and from under these heavens.' He has made the earth by His power, He has established the world by His wisdom, and has stretched out the heavens at His discretion" (Jer. 10:11, 12).

Wrote the psalmist, "For the Lord is great and greatly to be praised; He is to be feared above all gods. For all the gods of the people are idols, but the Lord made the heavens. Honor and majesty are before Him; strength and beauty are in His sanctuary. Give to the Lord, O families of the peoples, give to the Lord glory and strength. Give to the Lord the glory due His name; bring an offering, and come into His courts. Oh, worship the Lord in the beauty of holiness! Tremble before Him, all the earth" (Ps. 96:4-9). Psalm 96 is an Old Testament precursor to the three angels' messages, containing references to nearly every aspect brought to light in Revelation 14.

What could possibly be more appropriate than giving God the glory and worship that He is due by observing the day that is the divine reminder of His creatorship and thus declaring our loyalty through obedience to His commandments! Just as disobedience to God in the matter of worship results in the reception of the mark of the beast, the mark of authority claimed by the Papacy, so obedience to God in the matter of worship prepares one to receive the seal of God.

As we consider the expressions "mark of the beast" and "image of the beast," we see a parallel between the worship of the image of the beast and Old Testament idolatry. What is the essence of idolatry? It is the worship of an object made by human hands. "Your carved images I will also cut off, and your sacred pillars from your midst; you shall no more worship the work of your hands" (Micah 5:13). "Their land is also full of idols; they worship the work of their own hands, that which their own fingers have made" (Isa. 2:8). The book of Isaiah is especially saturated with the contrast between the worship of men's hands and the worship of the Creator-God (see Isa. 40:18-22; 42:5-8; 44:9-20, etc.).

Here are some questions to consider: Does it make any difference from heaven's point of view if human beings fall down before something they fashioned with their hands from wood or stone, or if they bow before an institution made by their own hand, specifically, the first day of the week proclaimed to be the sabbath? Is anyone less guilty for violating the fourth commandment than the second? Is not the violation of each a form of idolatry?

When Moses was absent from the camp of Israel longer than the patience of the Israelites could bear, the people induced Aaron to shape for them a golden calf. "And he received the gold from their hand, and he fashioned it with an engraving tool, and made a molded calf. Then they said, 'This is your god, O Israel, that brought you out of the land of Egypt!' So when Aaron saw it, he built an altar before it. And Aaron made a proclamation and said, 'Tomorrow is a feast to the Lord'" (Ex. 32:4, 5). Could it be that modern Christianity is doing the same thing? Could they be in the shoes of Aaron, announcing, "Tomorrow (Sunday) is a feast to the Lord"?

Marks and Signs in the Old Testament

Will the mark of the beast or the seal of God be visible to the human eye? Why is the mark of the beast spoken of as being received in the hand or forehead, while the seal of God is mentioned only as in the forehead?

We must remember that the book of Revelation, in which we find the prophecy of the seal of God and the warning against the mark of the beast, is a collage stitching together pictures of God's activities from throughout history. To try to understand the book of Revelation without being familiar with the Old Testament is like trying to read a map while being blindfolded.

What does the Old Testament tell us that can help us to grasp the matter of God's seal and the beast's mark? Three passages will assist greatly in our understanding. Going back to the book of Exodus, we find a remarkable passage that appears in the context of the instruction regarding the blood of the Passover lamb being splashed on the doorposts of the houses to save the firstborn males from the destroying angel. It tells how to respond when future generations would ask why God's people were observing the Passover. "And you shall tell your son in that day, saying, 'This is done because of what the Lord did for me when I came up from Egypt.' It shall be as a sign to you on your hand and as a memorial between your eyes, that the Lord's law may be in your mouth; for with a strong hand the Lord has brought you out of Egypt" (Ex. 13:8, 9).

A most important text, it introduces the concept of something being "as a sign" on our forehead and hand. Notice very carefully the word "as," given twice. "It shall be *as* a sign to you on your hand and *as* a memorial between your eyes." Did God intend for anyone to literally place such words on their hand and forehead? Again, when Revelation speaks of God's seal being in the forehead of the saints, or the mark of the beast being in the forehead or hand of the lost, will this be some kind of visible tattoo or bar code on their physical person? Not according to the evidence of Scripture.

Why was it to be as a sign on their hand? Because the hand represents what we do—our behavior and actions. Why was it to be as a memorial on the forehead, between the eyes? Today we know that it represents where our thinking takes place. That's where remembering ("as a memorial") and decision-making happen. What was the overall purpose of this being "on the hand and forehead"? It was so "that the Lord's law may be in your mouth"—in other words, that they be in a right relationship with Him in obedience to His will.

What part of God's law stands as a "memorial" and stresses remembering? "Remember the Sabbath day to keep it holy. . . . For in six days the Lord made heaven and earth, the sea, and all that is in them" (Ex. 20:8-11). The "memorial" that God's people in the last days will have in their "foreheads" will be God's law. His Sabbath, which is a memorial of His Creation, will become the focus of attention, the last-day test, in contrast to the image and mark of the beast. We can see clearly, even in just the first occurrence of this idea, that what God is really saying by this is that His law will be remembered in how you think and characterized by what you do. That's it in a nutshell. It's not really that difficult. The concept is that His law will be the guiding principle in your thoughts and actions, your "ways and doings."

That phrase "ways and doings" appears some 11 times through the Bible. (We saw earlier that the phrase "ways and deeds" occurs another eight times.) "Ways and doings" is another way of saying "head and hand." It describes your thinking and actions. God desires that our minds be committed to Him, which will result in our behavior being righteous. If we have the principles of His kingdom written internally in our hearts and minds (the goal of the new covenant), then our external lifestyle will also exhibit godly features (Heb. 8:8-10). The fruitage of the life will be reflective of Christ living in the heart. Because of this emphasis on the thinking and decision-making aspect, the book of Revelation puts the stress on the seal of God being in the forehead. The companion phrase "in the hand" is not included, because if God's law is in our mind and heart, it will also demonstrate itself in our hands.

Why does Scripture describe the mark of the beast as being received on the forehead or hand, while only the forehead for the seal of God? It is because when the image of the beast is erected and Sunday worship becomes a matter of law with harsh proscriptions attached to it, some who will abide by the law and observe Sunday "with their mind"—that is, they will believe, erroneously, that they are doing the right thing. Agreeing mentally with the law, they will receive the mark in the forehead, because they have subscribed to the principle of it in their minds. As for the ones who receive the mark in their hand, we'll deal with them shortly.

Before we do that, however, we must consider still another question: if they, the ones who receive the mark in their forehead, really believe that this is right, how can God be fair in punishing them? It is something that deserves our attention. In times of ignorance "God winked." (Acts 17:30, KJV). That is, God does not hold people accountable for what they do not know. James says, "To him who knows to do good and does not do it, to him it is sin" (James 4:17). Jesus stated, "If you were blind, you would have no sin; but now you say, 'We see.' Therefore your sin remains" (John 9:41). He later declared, "If I had not come and spoken to them, they would have no sin, but now they have no excuse for their sin" (John 15:22). The punchline of Daniel's interpretation of the cryptic letters on Belshazzar's palace wall that indicted Babylon was "You . . . have not humbled your heart, although you knew all this" (Dan. 5:22). With knowledge comes accountability.

But what if a person chooses to remain ignorant? Will that provide an excuse? No. There is a clear difference between mere ignorance and willful ignorance. Peter describes the scoffers of the last days as being "willingly . . . ignorant" of the Creation and the Deluge (2 Peter 3:5, KJV). The NKJV says that "they willfully forget." Those who of their own volition choose to remain in darkness when God has made available a flood of light will be held responsible for the truth they could have acquired. Concerning those who will be swept away by Satan's last delusions, Paul wrote that they will perish because "they refused to love the truth and so be saved" (2 Thess. 2:10, NIV).

God is just in condemning them because He has revealed to all His truth in His holy Word. Today many are still unaware of the messages of the three angels. But the time will come when everyone on earth will have had an opportunity to know the issue at stake. In fulfillment of the text, the message will reach "to every nation, tribe, tongue, and people." At that time in our world's history, every single person on the globe will have had a chance to make a decision on this great issue of God's commandments and the day of worship. At that time it will be abundantly clear that to choose the first day of the week and honor it as a holy day is contrary to the express will of God, written by His finger in stone within the Ten Commandments. Without question the choice is between God's Word and humanity's word; God's commandments and humanity's commandments; God's day, the Sabbath, or humanity's day, Sunday.

What about those deceived by Satan? Is God fair to judge them if they have been tricked by the devil's sleight of hand? Yes. Paul tells us that in the Garden of Eden, Eve was "deceived" but "fell into transgression" (1 Tim. 2:14). Just because she was tricked didn't excuse her sin. That is because she had heard the word of God but didn't obey it. She put her faith in another source, the talking snake, rather than the Creator-God.

Thus it will be at the end. God reveals to us His truth, which will be a shield against the deceptions of the devil. If we fail to take up the shield and use it—if we fail to study and receive the warnings and promises of the Scriptures—we will be left to the whims and wiles of the evil one. At the end of time, to willfully and knowingly, or by deception, choose Sunday over Sabbath will bring to full and complete fulfillment the prophecy of the apostle Paul, who wrote: "For the mystery of iniquity is already at work; only He who now restrains will do so until He is taken out of the way. And then the lawless one will be revealed, whom the Lord will consume with the breath of His mouth and destroy with the brightness of His coming. The coming of the lawless one is according to the working of Satan, with all power, signs, and lying wonders, and with all unrighteous deception among those who perish, because they did not receive the love of the truth, that they might be saved. And for this reason God will send [or allow to come to] them strong delusion, that they should believe the lie, that they all may be condemned who did not believe the truth but had pleasure in unrighteousness" (2 Thess. 2:7-12).

In his letter Paul clarifies why it is that some who "sincerely" believe something that is false will still be lost. Notice carefully the usage of the article "the" in Paul's writing. We find that there is a contrast between "the truth" and "the lie." These people are lost because they "did not receive the love of *the truth*." "The truth" in this context includes all the revealed will of God, but it emphasizes and highlights "the truth" brought to light by the messages of the three angels, which includes the invitation to "worship Him who made," and warns against receiving the "mark of the beast."

They are lost because they "did not believe *the truth* but had pleasure in unrighteousness." God did reveal "the truth" to them. The Lord made it plain before their eyes, but they chose to believe "the lie," the instrument of deception. Satan has been the disseminator of falsehood from the beginning. He is the "father" of lies (John 8:44). "The lie" that he has promoted among the human family denies God's existence, His ways, and His law. In advancing "the lie," the devil has been remarkably successful.

At the time of the end, with the issue drawn in such clear and distinct lines, those who choose to believe "the lie" and refuse to accept and love "the truth" will exclude themselves from divine favor. They will place themselves under the dark banner of the general of wickedness, Satan. In so doing they will receive the mark of the beast in the forehead. Even though they sincerely believe what they are doing, they will stand judged as being wicked because the knowledge of "the truth" was made available to them and yet they preferred "the lie." Neither willful ignorance, sincerity, nor deception will provide an excuse for them on that day.

In the end all the lost will fall into two great categories. First will be those who have been deceived into disobedience, actually thinking that they are right, and second, those who know they are rebelling but choose to do so anyway. The story of sin began with those two classes in Eden, and it will conclude that way at the end of time. The Bible tells us that the serpent "deceived" Eve. Satan tricked her into believing that she was on a course that would bring her great benefit. But though tricked, she was still responsible for what she did, because she had opportunity to find out the truth. Her failure was a lack of faith—of not believing the express Word of God. She accepted the word of a talking snake that had done nothing for her rather than the Creator-God who had done everything for her. "Whatever is not from faith is sin" (Rom. 14:23). Many will, like her, let themselves be beguiled by the crafty serpent, but who nevertheless will still be accountable for their transgression, because they could have known the truth if they had wanted to.

Adam, on the other hand, "was not deceived" (1 Tim. 2:14). His failure, though, was likewise one of faith, for he did not believe that

God could rectify the situation in which he found himself. It seemed to him to be an impossible one. The woman he loved had transgressed. Adam knew that she had disobeyed, and he knew what God had said would be the consequences of such an act. But could he let her go? He could not face the future without her at his side. Nor could he imagine how God might fix the predicament. Instead, he decided to brave the consequences and bit into the forbidden fruit. As a result, he sinned with his eyes wide open.

During the last days there will be Adams who will know full well that they are disobeying the clear Word of God, but cannot discern how God can save them if they do His will instead of human demands. Adam's sin originated in idolatry (putting Eve ahead of God) and fear. He was afraid to obey God lest he lose his beloved Eve. And many will follow his course at the close of time. For some it will be concern about losing a job if they honor the seventh-day Sabbath, not trusting that God can and will provide for them. For others it will be the dread of abandonment by a spouse or other family member, or the loss of property or life. They cannot believe that God will give them in return something far greater.

A number of years ago I was privileged to work on the construction of the building of worship for our church, an edifice long anticipated by our congregation. One day I was busy in the kitchen section, while a worker from our local power supplier was upstairs in the room dedicated to electrical equipment. His assignment was to remove the stabilizing bars that came with the panel. Another team from his company had been there a day or two before, ensuring that power to the panel flowed properly. Since the new worker would be putting his hands in areas of potentially high voltage, I carefully warned him that I wasn't sure if they had left the power on or had turned it off. He assured me that it would be no problem, since he had equipment to check whether electricity flowed through it or not.

A few minutes later he rushed down the stairs and with an ashen face inquired whether we were supplying electricity ourselves to the system. Sensing something ominous, I replied no, knowing that our generator was busy churning power for a crew working on landscaping projects. When I asked him why he wanted to know, he told me that while he had his hands on the stabilizing supports, in direct contact with the buss bars, a large spark had jumped from the door of the panel, the nearest "ground," to his elbow. He couldn't understand it, since he had tested for electrical current and his equipment had registered none present.

I accompanied him back up the stairs as he again carefully probed with his tester. And again it did not indicate any. Then I think we both saw it at the same time. Amazingly, his testing device was set on "DC," not "AC"! There was not one volt of direct current within that panel, but there was plenty of alternating current, sufficient to produce instant death. I told him that this was a house of worship, and that God had been watching out for him that day. He agreed, and hastily went to shut off the 800 amps of current.

He was no doubt most sincere in his desire to be safe while working in a hazardous environment, but he could have been sincerely dead. The dial on his equipment was pointing to a wrong indicator, a mistake that could have easily cost him his life. The Holy Bible is the indicator of God's truth. Satan's desire is to "recalibrate" Scripture so that a misreading occurs.

On that last day many will have been deceived and sincerely believe that they are following the truth when they are in fact chasing the lie. They will assume that they are worshiping God when in fact they will be worshipping Satan. Such individuals receive the mark of the beast in their foreheads. On the other hand, some won't necessarily buy into the idea of worshipping God on the first day of the week, but to avoid the penalties that violating the law would bring—to be able to continue to buy and sell—they will do what the law requires, though their hearts are not fully in harmony with the legislation. They will go along with it though they don't believe the principles embedded in the new law. By so "doing," they will receive the mark of the beast in the hand.

To review: there have been instances when ignorance was excusable in God's sight and He judged people accordingly. But in the context of the last days, when this issue will be placed in an unavoidable and unmistakable spotlight, His truth will light the entire globe, and ignorance will no longer be acceptable. "Truly, these times of ignorance God overlooked, but now commands all men everywhere to repent, because He has appointed a day on which He will judge the world in righteousness by the Man whom He has ordained. He has given assurance of this to all by raising Him from the dead" (Acts 17:30, 31).

At that time no one will be unaware of the issue and the choice that it demands. If they are oblivious, it will be because they are willfully so. There will be no neutrality, no fence sitters. By refusing to assemble under the banner of Christ and His Sabbath, people will automatically have placed themselves under the flag of the enemy. "He who is not with Me is against Me, and he who does not gather with Me scatters abroad" (Matt. 12:30).

Does this mean that I can postpone making a decision on the Sabbath question until laws get passed to promote Sunday worship? No. When light comes to us we need to walk in it lest we lose the possibility. Besides, there is a great blessing in keeping His Sabbath holy. God made the Sabbath for humanity (Mark 2:27). Who would want to turn aside from a day of rest in which we can contemplate the great works of our Creator and draw closer to Him in fellowship? To refuse to apply truth, thinking that some other more convenient season will come, is very dangerous. The human mind has a way of rationalizing what is truth and turning light into darkness. Those who put off following God's commandments do so at their peril.

Two other passages in the Old Testament shed light on the concept of receiving a mark on head and hand. They come from the book of Deuteronomy, which contains Moses' farewell speech before he ascended Mount Nebo to lay his life's labors down. It's important to see that both texts appear immediately after the presentation of God's law (Deut. 5; 10). Following the giving of God's law in these chapters, we find material in Deuteronomy 6 and 11 that bears on our discussion.

"And these words [the Ten Commandments] which I command you today shall be in your heart. You shall teach them diligently to your children, and shall talk of them when you sit in your house, when you walk by the way, when you lie down, and when you rise up. You shall bind them as a sign on your hand, and they shall be as frontlets [a decorative headband] between your eyes" (Deut. 6:6-8). Notice again that God's law will be *as* a sign on their hand, and *as* frontlets on their forehead.

Though the Jews later took the divine admonition literally, that it was not God's intention is crystal clear. If it were, we would read that Jesus wore such objects, but no verse in the Bible tells us that He did. What we do read is that His testimony was, in the words of the psalmist, "Then I said, 'Behold, I come; in the scroll of the Book it is written of Me. I delight to do Your will, O My God, and Your law is within My heart'" (Ps. 40:7, 8).

Did Jesus live out the principle expressed in Deuteronomy 6? Was the law, the Ten Commandments, bound "as a sign on His hand" and "as a frontlet between His eyes"? Absolutely! But not in an overly literalistic way, as was too often the mistake of the Jews. They exhibited the externals of religion, but God's love was not in their hearts. "These people draw near to Me with their mouth, and honor Me with their lips, but their heart is far from Me. And in vain they worship Me, teaching for doctrines the commandments of men" (Matt. 15:8, 9).

Deuteronomy 11 repeats the admonition. "Therefore you shall lay up these words of mine in your heart and in your soul, and bind them as a sign on your hand, and they shall be as frontlets between your eyes" (Deut. 11:18). The key words are "as," revealing the symbolic nature of the instruction, "bind," emphasizing the close relationship between God's law and His people (the same word that describes Jonathan's heart being "knit" to the heart of David [1 Sam. 18:1]), and "sign," showing that obedience to God's law will be a special "mark" or "flag" indicating one's allegiance to the Creator. Many scriptures refer to the Sabbath as being God's special sign between Him and His people. "Surely My Sabbaths you shall keep, for it is a sign between Me and you throughout your generations, that you may know that I am the Lord who sanctifies you" (Ex. 31:13; see also Eze. 20:12, 20).

We have also the prophetic picture given in Ezekiel 9, in which God showed the prophet that those who "sigh and cry" for all the abominations done in "it" (Jerusalem, the professed city of God) will receive a mark on their foreheads placed by an angel. This mark will result in their being "passed over" by the destroying angels who will go through the city with sword in hand. The obvious lesson here is that those whose hearts beat in sympathy with God's; those who have developed a hatred of sin; those whose hearts are filled with sorrow for transgression, be it in the world, the church, or their own lives, will be the ones who receive the saving mark. They will exhibit the same humility as Daniel, who prayed in contrition for his people in the prayer recorded in Daniel 9.

Before we give more attention to what the "seal" is, we need to distinguish between the seal that is placed on a believer when he or she begins the Christian journey and the one mentioned in Revelation 7. They are two different things. When people first give their life to the Lord, He imparts a seal to them. Paul spoke of this when he wrote to the church in Corinth. "Now He who establishes us with you in Christ and has anointed us is God, who also has sealed us and given us the Spirit in our hearts as a guarantee" (2 Cor. 1:21, 22). In a similar way, to the Ephesian church he observed, "In Him you also trusted, after you heard the word of truth, the gospel of your salvation; in whom also, having believed, you were sealed with the Holy Spirit of promise, who is the guarantee of our inheritance until the redemption of the purchased possession, to the praise of His glory" (Eph. 1:13, 14).

Is this the same "seal" that Revelation speaks about? No. It is clear from these passages that there is a seal conferred on us when we believe and begin the Christian walk. Paul spoke of this seal in the past tense. He said that God "has sealed us," and "you were sealed." We might think of this seal as the "early rain seal," which confirms that a person has exercised their choice to receive Christ and start the journey toward the kingdom. Notice that the Holy Spirit is the active Agent in the placement of this seal.

However, the seal brought to view in Revelation 7 is different. We might think of it as being the "latter rain seal," given just before the second coming of Jesus to prepare God's people to receive the empowerment of the final outpouring of His Spirit. Revelation speaks of it as a future happening. "Then I saw another angel ascending from the east, having the seal of the living God. And he cried with a loud voice to the four angels to whom it was granted to harm the earth and the sea, saying, 'Do not harm the earth, the sea, or the trees till we have sealed the servants of our God on their foreheads'" (Rev. 7:2, 3).

It is evident that this seal is yet to be placed, and therefore should be distinguished from the seal referred to earlier by the apostle Paul.

As we think of what the Bible means when it speaks of the "seal of God," we turn to incidences and stories in Scripture to help us gain understanding. Seals in ancient times were typically of two types—a cylinder seal and a signet ring. A cylinder seal was an object of ivory, wood, or stone, perhaps one to one and a half inches in length, about three-fourths inches in diameter, and carved with a decorative pattern. Think of it as being a miniature rolling pin. A cylinder seal was hollow, like a straw, and with a leather cord passing through it, could be worn around its owner's neck. The intricacy and detail on such carved seals is often amazing. The major museums of the world have impressive displays of them, or you can do a search on the Internet and see them.

Such seems to be the case when Judah had an encounter with someone he thought was a prostitute who, unbeknown to him, was actually his daughter-in-law Tamar. Having nothing with him at the time to pay her, he asked what she wanted as collateral. She replied, "Your signet and cord" (Gen. 38:18). In the touching love story contained in Song of Solomon, the bride expresses a desire to be as close to her beloved as possible. See in your mind's eye a seal suspended around Solomon's neck as his lover says, "Set me as a seal upon your heart" (Song of Sol. 8:6). A similar expression of endearment regarding a signet ring occurs in Haggai. "'In that day,' says the Lord of hosts, 'I will take you, Zerubbabel My servant, the son of Shealtiel,' says the Lord, 'and will make you as a signet ring; for I have chosen you,' says the Lord of hosts" (Haggai 2:23).

When you rolled the cylinder seal over soft clay or warm wax, it would impart an image upon the material to be sealed. Ancient seals had such images as leaping gazelles or the portrait or name of reigning monarchs. Even today some important documents have seals that are embossed into them, and you can feel the raised surface as you run your fingers over them. My birth certificate has such a seal on it.

Beside the cylinder seal, people of the past also used a signet ring. We find numerous accounts in the Old Testament that refer to them. In order to obtain the vineyard of Naboth, the wicked queen Jezebel sent out letters setting him up for false accusations and execution.

"She wrote letters in Ahab's name, sealed them with his seal, and sent the letters to the elders and nobles who were dwelling in the city with Naboth" (1 Kings 21:8).

Likewise the unscrupulous Haman wrote a series of letters jeopardizing the lives of the Jews in Queen Esther's time. "These were written in the name of King Ahasuerus himself, and sealed with his own ring" (Esther 3:12, NIV). The lions' den into which Daniel was cast was sealed with the signet rings of King Darius and of his lords (Dan. 6:17). The tomb in which Jesus rested was "sealed" (Matt. 27:66).

As we reflect on this, here's an important point to consider. Could you make such an impression in hard stone or set concrete? That would be difficult, to say the least. Years ago when I was a young child, a road crew worked on the street in front of the house where we lived. Just as soon as the truck carrying the workers turned the corner and out of sight, I dashed out into the street to write my name in the still soft cement. Decades later the signature is still there. When the impression is made, the material must be soft and pliable. But after the document is sealed, it then becomes set and fixed, so that it doesn't change after that, just like the cement in front of my house. That's what happened when something was "sealed." What does this mean for us? That we must now be open to the impressions of the Spirit, as He remolds our characters into the likeness of the divine.

In other words, just as the medium on which the seal was rolled had to be soft and pliable, so the minds of the saints must be impressionable to the counsels of the Holy Spirit in order for the likeness—the image—to be transferred. It would do little good to try to place the seal on hard clay. Nor does it do any good for the Holy Spirit to attempt to make impressions on minds that are petrified and obdurate by the love of the world. If that is the case, we will be left to maintain the image of lost humanity. What should we be doing right now? We should be asking God, pleading with Him, to make us soft, pliable, and impressionable to the movements of the Spirit on our hearts and minds.

Yes, the material on which a seal is placed must be soft and pliable. But God can take the "heart of stone" from us and give us a "heart of flesh," according to the terms of the new covenant (Eze. 36:26).

Remember that His objective is to change the way we think so that our characters will reflect His image. The seal is a beautiful lesson of this. You can see how this beautiful and sublime truth of the gospel is lost if we regard the seal as a bar code or tattoo.

The seal operated as one's signature in ancient times. Because interest rates have reached historic lows, we recently refinanced our house. The notary public came to our home, and we signed what seemed to be a ream of papers. She would press her seal against them to affirm that our signatures were valid. But there was one paper that had a place for us to sign that had the word "seal" beside it, but lacked the other wording that usually went with the notary seal. I asked her about that. "Oh," she said, "I found that confusing too. Actually that's referring to your signature as being your 'seal.'" So even today it seems that a signature can be one's seal, just as it was in ancient times. The stories we previously noted of Jezebel and Haman illustrate the concept that sealed letters bore the "signature" of the king.

Back then, rather than signing your name as we are accustomed to do today, people placed their seal on a document or tablet, which was the same thing as signing their name. Remember what Revelation 14:1 tells us about God's people at the end of time? They have the "Father's name written on their foreheads." This is just another way of saying that they are "sealed," since the seal functioned as a person's signature. It is also true that the word "name" in the Bible often stands for "character." The sealed ones reflect God's character.

When we consider a signature in this context, we think of authorship, ownership, approval, and authority. The ones whom God seals at the end of time experience all of these. Paul mentioned that we are God's "epistle," or letter, "known and ready by all men; clearly you are an epistle of Christ, ministered by us, written not with ink but by the Spirit of the living God, not on tablets of stone, but on tablets of flesh, that is, of the heart" (2 Cor. 3:2, 3). God is writing His letter, His testimony, of how He can transform sinners into saints. When the letter is finished, He will sign His name.

It is God who composes the conversion story of every true Christian. He is the "author and finisher of our faith" (Heb. 12:2). It is His hand that inscribes on our hearts the principles of His kingdom.

When the writing is done, when the decision is made final, when the impressions of the Spirit have resulted in the likeness of Jesus, the image of the divine being impressed on the heart and mind, then God will sign His name.

The seal, like a signature, indicated ownership. When you have an object you treasure—a prized book for example—you write your name on it to let people know it belongs to you. God claims us as His own. But, someone might say, don't all people "belong to God." Yes, in a sense, we all do. We are all His by creation. Christ paid for the sins of everyone when He died on the cross (1 John 2:2). But not all choose to belong to God. It is only those who make a conscious decision to love, obey, and submit to Him that He will claim as His own when He comes in the sky.

They will have the insignia of God's ownership—His signature, His name—on their foreheads. In a special sense they belong to Him. "Those who are in the flesh cannot please God. But you are not in the flesh but in the Spirit, if indeed the Spirit of God dwells in you. Now if anyone does not have the Spirit of Christ, he is not His" (Rom. 8:8, 9). "Nevertheless the solid foundation of God stands, having this seal: 'The Lord knows those who are His,' and, 'Let everyone who names the name of Christ depart from iniquity'" (2 Tim. 2:19). Notice in the texts just quoted how Paul brings together the concepts of the Spirit removing sin from our lives, the seal of God, and our belonging to Him. "Then those who feared the Lord spoke to one another, and the Lord listened and heard them; so a book of remembrance was written before Him for those who fear the Lord and who meditate on His name. 'They shall be Mine,' says the Lord of hosts, 'on the day that I make them My jewels'" (Mal. 3:16, 17).

A seal not only indicates authorship and ownership but also approval. An artist who has finished a painting signs his or her name, indicating that "it is done," and has met with their approval. When Jesus returns in the clouds, He is going to point to the sealed ones still alive and declare, "Here is the patience of the saints; here are those who keep the commandments and have the faith of Jesus" (Rev. 14:12). They receive God's approval and will be modern-day Enochs, of whom it is written, "By faith Enoch was taken away so that he did not see death, 'and was not found because God had taken him'; for before he was taken he had this testimony, that he pleased God" (Heb. 11:5). Each will hear His words, "Well done."

In Christ's parable of the talents, on the day when accounts were audited those who had made proper use of what God had given them received His word of approbation. "His lord said to him, 'Well done, good and faithful servant; you were faithful over a few things, I will make you ruler over many things. Enter into the joy of your lord'" (Matt. 25:21). Some time ago it was pointed out to me that the word "done" in the Lord's commendation is supplied. Actually the sentence begins with one of the shorter Greek words, *eu,* which many times is attached as a prefix to words such as "eulogy" and "euphoria." One pastor translates this word *eu* as "Wow!" Wouldn't it be wonderful to hear our Creator-God express His approval over us? Could there be sweeter music than to hear His word of commendation? The seal of God expresses His approval. A popular magazine manifests its commendation on products by issuing a "seal of approval," and today the designation *"Good Housekeeping* seal of approval" has taken on a life of its own.

The seal also conveyed authority. Bearing the impress of the monarch's seal, all the backing of Ahab's throne stood behind the letters that Jezebel wrote concerning Naboth. All the power of Ahasuerus' kingdom bolstered the letter that Haman composed. To bear the seal indicated that something had authority and power. Likewise, the sealed ones will be conferred with divine authority as they, in God's name, proclaim the last message of warning to Planet Earth. With conviction and power, exceeding even the events of Acts 2, they will be embued with a competence that the world has never before witnessed, as they declare the messages of the three angels by divine strength.

Another lesson taught by the seal is that of preservation. To countermand the edict of the wicked Haman, another letter was authorized through the ministry of Queen Esther. The king told her and Mordecai, "You yourselves write a decree concerning the Jews, as you please, in the king's name, and seal it with the king's signet ring; for whatever is written in the king's name and sealed with the king's signet ring no one can revoke" (Esther 8:8). One of the primary features of the laws of the Medes and Persians is that once signed, once sealed, they could not be rescinded. This underscores the fact that the saints, once sealed (with the latter rain seal, as revealed in Revelation 7), are saved for eternity. Their destiny is sealed forever. They will not be contaminated by sin from that point onward, forever. It doesn't mean that things will be easy for them. Persecutions and martyrdoms will occur during this time period before the general close of probation. But their futures are safe with God forever.

One of my church members gave us some wonderful berry jam sealed in a glass jar. Why do you "seal" that jar of jam? It's to preserve the contents, isn't it? We even refer to what they contain as "preserves." It's to ensure that no change will take place—specifically that no impurity will get in or spoiling will occur. That's the purpose of the seal. Railroads seal their freight cars to indicate that "no change in transport" has happened. When God's people are sealed, likewise they will be preserved from the contamination of sin from that point forward. Though they may not know it, their probations have closed. They will be like Noah in the ark when "the Lord shut him in" prior to the falling of the rain (Gen. 7:16).

A second phase of protection will benefit the sealed ones following the general close of probation, the event that shuts the door of salvation for the world at large. During the seven last plagues of Revelation they will receive God's special safeguarding, as did Israel in Egypt's "seven last plagues." (Ten plagues struck Egypt, but after the first three, God sheltered Israel [Ex. 8:22]). After this point, no child of God will become a victim of martyrdom, as it would serve no evangelistic purpose. The blood of the saints will no longer be the seed of the gospel since all decisions have become finalized.

Psalm 91 will become fulfilled as "a thousand may fall at your side, and ten thousand at your right hand; but it shall not come near you. Only with your eyes shall you look, and see the reward of the wicked. Because you have made the Lord, who is my refuge, even the Most High, your dwelling place, no evil shall befall you, nor shall any plague come near your dwelling" (Ps. 91:7-10).

Psalm 124 will become precious to these sealed ones. "If it had not been the Lord who was on our side, when men rose up against us, then they would have swallowed us alive, when their wrath was kindled against us; then the waters would have overwhelmed us, the stream would have gone over our soul; then the swollen waters would have gone over our soul. Blessed be the Lord, who has not given us as a prey to their teeth. Our soul has escaped as a bird from the snare of the fowlers; the snare is broken, and we have escaped. Our help is in the name of the Lord, who made heaven and earth" (Ps. 124:2-8). Let your mind reflect on the familiar phase "signed, sealed, and delivered" as it pertains to God's seal.

Sociologists are fond of putting labels on different segments of society. They speak of "baby boomers" and "generation X." Those who live for and walk with God, who receive His seal and will be ultimately translated to heaven without seeing death, we could likewise identify. They will be "Generation Enoch." Like the patriarch who exemplified God's love to a world that was dying, those who live in this last generation will follow his pattern of life and his ultimate triumph. Pray to be among that group!

By way of review, the Bible issues its most solemn warning against receiving the mark of the beast. We have seen clearly that the beast mentioned is the first beast of Revelation 13, the historical Papacy. By the mouth of no less than seven witnesses, Scripture unveils the identity of the power that would "fall away" and corrupt biblical teaching and even have the audacity to attempt to change God's holy law, His Ten Commandments. But the Papacy is not embarrassed about what it has done in this area, but rather points to it and the honor given to Sunday as a day of worship, kept by nearly the entire Christian world, as the mark of its authority in ecclesiastical matters.

When the observance of Sunday as a holy day becomes a law, the "image of the beast" will have been established. At that time the issue will be crystal clear before the whole world. It will be understood that to bow to the Sunday image will be to reject God's sacred Decalogue, to accept the word of humanity instead of the Word of God.

When this issue has been made plain to every mind, at that time to turn one's back on God, His Word, His law, and His Sabbath and accept the day of worship erected by human authority will result in acquiring the mark of the beast. People can receive it in the hand by going along with it to escape the penalties accompanying the violation of the law, or it can be placed in the forehead, meaning that one erroneously believes that he or she is doing God's will. What did Jesus say to His followers? "The time is coming that whoever kills you will think that he offers God service" (John 16:2). God is fair and righteous to judge those who "sincerely believe" that they are doing right, because they did not "receive the love of the truth" but believed "the lie." Can you see how important it is not to be diverted by the idea that the mark of the beast is some sort of tattoo, bar code, computer tracking chip, or anything else of that kind? These concepts completely miss the issue of allegiance to God.

On the other hand, those who face the severe test of the image of the beast—those threatened with loss of property or life if they refuse to comply with the Sunday law and instead honor the day of God's appointment, His sacred Sabbath, the only day Scripture warrants as receiving His blessing—will receive the seal of God in their forehead, the seat of thinking and decision-making. The gospel promise will have been fulfilled for them, in that they have been transformed by the renewing of their minds. God's Spirit has written His law on their hearts and His name on their foreheads.

Their hearts were soft and pliable so that the impressions of His Spirit could form the likeness and image of Jesus in their lives. They are sealed. He acknowledges them as His own, the product of His authorship and the recipients of His authority to proclaim the three angels' messages with unprecedented power and conviction. Being sealed, they will be protected from the contamination of sin and, following the close of probation for the world at large, from death. Pray to be among those sealed by God! What a great privilege will be accorded those who stand firm for God's truth and His kingdom!

---

[1] See L. E. Froom, *Prophetic Faith of Our Fathers*, vol. 2, pp. 477, 478.
[2] *Catholic Record*, Sept. 21, 1923.

CHAPTER 21

THE "WRATH OF GOD" AND THE "CUP OF HIS INDIGNATION"

Then a third angel followed them, saying with a loud voice, 'If anyone worships the beast and his image, and receives his mark on his forehead or on his hand, he himself shall also drink of the wine of the wrath of God, which is poured out full strength into the cup of His indignation. He shall be tormented with fire and brimstone in the presence of the holy angels and in the presence of the Lamb" (Rev. 14:9, 10).

We see a contrast between the cup of the wine of the wrath of the beast (featured also in Revelation 17 and which symbolizes the penalty for violating the religious dogma enforced by the state) and the cup of God's wrath. Babylon will have its cup of wrath. It will cost something to stand up for God and disobey the law of the land. The choice will be between something that is visible and obvious (receiving temporal punishment for violating the law put forth by the beast) or seeing by the eye of faith the punishment that befalls one who rejects the law of the invisible God. Whichever side you choose to be on will involve "wrath."

Let's focus for a moment on the wrath of the beast. The beast will establish laws that contain penalties for those who disregard them, including economic boycott and a death decree (Rev. 13:15, 17). Revelation 13 relates latter-day Babylon's wrath against those who chose to reject its laws. Back in the days of King Nebuchadnezzar those who refused to bow to his "image" were told they would be cast into a burning furnace. Israelites Hananiah, Azariah, and Mishael, knowing that to worship the image of Nebuchadnezzar would be to violate God's holy law, stood boldly and defied the king's commandment.

"Then Nebuchadnezzar, in rage and fury, gave the command to bring" them forward (Dan. 3:13). His wrath grew even more intense when the king gave them another chance to bow to his image and they refused. At that time he "was full of fury, and the expression on his face changed" toward them (verse 19). God's people experienced the wrath poured out by Babylon. But the Lord honored their obedience by rescuing them in the flames.

Later Daniel faced a similar choice and similar wrath as his enemies plotted against him and manipulated King Darius to issue a decree prohibiting the free exercise of religion, on pain of being thrown into the lions' den. The Hebrew prophet defied the decree and as was his custom prayed toward Jerusalem three times a day, but by doing so he incurred the penalty attached to the law of the kingdom. God likewise spared the life of this saint, shutting the mouths of the lions (Dan. 6).

Notice that God didn't spare Daniel from the den, but in the den. The three Hebrews did not avoid the flames but were rescued from the flames. Israel wasn't escorted from Egypt before the plagues, but was protected during her seven last plagues. Only then did deliverance come. God's people will not be raptured away and be exempted from the last great trial, but will be preserved within the trial.

At the end of time every human being will have to decide whether to receive the wrath of the beast or the wrath of God. Everyone will experience one or the other. When the choice has to be made before the falling of the seven last plagues, one wrath will be seen by the visible eye, the other through the eye of faith. For the true Christian, the one who loves God supremely and would rather die than break the heart of the Father by committing sin, the decision will not be difficult. Like the three Hebrew worthies who refused to bow to the image, their answer will be, "We don't have to rethink this." Knowing where they stand, they will put their entire trust in the God of Abraham, Isaac, and Jacob.

What is the "wrath of God"? What is the "cup of His indignation"? How can we reconcile God's wrath with His character of love and benevolence? Will God really punish men and women? Isn't that contrary to His nature?

The modern world has no appetite to hear about God's justice. Many say, "Tell us about grace, mercy, forgiveness, but not of justice and retribution." If you read the whole Bible, however, you will see that both are components of the divine character. They cannot be separated. Read the second commandment if you have any doubts about that. There you find both love and justice, and it's weighted toward love. But it would be a foolish mistake to ignore the part of God's character that deals with sin. "For I, the Lord your God, am a jealous God, visiting the iniquity of the fathers on the children to the third and fourth generations of those who hate Me, but showing mercy to thousands, to those who love Me and keep My commandments" (Ex. 20:5, 6).

Sometimes when I take a walk I find myself on a street called Thunder Drive, and I let my mind reflect on its meaning. Interestingly, another street called Serenidad Place ("Serenity Place") intersects it. Thunder Drive meets Serenity Place. In the same way there is an aspect of God's character that deals with judgment and justice—Thunder Drive, if you please. But His character also is one of love and mercy—Serenity Place, if you can see it that way. The two intersect. Yes, God's character is one of love and benevolence. But to ignore the aspect of God that deals with judgment and justice would be a gross mistake.

Sin must be dealt with. It is the grit in the gears of all relationships. God's holy nature cannot coexist with sin. "You are of purer eyes than to behold evil, and cannot look on wickedness" (Hab. 1:13). His nature is as a consuming fire, the Bible says in Hebrews 12:29. That leaves us with a choice. We can either allow Him to consume sin within our lives and be cleansed from it, or we can cling to evil and be consumed in our lives of sin. Either way, God must destroy sin. No, I am not Jonathan Edwards, and this study is not "Sinners in the Hands of an Angry God." Jesus wants to cleanse us, purify us of all sin so that we can enter the joy of the Lord and be free from the entanglements of iniquity.

It is absolutely true that our God is a Deity of love. The way that the Bible expresses it is emphatic. Scripture frequently reminds us that "God loves." One of the most familiar is: "For God so loved the world that He gave His only begotten Son, that whoever believes in

Him should not perish but have everlasting life" (John 3:16). But it goes beyond this. Love is not merely an act that God performs. Nor is it something that He merely does. Not only does "God love," but "God *is* love" (1 John 4:8). He is the very essence and epitome of agape love.

At the same time He values freedom of choice supremely. He could have designed us as robots, but instead He conferred on His subjects the opportunity to evaluate and choose. Thus He created us as free moral agents. Because God refuses to force anyone, He allows us to make up our own minds. The universe can exist in harmony in only one way, and that is by adhering to the principle of selfless love, a conclusion made undeniably clear by our world's sad history. As a result, God must take radical and severe action in order to preserve the equanimity and safety of the universe. He must deal with sin.

The Lord gives the power to choose to everyone, just as He did to Adam and Eve in the garden. But ultimately, only upon those who subscribe to the principle of agape love and allow that principle to be written in their hearts, will He confer the gift of eternal life. Sin produces nothing but misery, and God will not force sinners to live out an eternity of misery. It is in mercy to the sinner that life is temporary. Neither the universe as a whole nor individual sinners would benefit from their miserable lives being perpetuated forever. In mercy and love unparalleled, God has given to humanity a second opportunity—no, a million and more opportunities—to choose His way. But there are limits even to divine mercy. God cannot allow sin to continue without end.

The act of destruction is foreign to the heart of the Life-giver. Because it goes against His nature, it is His "unusual act" (Isa. 28:21). But like a surgeon, God must excise the cancer of iniquity for the safety of the universe. We can allow that surgery to take place in our hearts right now, and He will remove sin from us, or if we cling to sin, we will suffer the consequences of our choice as He will forever remove sin and sinners from the universe.

God's "wrath" is not like human anger. When we become angry, our faces turn red and the hair on our necks stands on end. Our voices become tense and high pitched. We tend to set reason aside and let our emotions have command. But that is not what God's "anger" is like. The Bible presents to us a clear picture of His wrath. It is when God, who prizes freedom of choice, in sadness and after exercising divine forbearance to the limit, allows His rebellious creatures to reap the consequences of his or her own decision, though it result in pain and death. The seeds of death are in sin itself. If the creature will not relinquish sin, the natural consequence of that decision is annihilation. God's "wrath" is His allowing the sinner to reap what he has sown (Gal. 6:7, 8).

Paul reports that the "wrath of God is revealed from heaven against all ungodliness and unrighteousness of men" (Rom. 1:18). Notice the present tense of the verb in this passage. The wrath of God "is revealed." It is an ongoing process, in which God withdraws from those who reject Him and leaves them to their fate. We must point out, however, that this "wrath" is of less intensity than will be measured out on that final day, when it is poured out in full strength. So far, God has mingled with mercy the cup of His indignation, but that will change in the future. The seven last plagues will be an exhibition of God's wrath, and the second death—eternal separation from God—will write the final chapter in this regrettable account of God giving up the lost sinner.

Paul had still more to say in Romans 1 about those who rejected God and chose their own way, worshipping the works of their own hands. Notice, incidentally, how he phrases it as exchanging "the truth" for "the lie," something we discussed previously. Notice the thrice-repeated expression that "God gave them up," or "God gave them over." (The phrases are all translated from the same Greek verb *paradidomi*, "to deliver" or "to give over.")

The apostle declares, "For since the creation of the world His invisible attributes are clearly seen, being understood by the things that are made, even His eternal power and Godhead, so that they are without excuse, because, although they knew God, they did not glorify Him as God, nor were thankful, but became futile in their thoughts, and their foolish hearts were darkened. Professing to be wise, they became fools, and changed the glory of the incorruptible God into an image made like corruptible man—and birds and four-footed beasts and creeping things. Therefore God also *gave them up* to uncleanness, in the lusts of their hearts, to dishonor their bodies among themselves, who exchanged the truth of God for the lie, and worshiped and served the creature rather than the Creator, who is blessed forever. Amen. For this reason God *gave them up* to vile passions. . . . And even as they did not like to retain God in their knowledge, God *gave them over* to a debased mind, to do those things which are not fitting" (Rom. 1:20-28).

The Scriptures are saturated with examples of how God struggled to reach the point of letting an unrepentant sinner go. "How can I give you up, Ephraim? How can I hand you over, Israel? . . . My heart churns within Me; My sympathy is stirred" (Hosea 11:8). Yet, if ignored too long, God will reluctantly leave the sinner to his or her fate. When we push God away, we relinquish His protecting presence, and we find ourselves left to fend off the enemy in our own strength. Satan, whose powers greatly exceed ours, is only too happy to harass, deceive, and destroy when this happens. We find an instructive illustration of this in God's relationship with His people in the past.

The poignant story of Hosea's love for an unfaithful wife mirrored the conduct of Israel toward their Husband. For this reason He was forced to let them go. "My people are destroyed for lack of knowledge. Because you have rejected knowledge, I also will reject you from being priest for Me; because you have forgotten the law of your God, I also will forget your children" (Hosea 4:6). "Ephraim is joined to idols, let him alone" (verse 17). "With their flocks and herds they shall go to seek the Lord, but they will not find Him; He has withdrawn Himself from them. They have dealt treacherously with the Lord, for they have begotten pagan children" (Hosea 5:6, 7). "I will pour out My wrath on them like water. Ephraim is oppressed and broken in judgment, because he willingly walked by human precept" (verses 10, 11). "Yes, woe to them when I depart from them!" (Hosea 9:12). "My God will cast them away, because they did not obey Him; and they shall be wanderers among the nations" (verse 17). Think of how relevant that one verse is, as applied to apocalyptic Babylon: "Ephraim is oppressed and broken in judgment, because he willingly walked by human precept." For this, God will have to let Babylon go.

Speaking of Jerusalem when God stepped back and allowed Nebuchadnezzar to attack it, the prophet Ezekiel observed: "She revealed her harlotry and uncovered her nakedness. Then I alienated Myself from her, as I had alienated Myself from her sister" (Eze. 23:18). The "sister," of course, was the northern nation of Israel, which fell to the Assyrians in 722 B.C. "People will call them rejected silver, because the Lord has rejected them" (Jer. 6:30). " 'Cut off your hair and cast it away, and take up a lamentation on the desolate heights; for the Lord has rejected and forsaken the generation of His wrath' " (Jer. 7:29). "I will hand them over to trouble, to all kingdoms of the earth, because of Manasseh the son of Hezekiah, king of Judah, for what he did in Jerusalem" (Jer. 15:4). "I will give up Zedekiah the king of Judah, his princes, the residue of Jerusalem who remain in this land, and those who dwell in the land of Egypt. I will deliver them to trouble into all the kingdoms of the earth" (Jer. 24:8, 9). God exhibited His wrath when, after the persistent disobedience of His people, He withdrew and allowed them to reap the consequences of their choices.

Scripture has much to say on this topic. Second Kings 17:5-18 explains why God allowed Israel to be attacked and concludes, "Therefore the Lord was very angry with Israel, and removed them from His sight" (2 Kings 17:18). The chronicle of Judah's subsequent fall appears a few chapters later. "I will forsake the remnant of My inheritance and deliver them into the hand of their enemies; and they shall become victims of plunder to all their enemies, because they have done evil in My sight, and have provoked Me to anger since the day their fathers came out of Egypt, even to this day" (2 Kings 21:14, 15). "Because of the anger of the Lord this happened in Jerusalem and Judah, that He finally cast them out from His presence" (2 Kings 24:20).[1]

Listen to the plea of the prophet during the apostasy of Joash. "Therefore they left the house of the Lord God of their fathers, and served wooden images and idols; and wrath came upon Judah and Jerusalem because of their trespass. Yet He sent prophets to them, to bring them back to the Lord; and they testified against them, but they would not listen. Then the Spirit of God came upon Zechariah the son of Jehoida the priest, who stood above the people, and said to them, 'Thus says God: "Why do you transgress the commandments of the Lord, so that you cannot prosper? Because you have forsaken the

Lord, He also has forsaken you"'" (2 Chron. 24:18-20). For his faithful ministry, Zechariah was stoned.

The record is clear. Because of their disobedience, God removed His protection from the people called by His name, and permitted the ancient Babylonians to attack. Shortly beforehand, in words impossible to misunderstand, the prophet Azariah had said to King Asa, "Hear me, Asa, and all Judah and Benjamin. The Lord is with you while you are with Him. If you seek Him, He will be found by you; but if you forsake Him, He will forsake you" (2 Chron. 15:2). The events of our world are complex and should not be over simplified, as the book of Job illustrates. But at the same time, the cause-and-effect relationship between our clinging to God and receiving His blessing, or of our shoving Him away and forfeiting it, so clearly enunciated in Scripture, often gets overlooked or deemphasized. It is a general principle revealed by God's Word that if we push God away, we relinquish His blessing and His protection. That process constitutes His "wrath."

The introduction to Daniel's book declares: "And the Lord gave Jehoiakim king of Judah into his hand" (Dan. 1:2). Could God have protected the people of Judah? Absolutely! We have the record of how one angel slew 185,000 Assyrian troops as they were about to assault Jerusalem back in King Hezekiah's reign (2 Kings 19:35). Could God have defended His city when Babylon advanced against her? Without question He could have fulfilled the promise, "He shall cover you with His feathers, and under His wings you shall take refuge" (Ps. 91:4).

With the words of that beautiful psalm in mind, notice what Jesus said as He spoke to this critical issue of the withdrawal of divine protection. "O Jerusalem, Jerusalem, the one who kills the prophets and stones those who are sent to her! How often I wanted to gather your children together, as a hen gathers her chicks under her wings, but you were not willing! See! Your house is left to you desolate" (Matt. 23:37, 38). This same principle of the removal of God's gracious hand of protection again manifested itself as the Jerusalem of the first century, having pushed God away and having crucified His Son Jesus, reaped the consequences of their choice in the assaults of the marauding armies of Titus the Roman four decades after Jesus' death.

"My people would not heed My voice, and Israel would have none of Me. So I gave them over to their own stubborn heart, to walk in their own counsels. Oh, that My people would listen to Me, that Israel would walk in My ways! I would soon subdue their enemies, and turn My hand against their adversaries" (Ps. 81:11-14). One would have to be blind to read Scripture and not see the concept of a loving God pleading with the people to whom He had given freedom to choose, then stepping back and withdrawing His presence after exercising "second-mile" forbearance. This is what the Bible presents as God's wrath.

Jesus characterized lost sinners as weeping and gnashing their teeth on that last day (Luke 13:28). They knew that there was a loving and eternal God who provided salvation and life, yet they turned Him down. The feeling of abandonment and rejection felt by the one who has refused God's grace will be immeasurable! His wrath will be poured out in the final destruction of the lost as He lets them go into eternal oblivion. What a sad, tragic, and unnecessary event! Remember, God prepared hell for the devil and his angels (Matt. 25:41). He never intended that one single human being should be destroyed in it. Did not Christ pay for the sins of all humanity when He died on the cross? Yet, honoring the choices of His creatures, those who refuse Him will be cast into the lake of fire.

The "wrath of God" is contained in the "cup of His indignation." The Bible has much to say about the imagery of "cup." Let us see how Scripture uses it in a symbolic sense. "Upon the wicked He will rain coals; fire and brimstone and a burning wind shall be the portion of their cup" (Ps. 11:6). "For in the hand of the Lord there is a cup, and the wine is red; it is fully mixed, and He pours it out; surely its dregs shall all the wicked of the earth drain and drink down" (Ps. 75:8). The "cup," figuratively speaking, holds God's judgments.

Because of Judah's sins, the Lord would remove His protection and allow them to go into captivity. "Awake, awake! Stand up, O Jerusalem, you who have drunk at the hand of the Lord the cup of His fury; you have drunk the dregs of the cup of trembling and drained it out" (Isa. 51:17). God would dispense the same cup of judgment to other rebellious nations as well as Judah. "For thus says the Lord God of Israel to me: 'Take this wine cup of fury from My hand, and cause all the nations, to whom I send you, to drink it. And they will drink and stagger and go mad because of the sword that I will send among them.' Then I took the cup from the Lord's hand, and made all the nations drink, to whom the Lord had sent me" (Jer. 25:15-17).[2] The cup symbolizes the concepts of punishment, judgment, guilt, sorrow, and woe.

In addition, the cup represents an ordeal, an unpleasant experience. Said Jesus to the mother of Zebedee's sons, who had asked that James and John receive places of honor in the new kingdom, "You do not know what you ask. Are you able to drink the cup that I am about to drink, and be baptized with the baptism that I am baptized with?" (Matt. 20:22). While in Gethsemane, Jesus prayed that He might be spared from drinking that cup, but closed His prayer by saying, "Your will be done" (Matt. 26:42). To provide salvation, He must go through the ordeal; He must drink from the cup of guilt and sin. And He did, because He loves us so much. He volunteered to drink the cup of woe on our behalf so that we wouldn't have to.

The Bible speaks of the "cup of His indignation." The word "indignation" deserves a moment of attention, as it seems to have special relevance to the outpouring of God's judgments that culminate in the seven last plagues. The Lord set forth the principles of His kingdom within the relationships that He sustained with the nations of the past, including Israel and Judah when they suffered the assaults of Assyria and Babylon. They experienced in a limited way the "day of the Lord" as God removed His protective hand and allowed the enemy to conquer. Thus we find that His dealings with the kingdoms back then were a type, an illustration—though it might have been a partial one—of His dealing with the whole world as the story of Planet Earth reaches its climactic end at the return of Christ.

In this sense God poured His "indignation" upon the empires of ancient times. They experienced, in a limited way, the "Day of the Lord." The biblical accounts serve as examples of what will take place at the close of earth's history, when the ultimate "Day of the Lord" comes to pass.

Before the children of Israel entered Canaan, Moses laid out clearly to them the consequences of rebelling against the Lord and bowing before false gods. "Then the anger of the Lord was aroused against this land, to bring on it every curse that is written in this book. And the Lord uprooted them from their land in anger, in wrath, and in great indignation, and cast them into another land" (Deut. 29:27, 28).

In one of his "imprecatory psalms," David prayed, "Pour out Your indignation upon them, and let Your wrathful anger take hold of them" (Ps. 69:24). Notice how another psalm employs the word "indignation" in connection with the 10 plagues that fell on Egypt, an obvious type of the seven last plagues. The poet Asaph wrote, "He cast on them [inhabitants of Egypt] the fierceness of His anger, wrath, indignation, and trouble, by sending angels of destruction among them. He made a path for His anger; He did not spare their soul from death, but gave their life over to the plague, and destroyed all the firstborn in Egypt" (Ps. 78:49-51).

In reading the following passages, keep in mind how Revelation describes the circumstances that accompany Christ's return, including the assault of great hailstones and the violent earthquakes. They are the "weapons of His armory" that He will wield at the Second Coming. "The Lord will cause His glorious voice to be heard, and show the descent of His arm, with the indignation of His anger and the flame of a devouring fire, with scattering, tempest, and hailstones" (Isa. 30:30). "For the indignation of the Lord is against all nations, and His fury against all their armies" (Isa. 34:2). "The Lord is the true God; He is the living God and the everlasting King. At His wrath the earth will tremble, and the nations will not be able to endure His indignation" (Jer. 10:10). "The Lord has opened His armory, and has brought out the weapons of His indignation" (Jer. 50:25). "Who can stand before His indignation? And who can endure the fierceness of His anger? His fury is poured out like fire, and the rocks are thrown down by Him. The Lord is good, a stronghold in the day of trouble" (Nahum 1:6, 7).

Yet, the Lord speaks kindly to His people so that they may trust in Him during the tempest of the plagues, when the cup of His fury is poured out. "For yet a very little while and the indignation will cease, as will My anger in their destruction" (Isa. 10:25). May we be sheltered in Christ when that day arrives! May we experience what God spoke of when He said, "Come, My people, enter your chambers, and shut your doors behind you; hide yourself, as it were, for a little moment, until the indignation is past. For behold, the Lord comes out of His place to punish the inhabitants of the earth for their iniquity; the earth will also disclose her blood, and will no more cover her slain" (Isa. 26:20, 21).[3]

The book of Revelation tells us that Babylon will indeed drink of the "cup" someday. "Render to her just as she rendered to you, and repay her double according to her works; in the cup which she has mixed, mix double for her" (Rev. 18:6). "Now the great city was divided into three parts, and the cities of the nations fell. And great Babylon was remembered before God, to give her the cup of the wine of the fierceness of His wrath" (Rev. 16:19).

To review briefly: what does it mean when it says that those who receive the mark of the beast will drink of the wine of the wrath of God poured out full strength into the cup of His indignation? These solemn words affirm a universe of accountability and responsibility. God has given to all freedom to choose and will force no one. But if anyone determines to reject God no matter what, He will remove His protecting grace, and, unsheltered, such individuals will reap the consequences of their choice. By separating themselves from the Source of life, the inevitable result will be death.

Today we see the "wrath of God" revealed in a limited way as He withdraws and allows unrepentant sinners to receive the consequences of their choices. But today mercy still mixes with such judgment. Human beings do not feel the full measure of their guilt today, for if they did, they would be crushed to death by its weight. In mercy, God allows our consciences to provoke us when we stray from the path of righteousness, to convict us of our sins. But we do not yet experience the full strength of what guilt really involves.

However, if a person persists in the path of perversity, there will come a day that God will step aside and leave that individual to be on his own, a subject of Satan's cruel and despotic domination. More than that, during the falling of the seven last plagues, he or she will not receive the protection afforded to those who have put their trust in God and obeyed His commandments. Instead, they will experience God's wrath as His indignation is poured out. Finally at the last judgment, they will be let go into eternal oblivion. They will be cut off, removed from God's presence, and destroyed by the second death forever and ever. No one would wish to drink of that cup! How important to make sure of our salvation and follow the clear teachings of God's sacred Word!

Revelation 14 contains strong and stern language. Some might wonder if we can possibly reconcile them with the God of love that Scripture portrays. Is it possible to see God's love in the teaching of His wrath? Yes! The Bible's revelation of God's character demonstrates that although He is sovereign of the universe, He allows each person to choose for themselves. That is love. Though He knows what is best, He never forces. That is love. Anyone determined to cling to sin would find the purity and holiness of heaven to be intolerable. God will not compel those who love sin to endure the agony they would feel in God's righteous kingdom. That is love. Though we have sinned and deserve the just punishment of death—yes, the full measure of God's wrath—He came here Himself to take upon Himself our punishment so that we could live. He accepted the curse that we deserved and gave us the life that He deserves. That also is love. Is this not the plain teaching of Scripture?

This mysterious cup containing the wine of the wrath of God was held in the hand of our Savior that Thursday evening in Gethsemane. It was undiluted—full measure, unmixed with mercy. His human nature recoiled from feeling the consciousness of guilt and sin. Jesus didn't just bear a physical cross to Golgotha—it was the burden of our guilt, our sins. "Surely He has borne our griefs and carried our sorrows" (Isa. 53:4). The purity of His divine nature recoiled from the malignity of the iniquity being placed on His untainted shoulders as He, "who knew no sin [was made] to be sin for us, that we might become the righteousness of God in Him" (2 Cor. 5:21). In His human nature He sought relief from the sense of His Father's rejection. Yet He still drank the cup of sorrow and drained it to the bottom.

Behold the spotless Son of God fallen prostrate on Gethsemane's floor exclaiming, "My soul is exceedingly sorrowful, even to death" (Matt. 26:38). Then with anguish we'll never comprehend He cried out, "O My Father, if it is possible, let this cup pass from Me; nevertheless, not as I will, but as You will" (verse 39). The amazing truth is that

Jesus drank the cup of God's wrath in our behalf. He felt the woe and dejection that the lost sinner will experience on that last day. On the cross, weighed by the sins of the whole world, feeling the rejection of God to the fullest measure, He cried out, " 'Eli, Eli, lama sabachthani?' that is, 'My God, My God, why have You forsaken Me?' " (Matt. 27:46).

Paul affirmed the beauty of this truth when he wrote, "He who did not spare His own Son, but delivered Him up for us all, how shall He not with Him also freely give us all things?" (Rom. 8:32). The verb "delivered up" is the same Greek word *(paradidomi)* that Paul used earlier in this same letter to describe God's wrath in giving up lost sinners.

The amazing truth is that Jesus took every curse mentioned in Eden's indictment upon Himself as our Savior and sin-bearer. He sweat drops of blood to fashion the bread of life (cf. Gen. 3:19). He experienced pain in giving birth to salvation (cf. verse 16). He wore as a crown the thorns of the curse (cf. verse 18), becoming by imputation the "King of sinners." He drank the cup of woe, and gave to us the "cup of blessing" of which we partake in the Lord's Supper, a reminder of His great sacrifice (1 Cor. 10:16; 11:23-26). He drank the cup of wrath but gave to us the "cup of salvation" (Ps. 116:13). Yes, even in a study of God's wrath, His love shines through.

Some time ago I did some shopping at Costco. When I came up to the cash register, I pulled from my wallet a card that said "American Express" on it. Actually, it said more than that. It bore the words "American Express Prepaid Gift Card." My church family had given it as a birthday present.

But let's say, just for sake of illustration, that, thinking that I am using my American Express credit card, I pull this one out, not realizing exactly what it is. When the cashier rings up the final purchase, I swipe the card and insist on paying for my purchases. The cashier tries to explain that I don't have to pay for them. The credit on the card has already been applied, and the items are "free" to me since it's a prepaid gift card. Suppose that I continue to insist that I must pay. After all, you should pay for your groceries when you go to Costco.

She tries again to explain to me that because of the credit on this special card I don't owe anything. It's been paid for already and the credit is "on deposit." By now the people behind me have strange expressions on their faces as they shift their weight from one foot to the other. Totally frustrated, I refuse to believe what she has said. Leaving my basket there with all its contents, I walk out with my mind spinning.

Let me ask you a question. Do you think that what I've just told you would happen in real life? Would anyone in the entire world do what I've just described in this hypothetical situation? And yet Jesus has given us something more valuable, more lasting than anything you buy at Costco. That day I went shopping I bought, among other things, salad and bananas. They're long gone. What Jesus has given us will last for eternity! Yet how many people don't value the Gift! How many refuse to believe it's genuine. How many are standing figuratively at the cashier's counter arguing whether it's really true that the Gift means they don't have to hand over any money. How many are trying somehow to render compensation for their sins when they've already been taken care of. How many don't realize that Jesus drank the cup for us, and that if we believe and follow Him, we won't have to.

---

[1] See also Num. 32:15; Neh. 13:17, 18; 1 Kings 14:16; 2 Chron. 12:5, 12; 30:7-9; 34:24, 25; Eze. 16:27; 20:25.

[2] See also Jer. 49:12; Lam. 4:21; Eze. 23:31.

[3] See also Isa. 30:27; Eze. 21:31; 22:31; Zeph. 3:8.

CHAPTER 22

"THE SMOKE OF THEIR TORMENT ASCENDS FOREVER"

We turn our attention to what the third angel said further to John. "He [the one who receives the mark of the beast] shall be tormented with fire and brimstone in the presence of the holy angels and in the presence of the Lamb. And the smoke of their torment ascends forever and ever; and they have no rest day or night, who worship the beast and his image, and whoever receives the mark of his name" (Rev. 14:10, 11). How do we understand such words in the light of God's character of love?

Some have taken the passage to mean that the lost will burn in a never-ending fire. Many believe that God will perform a miracle of preservation like He did with the burning bush that caught Moses' attention as it burned but was not consumed (Ex. 3:2). The wicked will burn as "sinners in the hands of an angry God," as Puritan pastor Jonathan Edwards preached on July 8, 1741. Is this what the Bible teaches? How do you reconcile Revelation 14:10, 11 with other passages that teach that the wicked will suffer the second death and will be no more? Many have turned away from a God pictured in this light. They have rejected the Bible on the basis that a God who punishes forever for the sins of a lifetime cannot be loved and appreciated. As a result, Satan, the deceiver from the beginning, has won a victory. He has superimposed his character of cruelty on the portrait of a loving God.

Let's start by noting that we must distinguish between eternal punishment and eternal punishing. Do you see the difference between the two terms and the concepts they convey? The first speaks to a confined and limited event, of which the effects are eternal, while the second embraces the idea of a never-ending process. Which term does the Bible use? "Then He will also say to those on the left hand, 'Depart from Me, you cursed, into the everlasting fire prepared for the devil and his angels . . .' And these will go away into everlasting punishment, but the righteous into eternal life" (Matt. 25:41-46). The effect of the act of punishment will last eternally, not the process itself. There's a huge difference.

Are we not encouraged to "rightly [divide] the word of truth" (2 Tim. 2:15)? Are we not warned that it is possible to "twist the Scriptures, to [our] own destruction" (2 Peter 3:16)? We must not fall into the trap of Job's friend Eliphaz. The Lord reproved him when He said, "My wrath is aroused against you and your two friends, for you have not spoken of Me what is right" (Job 42:7). To "charge God falsely" with the crime of torturing sinners in a never-ending hell is a serious matter!

How shall we understand the words and phrases we find in Scripture concerning God's dealing with the lost? Fortunately, by comparing Scripture with Scripture we can come to an understanding that weds the portrait of God's love and mercy with the picture of His justice and retribution. In God's Book "Thunder Drive" does indeed intersect "Serenity Place." "Mercy and truth have met together; righteousness and peace have kissed" (Ps. 85:10). If read carefully and responsibly, the Bible presents a harmonious and consistent whole.

For one thing, we can see that the word "ever" and "forever" in the languages of the Bible don't have the precise meanings that our modern words do. The word in the Old Testament *olam* means "as long as it lasts." Hannah lent her son Samuel to the Lord "forever" (1 Sam. 1:22), then explained, "as long as he lives he shall be lent to the Lord" (verse 28). Jonah said that he was in the belly of the great fish "forever" (Jonah 2:6), which Scripture documents as "three days and three nights" (Jonah 1:17).

The New Testament word is *aion,* from which we get our word "eon," which means "age."* How long is that? What exactly is an "eon"? It depends on the context. We speak of the "atomic age" or the "computer age." These terms are not necessarily meant to be definite periods of time. So when we read of the punishment of the wicked we need to bear in mind the differences between our word "forever" and the Hebrew *olam* or the Greek *aion*.

Let's look at some of these terms and see how Scripture employs them. The Bible speaks of "everlasting burnings" (Isa. 33:14). Are we to understand from this that the fires of hell will be stoked throughout the ceaseless ages of eternity? No. We find clear indication as to what "eternal fire" means from passages that appear elsewhere. "As Sodom and Gomorrah, and the cities around them in a similar manner to these, having given themselves over to sexual immorality and gone after strange flesh, are set forth as an example, suffering the vengeance of eternal fire" (Jude 7).

Do you want to know what "eternal fire" is? Study the history of these cities. They are "set forth as an example" for this purpose. None should be misled as to what God is saying. Did Sodom and Gomorrah suffer the fires of divine judgment? Absolutely. Are they burning today? No. However, even though flames are not rising today from these reprobate cities, the effects of that destruction were "forever." This is what the Bible is telling us will happen when the wicked are destroyed. It will be a forever destruction, not a forever destroying.

The Bible speaks of "unquenchable fire" (Matt. 3:12). What does it mean? Notice the warning the prophet Jeremiah gave to Jerusalem: "But if you will not heed Me to hallow the Sabbath day, such as not carrying a burden when entering the gates of Jerusalem on the Sabbath day, then I will kindle a fire in its gates, and it shall devour the palaces of Jerusalem, and it shall not be quenched" (Jer. 17:27). The city faced unquenchable fire if its people did not follow the Lord.

Did it happen? Yes. Concerning the destruction brought by King Nebuchadnezzar in 586 B.C. we read: "He burned the house of the Lord and the king's house; all the houses of Jerusalem, that is, all the houses of the great, he burned with fire" (2 Kings 25:9). Notice how the author of Chronicles connects the dots for us and makes it clear that the destruction fulfilled Jeremiah's prophecy. "Then they burned the house of God, broke down the wall of Jerusalem, burned all its palaces with fire, and destroyed all its precious possessions. And those who escaped from the sword he carried away to Babylon, where they became servants to him and his sons until the rule of the kingdom of Persia, to fulfill the word of the Lord by the mouth of Jeremiah" (2 Chron. 36:19, 20). Penned the prophet Jeremiah: "The Lord has given full vent to his wrath; he has poured out his fierce anger. He kindled a fire in Zion, and it has consumed her foundations" (Lam. 4:11, NIV).

So Jerusalem felt the flame of "unquenchable fire." The prophecy was fulfilled, but is the city still burning today? No, the "unquenchable" flames eventually died out. What we must conclude, then, is that "unquenchable fire" means that it can't be stopped while it's burning, but when it has finished its job, it will cease. We've had some fires in southern California in the past few years that were literally unquenchable. Skilled and trained firefighters could do little but watch as the flames leaped across 12 lanes of the Interstate 15 freeway on their destructive journey. But those fires, thankfully, eventually went out. So too will the "unquenchable fire" that devours the wicked.

What about the matter of "the smoke of their torment ascending forever and ever"? Keep in mind that the book of Revelation draws heavily on the stories and accounts of the past in describing what God has in store for the future. That's His preferred method of teaching us. This particular phraseology derives from the Old Testament prophecy concerning the Edomites, the descendants of Esau, Jacob's brother. Edom rejoiced in the afflictions of their "brother" nation when Babylon attacked it. It looted Judah's possessions, cut off its escape routes, and delivered to Nebuchadnezzar any who attempted to flee (see Obadiah 10-14).

Unhappy with Edom, God predicted its fall. "For My sword shall be bathed in heaven; indeed it shall come down on Edom. . . . For the Lord has a sacrifice in Bozrah, and a great slaughter in the land of Edom. . . . For it is the day of the Lord's vengeance, the year of recompense for the cause of Zion. Its streams shall be turned into pitch, and its dust into brimstone; its land shall become burning pitch. It shall not be quenched night or day; its smoke shall ascend forever" (Isa. 34:5-10).

Did that happen? Yes, it did. Is Edom still burning? No. Notice not only that the passage also includes not only the thought that Edom would experience fire that could not be quenched, but also something of special interest as we read Revelation 14. Does the fact that the fires of Edom would not be quenched "night or day" mean that they would last forever? No. Keep that thought in mind as you ponder the expression in Revelation 14:11: "The smoke of their torment ascends forever and ever; and they have no rest day or night, who worship the beast and his image, and whoever receives the mark of his name."

When the fires burn, there will be no rest, no escape from them. But the description does not require us to believe that such fire will continue throughout eternity. The biblical examples portray a fire unstoppable and inescapable while in the process of actually burning. The flames that annihilate the wicked cannot be stopped as long as they burn, and the lost will have no rest "day or night" while the destroying fires do their work. But the fire that consumes the wicked will be as the one that destroyed Edom. Even though the fires could "not be quenched night or day," Edom no longer burns today. We see then that as in the case of Edom the phrase "its smoke shall ascend forever" does not in any way indicate a continuous never-ending torment. The biblical example clearly means that the effect of the destruction is eternal.

Other prophets draw on the figure of speech of rising smoke to depict the final punishment of the lost. "Therefore they shall be like the morning cloud and like the early dew that passes away, like chaff blown off from a threshing floor and like smoke from a chimney" (Hosea 13:3). "Do not fret because of evildoers, nor be envious of the workers of iniquity. For they shall soon be cut down like the grass, and wither as the green herb" (Ps. 37:1, 2). "The wicked shall perish; and the enemies of the Lord, like the splendor of the meadows, shall vanish. Into smoke they shall vanish away" (verse 20). In the poetic lament concerning the fall of apocalyptic Babylon we read, "The kings of the earth who committed fornication and lived luxuriously with her will weep and lament for her, when they see the smoke of her burning" (Rev. 18:9). Such expressions seek to depict a complete and thorough destruction.

When it speaks about the destruction of the wicked, Scripture uses such emphatic verbs as "consume," "devour," and "burn up" to convey the idea of total destruction (see Isa. 33:14; Dan. 2:44; Zeph.

1:2, 3; Mal. 4:1; Rev. 20:9). It's a picture of total annihilation. When you "devour" what's on your dinner plate, there's nothing left. The wicked, including the author of sin himself, will "be no more" (Ps. 37:10, 36; Eze. 28:19). "May sinners be consumed from the earth, and the wicked be no more" (Ps. 104:35). "The wicked are overthrown and are no more" (Prov. 12:7). "They shall be as though they had never been" (Obadiah 16). "They will be consumed like dry stubble" (Nahum 1:10, NIV). The language couldn't be clearer.

Figuratively speaking, the wicked will be "ashes under the feet" of the saints. "'For behold, the day is coming, burning like an oven, and all the proud, yes, all who do wickedly will be stubble. And the day which is coming shall burn them up,' says the Lord of hosts, 'that will leave them neither root nor branch. But to you who fear My name the Sun of Righteousness shall arise with healing in His wings; and you shall go out and grow fat like stall-fed calves. You shall trample the wicked, for they shall be ashes under the soles of your feet on the day that I do this,' says the Lord of hosts" (Mal. 4:1-3).

Let's include in our analysis some other considerations from the Bible that bear on the question of the fate of the wicked. Notice the strong contrast contained within these two familiar texts. "For the wages of sin is death, but the gift of God is eternal life in Christ Jesus our Lord" (Rom. 6:23). "For God so loved the world that He gave His only begotten Son, that whoever believes in Him should not perish but have everlasting life" (John 3:16).

If it were really true that God burned sinners in a never-ending hell, then the texts need serious revision. The text in Romans should read, "The wages of sin is eternal life in hell, but the gift of God is eternal life in Christ Jesus our Lord." Is that what it says? No! The conjunction "but" clearly indicates the contrast between the words "death" and "life." By this same reasoning John's passage should state: "Whoever believes in Him should not live in hell forever, but have everlasting life." Again, is that what Scripture is trying to tell us? Is that consistent with the rest of biblical teaching on the subject? Isn't it simpler just to read it the way that it says?

We must also consider the matter of the geographical impossibility of a never-ending hell. It isn't something that takes place in some ill-defined nether region, and it's not going on now. The wicked are reserved for the day of judgment (2 Peter 2:9). The Bible tells us that "hell" will take place right on the surface of Planet Earth. "They [the wicked] went upon the breadth [or surface] of the earth and surrounded the camp of the saints and the beloved city. And fire came down from God out of heaven and devoured them" (Rev. 20:9). The destruction that "devours" the wicked is an event that happens on, not beneath, the earth.

Furthermore, remember that Jesus promised that the "meek shall inherit the earth" (Matt. 5:5). Reading Revelation 20 and 21, we find that following the period of 1,000 years God brings the Holy City, the New Jerusalem, the city that He has prepared for those who love Him, down to our earth. The wicked, who have been dead during the 1,000-year period, are brought back to life and are seduced by their leader, Satan, to attack the New Jerusalem (Rev. 20). It appears to them that they outnumber those within the walls of God's city. In one last and final demonstration of their terminal disease of wickedness they mount an assault against the camp of the saints. All this takes place on the soil of our planet. It is at this point that God sends fire from heaven that "devoured them" (Rev. 20:9).

Following this, according to His promise, He will make a "new heaven and a new earth" (Rev. 21). He will cleanse our planet and wherever sin has polluted our solar system and then re-create this earth in the beauty it enjoyed before the Fall. Earth will be the permanent abode of the saints. Then will come to pass Jesus' promise, a quotation from Psalm 37:11: "The meek shall inherit the earth."

Notice, then, the geographical impossibility of a never-ending hell. If it takes place on this earth, as Scripture emphatically teaches, and if the earth will be made new and become the home of the saved, how could it possibly be that hell would last throughout eternity? Exactly what would that entail? Could heaven and hell coexist in the same place? Would the Southern Hemisphere be the abode of the wicked in fiery conflagration, while the Northern Hemisphere comprised the Canaan of the saints? Ridiculous! The simple truth is that God will destroy sinners with fire that will cleanse the planet of all the effects of evil. He will then make our earth new, and it will be the eternal home of the redeemed. God's plan is simple, beautiful, and easy to understand.

The book of Revelation contains the beautiful promise: "And God will wipe away every tear from their eyes; there shall be no more death, nor sorrow, nor crying. There shall be no more pain, for the former things have passed away" (Rev. 21:4). Here's an important question: will there arrive a time when He will fulfill it? Yes, we believe so. God is not in the practice of lying. Then, if it is true that the wicked suffer throughout eternity, when would the promise ever come to pass? Should sinners burn in hell forever, there would always be sorrow, crying, and pain, wouldn't there? It would be a confession that God doesn't really have the power to fix the sin problem permanently.

But we believe that God does mean this beautiful promise, and that it will happen. Yes, there will be tears and crying at the destruction of the lost. Christ will weep over the ones who rejected His mercy. But the Lord will have dealt with sin and sinners once and for all and expunged the universe of all evil. The Bible tells us that "He will make an utter end of it. Affliction will not rise up a second time" (Nahum 1:9).

Consider another thing: the doctrine of eternal torment is a theological impossibility. How is that so? Think of it this way: Jesus paid for our sins by dying on the cross, enduring the penalty for sinners that we might have eternal life—and not just for those who would repent, but for the sins of the whole world (1 John 2:2). Jesus suffered the fate of all lost sinners. It's the only way He can be our Savior, the only way we can receive salvation. The scales of divine justice must balance. He took our place. When the Father looked at the Son, bearing our sin, He saw ugliness. Jesus (and we say it reverently) "became" the world's greatest sinner, not by His own sins, since He was perfect, but by substitution—His acceptance of our guilt. Paul may have styled himself the "chief" of sinners (1 Tim. 1:15), but by being our Savior and bearing our sins, Jesus became the "king of sinners"!

The Bible declares that "the Lord has laid on Him the iniquity of us all" (Isa. 53:6; the margin of the KJV has that the Lord "caused to meet" on Him all our sins). All the sins, before or after Calvary, were brought together and heaped on Him.

Because of this, when the Father looked at the Son on the cross, He saw the total repulsiveness of sin. Do you remember the picture that God gave Isaiah of Israel's condition? "From the sole of the foot even to the head, there is no soundness in it, but wounds and bruises and putrefying sores; they have not been closed or bound up, or soothed with ointment" (Isa. 1:6). "But we are all like an unclean thing, and all our righteousnesses are like filthy rags" (Isa. 64:6). In vision Zechariah saw the high priest Joshua "dressed in filthy clothes" (Zech. 3:3, NIV). Speaking of the Laodicean church, Jesus said, "You are wretched, miserable, poor, blind, and naked" (Rev. 3:17). This is what sin looks like to a pure and holy God. And it is what Jesus took upon Himself when He "became sin for us."

As we consider the list of sins that Jesus bore, perhaps the single most wicked act in human history was that of putting God's Son on the cross. Could we imagine a greater transgression in the history of iniquity than crucifying Jesus, God incarnate? And could there be a sin greater in the annals of wickedness than the act of taking the life of the Life-giver? Yet we know that the Savior accepted even the guilt of that sin, because He prayed specifically in behalf of His persecutors and crucifiers, saying, "Father, forgive them" (Luke 23:34). He was speaking specifically of those who nailed Him to the tree.

The forgiveness of those who voted His death, wielded the whip, drove the spikes, and planted the cross could be possible only if He bore their guilt. In other words, Christ not only suffered and endured the tortures of the Crucifixion, but He accepted the responsibility for it also! When the Father looked down at Jesus, among the sins He saw placed upon Him was that of causing His Son's death! If you were a parent, how would you feel toward the murderer of your child? Yet Jesus was willing to bear all our sins.

What does all this mean in the context of the destruction of the wicked? Let's put it together this way. If it is true that Jesus endured the punishment for all the sins ever committed (and we believe the Bible says that He did), and if He took our place on the cross and accepted the penalty that we deserve (and we believe He did), then what does this say about the final judgment against individual sinners? Jesus indeed assumed the place of lost sinners and suffered the fate of the lost. Thus He bore not the guilt of one sinner, but all sinners—the total sum of all human iniquity. But notice carefully that His death took place within the time limitations of that Friday. So here's the question we have to think about: if Jesus suffered the penalty for all the sins of the world and accomplished that on that one day, why would it make sense then that those individuals who refuse the Gift and demand to pay for their own sins would be required to suffer for eternity? It just doesn't add up.

Or to view it from the other side of the coin, if it does indeed require an eternity's worth of suffering to pay for sin, even the sins of one single person (essentially what those who subscribe to the teaching of eternal torment believe), then Jesus must remain on the cross also for that length of time to pay for the sins of even one saved individual. He must stay on the cross throughout eternity to satisfy the requirements of divine justice and procure salvation, especially so if He is dealing with the sins of the whole world and not just for one person. Otherwise the debt would never completely be covered. Obviously He is not still on the cross, and equally obvious His sacrifice was sufficient to ransom humanity from sin and its penalty. When He breathed His last, He said, "It is finished" (John 19:30). His work of sacrifice was completed, the offering satisfactory.

This is not to minimize the horrific trauma of what Jesus experienced on the cross nor the final separation from God that sinners will experience at the last day. It was terrible for Christ, and it will be terrible for the lost. Jesus drank the cup of woe to its bottom. Our guilt and the rejection of His Father broke His heart. Likewise, weeping and gnashing of teeth will characterize the wicked as they see the glory of the kingdom they rejected and the benevolence of a loving God they despised. To realize all that God provided and yet in stubborn and insane obstinacy to know that they turned their back on it will crush the hearts of all sinners. No agony equals the pangs of regret! To feel the full weight of guilt in knowing that they trampled on the law of liberty and violated the principles of God's holy law will produce a burden of sorrow and woe from which they will desperately desire relief.

They have spurned the Voice that patiently spoke to them. Although they had ample opportunity to respond to God's gracious

Spirit who whispered to them of Jesus, they responded in their minds, "We will go our own way. We will not have this Man to rule over us." The full realization of these things, brought to view in unadulterated clarity on that last day in the light flashing from the eternal city, will send arrows of horror through the hearts of the lost. There looms the beautiful kingdom, the city of gold, and they are on the outside of its glorious walls, forever doomed! While they could have been inside, they made a different choice, and now the sun has set on their day of salvation. What woe and agony to wrestle with these thoughts, now seen in stark reality. Allowing the wicked to perish will truly be an act of infinite mercy.

In fact, God's love shines within even the doctrine of the destruction of the wicked. Once we understand the full teaching of Scripture, rather than a picture of a vengeful God, as Jonathan Edwards preached, it portrays a benevolent Ruler. He must deal with sin as a cancer that must be excised for the sake of the serenity and safety of the universe. But He will not remove from His creatures the capacity to decide for themselves—the freedom of choice. While holding out the inducements of eternal life and the invaluable gift of His grace, He also shows to the sinner the results of wrong choices. Patiently He guides and counsels through His Spirit, hoping thereby to spark new life in the heart of the wanderer. God hopes to shine the light of truth on the Damascus road of each traveler through life.

Ultimately, however, He leaves the final choice to us. It is said that each of us finds ourselves in the midst of a gospel election. God has voted in favor of our salvation. The devil has voted in favor of our damnation. We cast the tie-breaking vote. Will we accept His plan and His way? His way is the only way the universe can operate. The principle of self-love, cherished in the mind of Lucifer, is the sand in the gears of all relationships. The only operating system that will promote happiness and peace is the principle of selfless love, the foundation of God's holy law. "Love is the fulfillment of the law" (Rom. 13:10). Eventually those who cling to an existence of self-love must be destroyed, though it breaks the heart of the Creator.

The essence of the three angels' messages is the true revelation of God's character, not the sinister portrait painted by the deceiver Satan, the master of smear and reputation assassination. It is the true picture of His generous heart of love and not the fiendish scene of a vengeful Deity delighting in the writhing of the lost in flames of agony, as taught by some fire and brimstone preachers. A kindly Sovereign anguishes over the decisions of the unsaved. If He truly gives freedom to choose, then He must honor those decisions, though it means the destruction of those who cling to sin.

David's lament over his wayward son Absalom, who tried to seize the kingdom from his father, will be amplified a million times as sinners perish in the lake of fire. It will be God who will be weeping as did King David, who said, "O, my son Absalom—my son, my son Absalom—if only I had died in your place! O Absalom, my son, my son!" (2 Sam. 18:33). The incredible irony will be that God did indeed die in the place of every sinner, but they refused His generous gift of salvation.

The tears that fall on that day will include those of a loving God who created and redeemed creatures destined for eternal life, but who now, because of their own choice, must suffer the results of their decisions. It will be God's "strange act" to destroy. But let sinners know that our God is not to be trifled with. Not an indulgent grandfather who will tolerate rebellion forever, He will bring to an end the saga of sin—an "utter end." Let us bow in thanksgiving for His mercy and grace. Let us pledge to yield our wills to His guiding Spirit, so that we can be on the inside of those jasper walls. God wants it so. Having died for our sins, He waits at the door of our hearts and knocks, hoping that we will open it to Him.

Having said all this, could it be that the teaching of a never-ending hell is in some way a form of refuge for the sinner—that is, even though the prospect of the torments of hell are not pleasant, they at least represent *some type* of existence? It hopes to avoid the dark oblivion of eternal death. Life in hell is preferable to no life at all. If that be the thinking of some, let it be stated that the Scriptures clearly tell us that sin and sinners will "be no more." Eternal death means exactly that—the total and permanent cessation of any conscious existence. But through Christ we can avoid that verdict.

In response to a number of recent tornado tragedies, a successful business has started making what it calls "safe boxes." They are metal containers that you can bolt down to a secure surface such as a concrete slab. Tests have shown that they can withstand wind forces up to 400 mph. You can purchase the smallest model, adequate for a person of slight build, for about $2,500. They go up in size and in price to accommodate groups of people. In the figurative language of the book of Revelation, the "storm winds" are about to blow. Right now the angels are holding them back, but soon they will be released, and calamities such as we've never before witnessed will strike the earth. Where will our safety be? Do you have a "safe box"? What, or who, will be your place of protection? Have you found your refuge in Christ?

---

* W. F. Arndt and F. W. Gingrich, *A Greek-English Lexicon of the New Testament*, pp. 26, 27.

CHAPTER 23

THE "COMMANDMENTS OF GOD AND THE FAITH OF JESUS"

The messages of the three angels close with an encouraging announcement. "Here is the patience of the saints; here are those who keep the commandments of God and the faith of Jesus" (Rev. 14:12). The word translated "patience" is the Greek *hupomone,* which means literally "remaining under" and has the idea of "endurance," "tenacity," or "perseverance."[1] It appears frequently throughout the pages of the New Testament. Quite obviously such "patience" is a vital component of the characters of the saints. Though translated by a variety of English words, it is this word that appears (in italics) in the following passages, the ones from the Old Testament being from the Septuagint (again we quote from the NKJV, which captures the essence of the Greek translation of the Old Testament passages).

The life of Jesus, the divine pattern, exemplified such patience. "Looking unto Jesus, the author and finisher of our faith, who for the joy that was set before Him *endured* the cross, despising the shame, and has sat down at the right hand of the throne of God. For consider Him who endured such hostility from sinners against Himself, lest you become weary and discouraged in your souls" (Heb. 12:2, 3).

Christians during all ages, those who follow the example of Jesus, have needed this "patience," but it will be especially required among those who live at the close of time. Amid His predictions of the fall of Jerusalem, an illustration of the circumstances at the end of the age, Jesus said, "By your *patience* possess your souls" (Luke 21:19). In this same discourse He said, "He who *endures* to the end shall be saved" (Matt. 24:13). Speaking of the coming kingdom, Paul wrote, "If we hope for what we do not see, then we eagerly wait for it with *perseverance*" (Rom. 8:25). In the book of Hebrews we read, "For you have need of *endurance,* so that after you have done the will of God, you may receive the promise" (Heb. 10:36).

James writes, "Knowing that the testing of your faith produces *patience.* But let *patience* have its perfect work, that you may be perfect and complete, lacking nothing" (James 1:3, 4). "Therefore be *patient,* brethren, until the coming of the Lord. See how the farmer waits for the precious fruit of the earth, waiting *patiently* for it until it receives the early and latter rain. You also be *patient.* Establish your hearts, for the coming of the Lord is at hand" (James 5:7, 8). God's counsel is "therefore wait for Me,' says the Lord, 'until the day I rise up for plunder'" (Zeph. 3:8). Those who cultivate such "patience" will look up one day and say, "Behold, this is our God; we have waited for Him, and He will save us. This is the Lord; we have waited for Him; we will be glad and rejoice in His salvation" (Isa. 25:9).

"Here is the patience of the saints." The word translated "saints" means "holy ones."[2] Is such holiness something they've developed on their own, a quality they've earned by their personal endeavors? Absolutely not! "And to her [Christ's bride, the last-day church] it was granted to be arrayed in fine linen, clean and bright, for the fine linen is the righteous acts of the saints" (Rev. 19:8). The word "granted" tells us that this is a gift—something given to the saints. But they must cooperate in this process. They must be willing to receive what God intends to provide.

"Here is the patience of the saints; here are those who keep the commandments of God and the faith of Jesus." There can be no doubt but that the "commandments of God" here refer to the Ten Commandments. When Jesus spoke to the scribes and Pharisees, questioning why, through their tradition, they transgressed the "commandment of God," He quoted from the fifth commandment: "For God commanded, saying, 'Honor your father and mother'" (Matt. 15:4). Jesus told the rich young ruler: "'If you want to enter into life, keep the commandments.' He said to Him, 'which ones?' Jesus said, 'You shall not murder,' 'You shall not commit adultery,' 'You shall not steal,' 'You shall not bear false witness,' 'Honor your father and your mother'" (Matt. 19:17-19). They are obviously references to the

Ten Commandments. Jesus then added the thought "You shall love your neighbor as yourself," because that principle summed up the second half of the Decalogue.

When Paul declared, "Therefore the law is holy, and the commandment holy and just and good" (Rom. 7:12), to what commandments was he speaking? Obviously the Ten Commandments, since just before this he said, "I would not have known covetousness unless the law had said, 'You shall not covet'" (verse 7). There can be no question that the "commandments of God" that the saints keep at the close of earth's history are indeed the Ten Commandments, God's holy law, the Decalogue spoken from Sinai and committed to writing by God's own finger. It has been the object of attack by the enemy from the beginning. He knows that if he can get God's people to disobey Him, they will forfeit His blessing. Satan accomplished exactly that on the borders of Canaan through the agency of Balaam and the seductive women at Beth Peor. Bewitched into idolatry and immorality, many suffered the divine judgment and perished (see Num. 25).

Just as it takes only one door to be violated for an entire building to be compromised, the breaking of only one of the commandments results in an individual being a transgressor of all. As we have seen, the special point of attack by Satan has been the Sabbath day, the subject of the fourth commandment. Seeing how it reveals the Creator-God, how it illustrates salvation by grace, how it testifies to His power to bring beauty from that which is "without form and void," the devil has erected his siege mounds and aimed his battering rams against this commandment as with no other. In Old Testament times he succeeded in getting God's people to treat the Sabbath with carelessness. Then, following the captivity, they overreacted and piled on it a mountain of useless and distracting regulations, obscuring the glory of what God had established.

Through his sophistry and the work of misguided teachers and ecclesiastics, Satan assaulted this commandment in the early centuries of Christianity, and has maintained his fierce warfare against it ever since. He substituted a common working day, the first day of the week, the day espoused by pagans in honor of the sun god, for God's sacred Sabbath. The man of sin, the horn power of Daniel, the beast from the sea that came to life in the historical ecclesiastical structure of the Papacy, sought to "change times and laws" and "cast truth to the ground." The highest church leadership elevated itself above "all that is called God" and aspired to evince its supernatural authority in the act of changing His eternal law. The Roman bureaucratic structure points with satisfaction to the millions (Catholic and Protestants alike) who follow its lead though there does not exist, by its own confession, a whisper of biblical evidence to support the notion that God or the apostles made such a change in His law.

A popular notion that has taken root lately is the concept that "Christ is my Sabbath." The reasoning goes something like this: "He is my Rest; He is my Sabbath. Therefore I don't have to literally keep the seventh day holy." Sometimes its proponents quote Hebrews 4:8-10 in support of the idea. This brings into discussion the very important relationship between concepts such as substance and form, what is spiritual and what is literal, grace and law, love and obedience, faith and works, and our relationship with God and our behavior.

Which is more important between any of those sets of terms? The answer is, of course, that both are important! It's not an either/or proposition. Obviously it is vital that we receive the rest that Christ provides. To attempt to keep the Sabbath without receiving Christ as personal Savior, without embracing the peace and rest that He gives us, would be futile and empty. That was the religion of the Pharisees who wouldn't lift a finger to help someone in need during the Sabbath and who taught that it would have been improper to seek healing from Jesus on the Sabbath. Because of this misconception, the sick and ill at Capernaum waited till after sundown to come to Him for help, though it was clear that He was willing to heal on the Sabbath, having just restored Peter's mother-in-law from her fever (Mark 1:29-34).

God wants us to have the peace and rest in Christ that He has so graciously provided, which is symbolized by the Sabbath. Those Christians who trust in Jesus for salvation have ceased from their labor to earn favor with God by their own righteousness. But to say that having received this rest I can now dispense with obeying His explicit commandment is absurd! It's a fallacy advanced by the devil to derail Christians from their walk of obedience to God's will.

Jesus acknowledged that the personal relationship component of religion was crucial. Those who are rejected will hear His sad words, "I never knew you" (Matt. 7:23). That phrase highlights the personal relationship aspect of Christianity. Knowing Christ is integral to the Christian life. But He also said in that same passage, in words so close that they could reach out and touch each other, "Not everyone who says to Me, 'Lord, Lord,' shall enter the kingdom of heaven, but he who does the will of My Father in heaven" (verse 21). Christ's declaration tells us that obedience has its place as well. Having a personal relationship and doing His will are both important! David admonished his son, "As for you, my son Solomon, know the God of your father, *and* serve Him with a loyal heart and with a willing mind" (1 Chron. 28:9). Knowing Jesus and following Him go together.

Think about this for a moment. Consider someone who lived back when God was about to deliver His people from the slavery of Egypt. The Lord told them to slay a lamb and splash the blood on the doorposts of their house. This would enable the angel of death to "pass over" the house and spare the firstborn son (Ex. 12:1-13). The lamb that was slain can represent only one being, and that is Jesus. "Christ, our Passover, was sacrificed for us" (1 Cor. 5:7). But what if a person said, "Yes, I believe in the Lamb! I believe that the lamb represents the Savior, but I won't bother to literally cover the doorposts of my house with its blood. My acknowledging the Lamb is sufficient to save me." Would the angel of death have passed over that house?

Or what if someone reasoned, "I believe that Christ died for my sins and rose from the grave, but I won't bother to literally be lowered into the waters of baptism." Would that be a safe way of thinking? Would the New Testament endorse that teaching? Of course not! To be baptized without a renewal of heart is meaningless—it would be "form" without "substance"—but to willingly refuse baptism is a serious transgression (see Mark 16:16). Another might argue, "I believe that God is the rightful owner of all that is in the earth, but I'll not bother with returning a faithful tithe." No! True faith always manifests itself through deeds of righteousness. Our works don't save us, but they reveal that our faith in Jesus is genuine. In the same way, having Christ as my "Rest" is vital—but refusing thereby to honor His day of rest, the Sabbath, would be disastrous.

The Bible tells us that God will have people who will honor His law and "keep the commandments" (Rev. 14:12). They will not do it in order to earn salvation—that's impossible. Only the blood of Jesus can save. But obedience is the fruit of genuine faith—the outgrowth of appreciation for God's gift of salvation and the product of Christian maturity. The result of the Spirit's writing His law on our hearts, it is the highest form of worship. To say "I love Him, but I refuse to obey Him" is utter blasphemy.

Doesn't Scripture declare that "God is love"? Yes, the Bible does say that (1 John 4:8). But it also reminds us that "love is the fulfillment of the law," and that the whole law hangs upon the principle of love (Rom. 13:10; Matt. 22:37-40). It follows, then, that since God is love, and since His law is love, God and His law are one and the same—they are indivisible. You can't separate them. They are a seamless garment.

Therefore it is impossible to profess allegiance to God and knowingly despise His law, because they are the same. The Jews of Jesus' day put the Son of God on the cross, and the Christian world abhors such an act of sacrilege. But is the Christian world any less guilty because they have put God's law on the cross? Is it any different in the eyes of the Father?

To say that one loves Christ but rejects His law is not only impossible—it is the essence of idolatry and anarchy. God cannot save the one who knowingly rebels. It would only perpetuate the sin problem. He must deal with sin. Therefore He can take to heaven only those who submit to His gracious law of love, for the sake of the harmony of the universe. Does it really make sense that He would take commandment-breakers to live with Him?

The saints at the end will be those who have chosen to obey God though it cost them goods, kindred, and even their very lives. The beast will have erected his image, the false sabbath. The command will have gone forth throughout the world to bow to it and worship it. But here is a company who refuse to bow to the image and who stand firm to the commandments of God. This raises the ire of the beast and his consorts, who attach the severest of penalties upon the violation of their laws. But God's people hold firm. They have tenacity, endurance, perseverance, and patience.

And they have something else, too. Notice that Revelation 14:12 speaks of the faith of Jesus, not faith in Jesus. It is true that we need both, but this text emphasizes the faith of Jesus. Most assuredly we are to believe "in" Him, and the Scriptures contain many admonitions addressing that principle. But there is a difference in the nuance when the passage reads "the faith of Jesus." Now given to the saints, it is the faith that belongs to Jesus, that kept Him faithful ("full of faith") all the way to the cross of Calvary. It is the faith that maintained His allegiance to the Father despite the afflictions and temptations that assailed Him in that last trying hour.

For the saints to have the faith of Jesus is most appropriate, since they will be required to walk a similar path as did Jesus. He Himself predicted that, just as He experienced, the saints of the last day would also endure prosecutions and court trials filled with false testimony. Jesus personally knew cruel mockery and taunts. Our Savior endured physical adversity heaped upon Him by the master of coercion. The saints will also know what it is to drink "the cup" and be "baptized with the baptism" of His experience (Matt. 20:23). They will have made their own journey from Gethsemane to Golgotha, enduring the hatred of God's enemies. Some, before the close of probation, will have shed their blood in martyrdom. Others, though they have been spared by the protecting hand of God, will have been judged worthy of death by human authorities.

All will need the faith of Jesus in order to survive such trials, and God will give it to them. How does it happen? Because they have received the "mind of Christ." With His mind comes His faith. The Pauline promise has been fulfilled in their lives: "Let this mind be in you which was also in Christ Jesus" (Phil. 2:5). Along with His mind, which means His way of thinking, they have received His faith— not merely faith about Him, or faith in Him, but His very faith. To withstand the horrific tribulations through which they must pass, God grants them "the faith of Jesus." Do you feel that your faith is weak, that it couldn't survive the trials of persecution? Would you like to have the faith of Jesus? He is willing to give it to you!

John wrote in his first epistle: "We know that the Son of God has come and has given us an understanding" (1 John 5:20). The word translated "understanding" is the Greek *dianoia,* often rendered in translations of the New Testament as "mind." The apostle is saying that "Jesus has come and has given us a mind," that is, a new way of thinking and a new way of believing. It is the same word that appears in texts such as "You shall love the Lord your God with all your heart, with all your soul, and with all your mind" (Matt. 22:37). "Therefore gird up the loins of your mind" (1 Peter 1:13).

God's saints, who have the "faith of Jesus," are the recipients of the blessings of the New Covenant, which includes the promise, "I will put My laws in their mind and write them on their hearts" (Heb. 8:10). Notice the perfect blending of "law and grace," of "obedience and faith," as revealed in God's way. It is His law being written in the minds of saints, along with His faith that makes obedience to His law possible. With His faith they can obey even though they are weak mortals. And instead of being to their credit, it is all to God's glory. Through their lives God produces evidence that His gospel, the "power of God that brings salvation," is capable of overcoming sin in the lives of willing and submissive people (Rom. 1:16, NIV).

Such saints have "put on the new man who is renewed in knowledge according to the image of Him who created him" (Col. 3:10). At the Creation, God said, "Let Us make man in Our image, according to Our likeness" (Gen. 1:26). But then came the Fall, marring the divine image. What's important to understand is that the intention of God as expressed in Genesis 1 has *never been withdrawn,* never been revoked or canceled. It is still today His proposal to "make man in Our image."

The word in Greek that appears in the text quoted from Colossians is *eikon,* the same word used in the Septuagint of Genesis 1:26. We get "icon" from that word, a term familiar to users of computers as well as members of the Greek and Russian orthodox faiths, who commonly paint pictorial representations on wooden panels that decorate the walls of their churches.

The word *eikon* means "image or likeness."[3] The ancients used, for example, it to describe the representation of the emperor on a coin. When questioned by the Pharisees and Herodians about paying taxes, Jesus said, " 'Show Me the tax money.' So they brought Him a denarius. And He said to them, 'Whose *image* and inscription is this?' " (Matt. 22:19, 20). It is also, we should note, the same word employed in the phrase "the *image* of the beast." Satan wants his followers to receive his image, his *eikon*. But through the gospel God wants to replicate the picture, the *eikon,* of His character in our hearts. This is what the three angels' messages are all about! Instead of physical *eikons* hanging on church walls, as beautiful as they may be, it's about His character and the way of thinking that controls our brains, so that we can reflect His *eikon*. That was God's design in creating Adam and Eve in the beginning. When the last chapter is written, each of us will either bear the image of God in our characters or of Satan—we will either have the *eikon* of Christ or that of the beast.

Having spent a number of years in building, I've always considered that new construction is preferable to remodeling. Some contractors may differ, but I've concluded that building something from scratch is easier. If you have to deal with older construction, you often find unpleasant surprises behind those walls. Older pipes have a tendency to break off, and older wiring isn't always safe to work with. The floor may not be very level or the wall not straight. You'll need to spend significant time just getting things prepared to work because of the need to remove the older components. It's harder to fix something that's decrepit and decayed than it is to begin fresh with new material.

So it is with humanity. God's work of restoration, the re-creation of His likeness—His *eikon*—in fallen humanity requires greater skill and power than what happened in Genesis 1 and 2. But our Lord is capable of doing just this! He has promised to make us, lost sinners, into "the *image* of Him who created him."

Throughout the centuries people have responded to His invitation to become new in Him—the Enochs and the Elijahs and the Josephs and Daniels. But now at the end there will be a "harvest," a representative group to whom He can point and say, "Here they are. Here are the ones who keep God's commandments and have the faith of Jesus. Here is the Generation Enoch that reveals My power and grace." I want to be among that number, don't you?

[1] W. F. Arndt and F. W. Gingrich, *A Greek-English Lexicon of the New Testament*, p. 854.

[2] Arndt and Gingrich, p. 9.

[3] Arndt and Gingrich, p. 221.

CHAPTER 24

SUMMARY AND CONCLUSION: PREPARING FOR THE COMING CRISIS

We have seen that God has a message of invitation and warning that must go to the entire world before He returns. The book of Revelation presents three angels who bring one message of God's love. The first angel's message includes a call to "fear God," which means to cultivate an attitude of deepest respect, humility, and obedience. It summons humanity to recognize that He is the sovereign Monarch of the universe, and that we as His creatures rightfully owe Him this homage. The call to "give Him glory" not only includes praising Him with our lips, but also honoring Him by how we live. Our lifestyle, our diet, and our life patterns should reveal that we are God's sons and daughters. "Whether you eat or drink, or whatever you do, do all to the glory of God" (1 Cor. 10:31).

That message has special urgency because the "hour of His judgment has come." Since 1844, the last date on the prophetic calendar, the process of the pre-Advent judgment, reviewing the books of record in heaven as described in Daniel 7, has been under way. It is a necessary precursor to the return of Jesus, since He comes "with His reward" that He will give to each individual.

This message commands that we "worship Him who made heaven and earth," a summons to return to the simple obedience of the Ten Commandments, the fourth of which declares that God's day of rest, the only day blessed and sanctified by Him, is the seventh day of the week. According to the testimony of Scripture and even Catholic theologians, the day has never been changed. It remains as God's sacred memorial of Creation. We are greatly blessed in keeping it, not as a way of earning God's favor, but in appreciation of all that

304

He's done. Furthermore, it not only points to Him as the Creator, but illustrates salvation by faith and evinces His ability to re-create us in His image, His *eikon*.

The second angel declares that "Babylon is fallen, is fallen." Babylon in Scripture is a symbol of God's enemies. Satan has worked through human agencies from the very beginning to bring about his deceptive policies. The Christian church, established in truth and purity, fell away as Paul predicted. By the Middle Ages the ecclesiastical structure had corrupted nearly every teaching of Jesus in some way, restricted access to the Bible to just a few, and persecuted those who chose to defy its authority.

Rising in protest, just before and then culminating in the sixteenth century, were stalwart pioneers who led the effort to return to Scripture as the source of religious authority. The Protestant movement, which understood clearly the prophetic symbols that pointed to the papal organization as the antichrist, though beginning with great promise, likewise drifted from its position of honor. Refusing to advance in the light given by Inspiration, the Protestant churches too "fell" and lost the momentum with which they had begun. They have discarded views cherished by their forefathers, including the deciphering of the prophetic symbols identifying the Papacy, and replaced them with a system of interpretation largely conceived in the minds of papal theologians for the very purpose of squelching Protestantism.

Satan's goal has been to marshal all the world under his banner of defiance and rebellion against God, epitomized by the false sabbath, Sunday. Though it has not yet come to be, someday soon it will be true that Babylon will make all nations drink the potion of its false teachings, including the worship of Sunday. Such a coercive policy will resurrect the practices of the past and will be enjoined by the arm of the state, forming an illicit relationship between church and government, a practice identified by Scripture as spiritual "fornication."

That will lead directly to the circumstance of which the third angel warns—the implementation of the mark of the beast. The "beast" is the first beast of Revelation 13, the historical Papacy. It has offered as the mark of its authority the change of the Bible Sabbath to the first day of the week, Sunday. When a person, with full knowledge, chooses to accept the word of human leaders instead of the Word of God; when a person decides to bow to the commandments of human beings instead of to those of God; when a person chooses to pay homage to the authority of the papal structure and give honor to the first day of the week instead of the Sabbath of the Lord, the seventh day of the week, then that individual will receive the mark of the beast. Although it has not yet come to pass, it soon will when legislation includes proscriptions against dishonoring the Sunday sabbath.

Conversely, those who choose to honor the day of God's designation, having walked in the light of God's Word and having been transformed by His Spirit, will receive the seal of God in their foreheads. Placed in the mind of those who are responsive to the Spirit's promptings and guidance, the divine seal is like God's signature, indicating His ownership, authorship, authority, and approval. It will protect His followers from the contamination of sin, and after the close of human probation, from death.

Such marks are not bar codes, tattoos, computer chips, or anything physical, but indicators seen by heaven that reveal the condition and choices of the human soul. The book of Revelation opens with the explanation that these important matters are communicated through "signs" (see Rev. 1:1). The forehead represents our thinking and decisions while the hand stands for what we do and how we behave. Through their patient endurance and unbending obedience to God's commandments and by the grace and faith of Christ, they have conquered the beast and his image.

It is character that God is interested in, not outward appearance. Ultimately, the first two words of Jesus' response to the Pharisees and Herodians who asked Him about paying tax ("Whose image?") will depict the two classes that comprise all of humanity at the close of time. Each person will either have the image, the *eikon*, of the beast, or the image, the *eikon*, that is the character of God. "Whose image" will you choose to bear? Let those two words burn their significance into your mind and encourage you to submit to the Holy Spirit's ministry.

Those who have allowed God to change their way of thinking so that they reflect the divine image will qualify to receive His name, which is a symbolic way of saying His character, on their foreheads

(Rev. 14:1). Solomon said, "A good name is better than fine perfume" (Eccl. 7:1, NIV). Through the saints, the perfume of God's name, His character of selfless love, will permeate through the world in one last exhibition of righteousness to call the world to a love relationship with Him, just as the aroma of Mary's ointment "filled" the house when she bathed the Savior's feet (John 12:3).

On the other hand, those who receive the mark of the beast will find themselves left unprotected when the seven last plagues fall, and they will endure the final outpouring of His "wrath," a word that means that He ultimately permits men and women to experience the consequences of their choices. Forever separated from the Source of life, they will perish in the lake of fire, the second death (Rev. 20). Sinners will not suffer torture from flames that never cease, but will be consumed and destroyed in the purifying fires that will go on to cleanse wherever sin has reached, in preparation of God's re-creating our planet into the "earth made new," the forever home of the redeemed.

As unthinkable as it might seem now, our country of America, founded on the twin themes of religious and civil freedom, will take a leading role in the implementation of the image and mark of the beast. It will pass laws enforcing the worship of the first day of the week, copying the behavior (that's what the "image" is) of the church of the Middle Ages. Following in quick succession will be the test given to God's people, whether to bow to the "image" (the copy) or face the consequences. God's faithful, gifted by the power of His Spirit, will say no to the temptation to yield and will stand firmly for God and His truth, just as the three Hebrews refused to bow to the image of Nebuchadnezzar 2,500 years ago.

Obtaining, through Christ's strength, victory in the test, God's people will be "sealed" and their sins "blotted out," and they will be invested with the Spirit's energy to declare God's truth in a more powerful way than ever before. Signs and miracles that even overshadow the evangelism of the Day of Pentecost recorded in the book of Acts will attest their efforts. Called the "refreshing," the "latter rain," or the "outpouring of the Holy Spirit," it enables the saints to give the "loud cry," which is the declaration of the three angels' messages, in a more complete way than ever before.

Satan, of course, will have engineered his own "revival," complete with false signs and wonders, even calling "fire down . . . from heaven" (Rev. 13:13). As a crowning touch, he will impersonate Christ to confirm the establishment of the false sabbath.

When all have had an opportunity to make an intelligent decision whether to serve and obey God, symbolized by the honoring of His true Sabbath, the seventh day of the week, or to reject the Word of God and accept the false sabbath, then all those who have decided for God will receive the "seal of God," and those who reject His message of last-day truth and follow the "beast" will receive his "mark." At that time probation for the planet will come to a close.

The world will then find itself hurled into chaos and calamity never seen before. It will be the time of the two harvests, when the saints will have fully matured into God's *eikon* of righteousness, and Satan's followers will have ripened into his *eikon* of wickedness. The Holy Spirit's restraining influence will withdraw from those who rejected Him. It will be the "time of trouble, such as never was" (Dan. 12:1), making the hundreds of ferocious and deadly tornadoes, the earthquakes, and tsunamis that we've seen recently seem tame. The seven last plagues will be poured out. It will be the time of God's "wrath," His "indignation." Though God's people will not have it easy, their lives will be protected. After the close of probation no child of God will lose his or her life. Then will come the great day of God's deliverance, the one to which His people have looked for centuries. Christ will split the sky, raising His dead children to immortality and changing and translating the still-living. All will meet Him in the air.

Preparing for the Coming Crisis

These awesome things are yet to be; but we are not far away from them. The question springs to mind, in view of all these stupendous and tremendous events looming ahead, How shall we prepare? What should we be doing now to become ready? It makes no sense to know what is coming if we don't do anything about them. At the moment we are now living in the time of "preparation," a word worthy of our study. First, we will look at several Bible passages containing that word. We may divide the concept of preparation into two categories:

God's preparation, with which we have nothing to do, and humanity's preparation, which God will accomplish in us if we surrender and comply.

What is God's preparation? Before Jesus died He said, "In My Father's house are many mansions; if it were not so, I would have told you. I go to prepare a place for you. And if I go and prepare a place for you, I will come again and receive you to Myself; that where I am, there you may be also" (John 14:2, 3). Jesus committed Himself to establishing a place in which the righteous will dwell.

Has that been done? Did He keep His promise? Only a few decades after this, Scripture declared of God's saints, "Therefore God is not ashamed to be called their God, for He has prepared a city for them" (Heb. 11:16). What does the tense of the verb tell us? Jesus promised to prepare a place, and the book of Hebrews notifies us that "He has prepared" the city. God has already finished His part, and it has been waiting our occupancy for centuries!

A wonderful parallel appears in the Old Testament. When God took Israel from Egypt and sent them on the way to Canaan, He told them, "Behold, I send an Angel before you to keep you in the way and to bring you into the place which I have prepared" (Ex. 23:20). Through Ezekiel He said that He was leading them to a land of milk and honey "that I had searched out for them" (Eze. 20:6). Before they left the land of bondage, God had already scouted out the area to which He would bring them and had "prepared a place" for them. What a wonderful comparison! In one of the psalms Asaph testified, "You have brought a vine out of Egypt; You have cast out the nations, and planted it. You prepared room for it, and caused it to take deep root, and it filled the land" (Ps. 80:8, 9). So God had "preparation" work to do, both for the Israel of old as they entered earthly Canaan, and for the Israel of today as we look forward to the heavenly Canaan. It seems that He has completed the preparation long ago!

The other category of "preparation" involves us. We'll look at three very brief snapshots that focus on preparation and illustrate where we are now in time and what our lives should be like in view of what's coming. The prophet Amos declared: "Prepare to meet your God" (Amos 4:12). It is wise counsel indeed!

First, Noah had a work of preparation to do before water destroyed his world. Peter reveals how God waited while Noah constructed the ark (1 Peter 3:20). Because of human wickedness, God sent a flood to wash the world of its filth. Yet God would provide salvation through the vessel that He commissioned Noah to build. The ark that Noah prepared was God's "safe box."

What can we learn from Noah's work of preparation? We see that the Lord gave him specific instruction regarding its design. God told Noah, "This is how you shall prepare it" (see Gen. 6:13-22). Preparation was needed for the coming crisis, and what Noah "prepared" carried him and his family from one "world" to the next. What are we to prepare? There's only one thing that we can take to the next "world"— our character. Not our bank accounts, not our real estate, not our titles or our looks, things on which the world spends so much of its time. Only our characters will go to heaven. Remember, when He returns He will change our bodies, not our minds (Phil. 3:20, 21). The work of transforming our minds is to take place now, before He returns (Rom. 12:1, 2). What exactly is our "character"? It is the sum of our thoughts and feelings. Those are the things that make us what we are. We should give much attention, time, and effort to this construction project, this preparation, in view of the final outcome that it determines.

What is the model in our character building? It is the life of Christ. Here's the lesson from the first story: Because his "world" was going to end, Noah received a "pattern" from above when he "prepared" the ark. He didn't make up the dimensions of the ark in his head. God gave them to him. The Lord also has provided us a "Pattern" from above: the life of our Savior. Jesus came to show us how to live as well as to pay for our sins, being both our divine Example and Sacrifice. Look to Jesus to find out how to live. Ponder carefully the episodes of His life journey. Not one flaw; not one mistake will you find in that record. His life is to be our life. "He who says he abides in Him ought himself also to walk just as He walked" (1 John 2:6).

Given the pattern, Noah then had a part to do. I'm sure he found his share of slivers and raised his share of blisters. He worked. He sweated. He invested all he had in the building project. Nor was it done in a day. It took 120 years, but when he finished, he had constructed a vessel that, with the Lord's protection, survived the Deluge. Noah's job was to "prepare" an ark with God's help, from the pattern he had received from above. Our job is to build character, through His grace, enabled by the Pattern from above.

Joseph also participated in a work of preparation. Though sold by his brothers into Egyptian slavery, because "the Lord was with him" (Gen. 39:3) he eventually became the prime minister of that country. Pharaoh had had dreams, and then the chief butler remembered that Joseph had successfully interpreted his dreams and those of the royal baker while the two officials were in prison. The king now summoned Joseph to hear his dreams. His dreams were similar and represented the same thing. One involved seven skinny cows that ate seven fat cows. The other depicted seven hearty stalks of grain eventually consumed by seven withered stalks of grain (see Gen. 41).

Through wisdom given him by God, Joseph interpreted the dreams to mean that Egypt would experience seven years of abundant harvests followed by seven years of extreme famine. He advised Egypt's monarch to appoint someone to gather the surpluses during the seven years of plenty and store the grain for the seven years of famine. Accepting both the interpretation given by Joseph and the wise counsel, Pharaoh appointed Joseph to be the one to carry out the project—to be the one to "prepare" for the coming famine. Does Genesis 41 speak to us today? Are we now living in a time of "plenty" to be followed by a "famine"?

We are living in a time of plenty now, in the sense that opportunities to learn about God and His truth abound. In many areas we have religious liberty, allowing us to study and pray in private or to worship together in public without fear of interference. The Scriptures are available to us in unlimited and unprecedented abundance. You can get the Bible in printed or electronic form, reading it on paper or on an ipad. Now is the "time of plenty," when we can "store up" knowledge of God's Word and His truth leading to a relationship with Him of faith strong enough to withstand the times of famine when religious liberty will vanish.

The prophet Amos said: "'Behold, the days are coming,' says the Lord God, 'that I will send a famine on the land, not a famine of bread, nor a thirst for water, but of hearing the words of the Lord. They shall wander from sea to sea, and from north to east; they shall run to and fro, seeking the word of the Lord, but shall not find it'" (Amos 8:11, 12). Are you taking advantage of this time of "preparation," during this time of "plenty"? Do you now appreciate the opportunities to build a relationship of love with your Savior through the study of His Word and through prayer?

Third, the story of the giving of the manna has much to tell us about preparation. A few centuries after Joseph's day God delivered the Israelites from Egypt's bondage, and His people found themselves in the wilderness. Before very long they had exhausted their food supplies. Immediately they complained to Moses that he had deliberately led them out into the desert to kill them (Ex. 16:3). "Then the Lord said to Moses, 'Behold, I will rain bread from heaven for you. And the people shall go out and gather a certain quota every day, that I may test them, whether they will walk in My law or not. And it shall be on the sixth day that they shall prepare what they bring in, and it shall be twice as much as they gather daily'" (verses 4, 5).

When the Israelites went out the next morning, they saw something on the ground. "What is it?" they asked. In Hebrew the way you express the question "What is it?" is *manna*. Thus that very question became the name for the miracle bread that sustained them during the next four decades. On the sixth day of each week (Friday), twice as much manna fell. Because none would appear on the seventh day, God's holy Sabbath (note that the Sabbath existed before the giving of the law from Mount Sinai recorded in Exodus 20), they received more on Friday. While on other days if they tried to collect and keep manna for the following day it "bred worms," the manna they gathered on Friday to "prepare" for the Sabbath did not.

Thus the sixth day became known to them as the "day of preparation," a designation that continued throughout their generations. When Jesus died on the cross, how does the Bible identify the day of His death? "That day [which we now call Good Friday] was the Preparation, and the Sabbath drew on" (Luke 23:54). His women followers "prepared spices and fragrant oils. And they rested on the Sabbath according to the commandment" (verse 56).

The New Testament was originally written in Greek, and the word "preparation" *(paraskeve)* has survived as the word for the sixth day of the week in the Greek language to this very day! How did it happen that the sixth day of the week in Greek received the name "preparation"? Do you know how much a word has to be used in order for it to become imbedded in a language?

I can remember the first time I heard the word "google," meaning to do a search on the Internet. Today it's firmly entrenched in our language, but only because of its widespread and frequent usage. So how did the *paraskeve*, "preparation," become the word for "Friday" in the Greek language, still retained today 2,000 years after Jesus was here? I wonder if people ask, "Why is Friday called the day of 'preparation'? What are we preparing for?" And "Why is the seventh day called 'Sabbath'"?

Here's the lesson for us. The Christian walk has three parts as reflected in the experience of ancient Israel. God has led us from the bondage of sin, represented by Egypt, and we're on our way to "Canaan," heaven, but we're not there yet. We're now in the "wilderness"—the "sixth day" of the "week," so to speak. A "sabbath" of rest is coming, a millennial "sabbath," but it hasn't arrived yet.

God has provided a large measure of "manna" for us now—a double portion. What is the manna? Jesus referred to the Israelites in the wilderness and said, "For the bread of God is He who comes down from heaven and gives life to the world" (John 6:33). "I am the Bread of life" (verse 35). "The words that I speak to you are spirit, and they are life" (verse 63). Jesus is the true manna, and we receive Him today through His Word, the Bible. We are now living in the world's "sixth day"—the "day of preparation." Now is when we need to be feeding on the true Manna, establishing a relationship with Him based on faith and love through His words, the Holy Scriptures. What did Jesus say? "When the Son of man comes, will He really find faith on the earth?" (Luke 18:8).

Eleazar, the son of Dodo, was one of the three leading mighty men of David. When others had retreated during a battle against the Philistines, Eleazar "arose and attacked the Philistines until his hand was weary, and his hand stuck to the sword. The Lord brought about a great victory that day; and the people returned after him only to plunder" (2 Sam. 23:10).

Eleazar battled against the Philistines so diligently that his hand "stuck to the sword." I believe here should be a picture of victorious Christians who engage the enemy of souls with the sword of the Spirit—the Bible. Their hands are "stuck to the sword," meaning that the principles of Scripture are so embedded in their minds that they are, as it were, "stuck" to their hands. In these last days that's what we need to be—so rooted in the teachings of the Bible that a "Thus saith the Lord" is the answer to the temptations and harassment that Satan brings against us. That's how Jesus defeated the devil.

"The Snorting of His Horses Was Heard From Dan"

Do we have any evidence that such things will soon become reality? The prophet Jeremiah, seeing by faith the "day of the Lord" in his time—the invasion of Nebuchadnezzar of Babylon—sounded a poetic alert: "The snorting of His horses was heard from Dan" (Jer. 8:16). He was speaking of the cavalry of Babylon on their way, now just at the northern border of Israel. Dan was the northernmost of Israel's tribes, and because of the way the travel routes went across Mesopotamia, most invaders approached Israel or Judah from the north. By saying "the snorting of His horses was heard from Dan," Jeremiah was speaking of their being on cusp, the edge of the territory of Israel. The invasion by Babylon was just around the corner. Though the popular prophets preached peace and safety, Jeremiah knew otherwise. Many felt that what he predicted seemed impossible, but already he could sense the approach of the enemy—hear the hooves announcing the coming invasion.

Likewise, what prophecy predicts today seems impossible to many. Could it really be, for example, that America would repudiate her heritage of liberty and enforce religious laws in cooperation with various religious leaders? Many would dismiss that prospect with a figurative wave of the hand. After all, we have constitutional guarantees of freedom, don't we? We have First Amendment rights.

Yet prophecy has spoken and the "Scripture cannot be broken" (John 10:35). The discerning ear can hear the "snorting of His horses" from Dan. Apocalyptic Babylon is mounting its attack. Its chariots clatter in the streets. But don't expect that Satan will show himself as he really is. He is much too wise and cunning for that. His specialty is the "behind the back" strategy; the swing of a dragon's tail.

How did he first tempt humanity? Do we read that he introduced himself to Eve with something like "Hello. My name is Lucifer. I'm the rebel angel you've heard about. I'm here to try to get you to disobey your Maker and eat of the fruit He has forbidden, though it will result in severe punishment." Satan knew that that approach wouldn't succeed. So here's the question: If Satan began his career of tempting others through subtlety, cleverness, and deception, will his last-day ploy be any different? No. He will cause it to be dressed in the finest clothes. The devil will make it appear that what he plans is good, even necessary for human survival.

Even now there is a movement to champion the "family day" of Sunday as being the logical choice to bring about a "cohesive society" through "synchronized free time." It's a day labor unions can support as a "worker rest day."[1] Already, amid the calamities of tornadoes, earthquakes, fires, and floods, combined with an economy teetering on the precipice of disaster and a society outdoing Sodom in vulgarity and immorality, we hear calls to "return" to the roots of our heritage.[2] Is it good to have calls to prayer and repentance? Yes, but be careful! Satan is lurking to deceive and lead unsuspecting minds into his pathway of rebellion.

At the same time, the world of atheistic humanism pushes its own agenda. God is being shoved out of the classroom, the public square, Hollywood, and much of America. Militant secularism has advanced its policies of unscriptural behavior and lifestyles. Godlessness, violence, immorality, injustice, and corruption of every type characterize our nation.

At some point, in the context of all these unsolvable problems, Satan will suggest to the minds of religious leaders that for the good of the country it is paramount that worship be encouraged, protected, and eventually enforced. Led by the master deceiver, it will be the worship of the beast—the elevation of the Sunday Sabbath—that will become the law of the land. Such a movement will gain swift and surprising momentum. Those not participating from a religious motivation will nevertheless acquiesce along the grounds of national unity, health, and safety or to avoid the harsh penalties attached to disobedience. Thus Satan will attempt to gather all on earth under his dark flag of defiant rebellion.

We must always keep in mind that the unfolding of last-day events and Christ's coming is inseparably linked with His people being ready to meet Him. Scripture brings this fact to our attention in at least three ways. The prophet John heard a triumphant shout ring through heaven at the announcement, "Let us be glad and rejoice and give Him glory, for the marriage of the Lamb has come, and His wife has made herself ready" (Rev. 19:7). The book of Revelation presents two "brides," and both must be "prepared." It describes the "city" and the "church" as "bride."

Revelation depicts the New Jerusalem as the "bride" of Christ, the city that He is to establish before returning (Rev. 21:9; John 14:1-3). But is this bride the subject of the shout "His wife has made herself ready"? No, that doesn't make sense. No city "makes itself ready." Rather, it is the city whose "builder and maker is God" (Heb. 11:10). Obviously the Creator who brought into being a world in a week would not experience 2,000 years of building delays.

The text specifically tells us that "His wife has made herself ready. And to her it was granted to be arrayed in fine linen, clean and bright, for the fine linen is the righteous acts of the *saints*" (Rev. 19:7, 8). It is the church as bride of Christ that must prepare before He returns.

When Scripture states that she has "made herself ready," is it teaching that we must in our own strength complete the preparatory work? No. But since it cannot happen without our cooperation through the surrender of our will, it is expressed as our doing. The New Jerusalem as bride has no choice in the matter. God speaks, and it is. But to human beings He has given the freedom to choose, which we must exercise in order for His Spirit to accomplish the soul preparation for His bride the church. Having officiated at many a marriage during my pastoral career, I can tell you that no wedding takes place until the bride is ready. Christ, the heavenly groom, waits longingly for His church, the bride, to experience transformation into

His likeness. We may lament the depravity of the present age, but until the "bride is ready," Jesus won't return, no matter how low the world declines morally.

Besides the marriage symbol, Jesus also employed an agricultural one to depict the growth of His followers in spiritual maturity. He said, "When the grain ripens, immediately he puts in the sickle, because the harvest has come" (Mark 4:29). Jesus here tells us that the "harvest," which is the "end of the world," won't take place until the "grain" is "ripe." And finally, what restrains the last-day "winds" of trouble and persecution from blowing? It is the completion of the sealing of God's servants (Rev. 7:1-3). All three illustrations teach the same truth.

True, the Bible declares that the last days will be evil ones, but as we saw earlier, Christ's coming is tied not to one but to two harvests in Revelation 14: the harvest of the grain representing the righteous, as well as the harvest of the grapes, symbolizing the wicked. Evil will continue to "wax worse and worse" as long as time continues, for that is its nature (1 Tim. 3:13, KJV). It may well be that Newton's second law of thermodynamics (that things tend toward decay) has a very real spiritual application. But until the marriage of the Lamb becomes reality, until His bride "has made herself ready," until the grain reaches its full ripeness and His saints are sealed, our Savior will not return to earth.

Today we need to be in the Word and in prayer. We need to be able to defend our beliefs from Scripture when asked. "Sow for yourselves righteousness; reap in mercy; break up your fallow ground, for it is time to seek the Lord, till He comes and rains righteousness on you" (Hosea 10:12). All of us need to pray for our hearts to be softened to receive the early rain so that when the latter rain falls we will be ready to receive it. Those who expect that they can procrastinate in the work of heart preparation until the Holy Spirit is poured out in Pentecostal power will be sadly deceived. His holy influences will run off the surface of their minds like rain on concrete.

Now we need to be repenting of our sins, asking God to search our souls and making true and complete confession. Now we need to ask Him to instill in us a hatred of sin, a loathing of anything corrupt or impure. We need to ask the Lord to give us a thorough change, a total

Three Angels, One Message

conversion by the renewing of our minds so that we can appreciate His truth and His ways. May God help us to surrender our lives to Him each day, to honor and vindicate His name by willing obedience.

The issue is clear—it has never changed. It was the same in heaven when Lucifer rebelled, in Eden when Adam and Eve fell, and it will be the issue as the story of Planet Earth comes to its grand climax: will the creature submit to the beneficent rule of a loving Creator? Will the creature obey the One who brought all into existence and maintains all through His power?

Those who have known the Sabbath truth, we encourage to walk in the light and develop now a deep and personal relationship with the Lord. The question of the Sabbath day is important, but it is much broader than being merely about a period of time just as the crisis in Eden was about much more than a tree and its fruit. We have to know the "truth" not as an abstract concept, but Truth as a living Being.

Those who have been unacquainted with God's Sabbath, we encourage to investigate, accept, and embrace this wonderful revelation of God's power and purpose. Observing His day brings a blessing not found anywhere else. Don't fall into the traps set by the devil, who says, "It doesn't matter that much." Could what God wrote in stone with His own finger be unimportant? And don't succumb to those who claim that observing the Sabbath is legalism. Loving obedience from a proper motivation is always appropriate. Is it "legalistic" to refrain from murder because you love others as yourself? Of course not. Nor is it legalistic to refrain from stealing the property of another or to avoid taking the name of our Lord in vain. Then why would it be legalistic to obey His command to worship Him on the day of His choosing, since you are doing it from the motivation of love and appreciation? "If you love Me, keep My commandments" (John 14:15).

Satan offers a host of other objections as to why Sabbathkeeping is outdated, irrelevant, or unnecessary. They all lack foundation. Solomon summed it up nicely: "Fear God and keep His commandments, for this is man's all" (Eccl. 12:13). Read His Word, follow His leading, obey His commands. They are promises of what we can become through Him.

"But concerning the times and the seasons, brethren, you have no need that I should write to you. For you yourselves know perfectly that the day of the Lord so comes as a thief in the night. For when they say, 'Peace and safety!' then sudden destruction comes upon them, as labor pains upon a pregnant woman. And they shall not escape. But you, brethren, are not in darkness, so that this Day should overtake you as a thief. You are all sons of light and sons of the day. We are not of the night nor of darkness. Therefore let us not sleep, as others do, but let us watch and be sober. . . . For God did not appoint us to wrath, but to obtain salvation through our Lord Jesus Christ, who died for us, that whether we wake or sleep, we should live together with Him" (1 Thess. 5:1-10).

The story of Planet Earth would have ended long ago if it hadn't been for God's indescribable and relentless love. The Lord created a perfect world and put a perfect pair, Adam and Eve, into it. But then a kidnapper came, a being of unbelievable and malignant hatred who, with insane delight, brought sadness into the picture. You and I are part of that picture today.

On the evening of August 4, 1987, a woman masquerading as a nurse slipped into the Harlem Hospital in New York and snatched 19-day-old Carlina White (who had been brought to the hospital because of a fever) and then disappeared. New York City detectives were unable to track her down, and years evaporated into mist. Joy and Carl, her parents, lost hope of ever seeing their daughter again.

Meanwhile in Bridgeport, Connecticut, a woman by the name of Ann Pettway was raising Carlina and now calling her Nejdra Nance. By the time she reached her sixteenth birthday, Nejdra began to suspect that maybe Ann Pettway wasn't her birth mother, and so she began to do a little detective work on her own. She began surfing the Web for information and located a site called "The National Center for Missing and Exploited Children" that helped her put the pieces of the puzzle together, and then she confirmed it all through DNA analysis.

In January of 2011, more than 23 years after being nabbed from her parents, and now a mother herself, Carlina arrived from Atlanta to be reunited with her birth parents. Joy White said that the DNA tests really weren't necessary. "As soon as I saw those pictures, I said, 'That's my daughter.' I saw myself in her."[3]

As painful as that separation was, and as joyful and emotional as the reunion decades later, her story doesn't come close to that of the kidnapping and rescue of Planet Earth. After all, Carlina initiated the reunion. It was her curiosity and efforts that led to the happy moment. Not so with Planet Earth! Wrenched from the Father's arms, humanity was in no condition physically or spiritually to effect a deliverance. Left to ourselves, it never would have happened.

But God took the initiative from the start. Seeking out Adam and Eve, who had run and hid, He took the first step in declaring His promise of salvation that very day. God first set the plan in operation. In the fullness of time "God sent forth His Son, born of a woman" (Gal. 4:4). What a miraculous, courageous and risky step that was! God put at risk not just the future of Planet Earth, but His entire kingdom in sending Jesus to our world. But Jesus came and conquered on the battlefield of sin, and His victory is promised to us, who believe in Him!

"And I saw something like a sea of glass mingled with fire, and those who have the victory over the beast, over his image and over his mark and over the number of his name, standing on the sea of glass, having harps of God. They sing the song of Moses, the servant of God, and the song of the Lamb, saying: 'Great and marvelous are Your works, Lord God Almighty! Just and true are Your ways, O King of the saints! Who shall not fear You, O Lord, and glorify Your name? For You alone are holy. For all nations shall come and worship before You, for Your judgments have been manifested'" (Rev. 15:2-4).

---

[1] See www.europeansundayalliance.eu.
[2] See www.theresponseusa.org.
[3] See www.newhavenregister.com/articles/2011/01/20/news/aa4kidnapped011911.txt.